JUST WHERE DO YOU
THINK YOU'VE BEEN?

JUST WHERE DO YOU THINK <u>YOU'VE</u> BEEN?

PAUL POWELL

A. H. & A. W. REED
WELLINGTON □ AUCKLAND □ SYDNEY □ MELBOURNE

First published 1970

A. H. & A. W. REED LTD
182 Wakefield Street, Wellington
29 Dacre Street, Auckland
51 Whiting Street, Artarmon, Sydney
357 Little Collins Street, Melbourne

© PAUL POWELL

ISBN 0 589 00449 2

Set in 11/12 point Times "Monotype"
by New Zealand Typesetters Ltd, Wellington
and printed by Dai Nippon Printing Co. (International) Ltd,
Hong Kong

To

Captain John Lort Stokes RN
of HMS *Acheron*

who in 1851 charted the South-West Fiords of
New Zealand, and, from seaward, first named Mount Cook.

Paul Powell: "Once upon a time no one knew I was an ass."

Judith Powell: "There's glory for you."

On my return from the Volta Glacier,
January 1965.

Contents

List of Illustrations

PHOTOGRAPHS

MAPS

Unless otherwise credited the photographs are by the author. The black and white sketches and the jacket design are by Jim Wakelin. The maps are by Margaret Ramsay. The endpapers are from a photograph by Murray Bolt.

Acknowledgments

I would like to thank the following: The New Zealand Alpine Club, the Canterbury Mountaineering Club, and the Tararua Tramping Club, for the use of their Journals as a supplement to my diaries.

The files of the *Dominion* and the *Evening Post* were invaluable sources of additional information.

My grateful acknowledgment is due to the New Zealand Alpine Club and the Lands and Survey Department for map information, to Mrs Anita Crozier and A. H. & A. W. Reed Ltd for allowing me to quote from *Beyond the Southern Lakes* (1950), and also to Arnold Wall for permission to quote from his father's poem, *The Old Botanist's Farewell to The Southern Alps*. John D. Pascoe kindly gave me permission to quote from one of his letters to me (1938).

I am indebted to the friends who have allowed me to use their photographs, and to Franz Barta and Allan K. Palmer for their expert assistance with photography.

I also acknowledge the valuable assistance of Mrs Margaret Ramsay, who drafted the maps, and Jim Wakelin, who designed the dust jacket painting and the line drawings.

I especially thank all those mountain friends, from the Tararua Ranges to Mt Tutoko, who have, over many years, shared their bivvy fires with me. Hills may be high or low, but only people and shelter give them meaning.

Paul Powell

Kenmure Road,
Dunedin
17 *January* 1970

Bivouac

There is an endless substance in the hills,
Three limitless dimensions, and the fourth's the mind.
Death's but the bridge to infinite adventuring.
Within them all a hillman
Lives his battle with himself, the peak, the storm,
But cannot add one cubit to the ringing names—
Fastness, Stargazer,
Moonraker and Main Royal:
Or conquer, where Aspiring stands
A jewelled pivot for the swinging stars,
The Cross, the Pleiades, Orion's burnished sword.
There is fulfilment of the mind
When wind shrills on the blizzard ridge
Or hail drumfires at dawn,
In sodden bivouacs where songs are sung,
At dusk, or time of peace
When bells of silence ring
And each slow dawn becomes a day
Perfect for journeying.

Paul Powell

1

Storm Over Ruth Flat

Would I were in an alehouse in London! I would give all my fame
for a pot of ale, and safety.
                                    —*Henry V*, Act 3, Sc 2

THERE WAS WIND, an insatiable fiendish wind, there was cold and
dark; and the cold was the worst for it bred the thoughts, and they
were no defence.

"Make your mind a blank," Geoff had said.

The cold was cunning. To resist it, you needed the very weapon
it used against you, and there was more cold than you, a whole
mountainside of it. The mountain had time and darkness and all
you had were thoughts.

It was the sixth night of continual Volta blizzard and the cold
was winning. The four of us huddled in wet clothes and sleepingbags
in the hole and the snow was all around us. We had been pinned
down on the rim of the Volta Icefield since we first climbed out of
the Cessna ski-plane. There had been time for a climb of Mt Fastness
and then the storm had come, turning our snug tent camp to flapping

ribbons. We had hurriedly dug an emergency snowcave and now we lay in the cold sodden darkness, our world of light and warmth and mountains shrivelled to a wormhole and we longed for shelter. Above everything we craved warmth. The thought obsessed our silence and dominated our talk. When the primus was lit and we propped ourselves up against the slippery smoothness at the back of the snowcave watching the red heart of its flame and hearing the burr of the burning gases we were comforted; we came to life and our universe expanded. The storm must die away soon and the mountains stand up clear in the morning and Aspiring soar resplendent over the wild glaciers and the green forest. Aspiring was only five miles away and the hut on its flank where other men were sheltering was infinitely beyond our reach. The storm possessed us and the ice in which we lay squeezed us in.

A mile below the lip in which we had excavated our emergency hole there was shelter, country where man had old allies in his struggle to survive: trees to build with and to burn, fern to strew thick under shelter rocks, grass to smell, and to touch. There was a living world down on Ruth Flat, even a hut tucked in against the toe of the bush at the end of the airstrip, but we couldn't get there; in the dark of the snowcave I wondered if we ever would. The eating cold was worst because it cut us from each other; it stilled and froze the linking of minds on which our morale and living grew. The ice was coldly silent and sterile. It had time to make us like itself and then one day might roll us down the black rock walls to the valley in a thunder of avalanche, too late for our caring.

Before the worst nights came, when we still talked hopefully into the pitch blackness of tomorrow and that other life in the city, we'd joked about our misery. A voice, I think mine, said, "What would you give for a night's lodgings if a hut suddenly materialised on the rocks above this cave?"

"A hundred quid," from Baylis.

"Two hundred," was Skinner's bid.

"Any advance on two hundred, gentlemen? Come now," I urged, "only two hundred for a night of warmth and cosy sleep? That's ridiculous. Just imagine—a roof over your head, a comfortable bunk and a warm sleepingbag under your backside. No lying on cold snow while it sucks the bleeding life out of you. A four-burner stove and gallons of fuel. Room to move around, not like this chilly bin where you can't sit up without banging your head on the ice. A wooden floor to walk on, chairs and a table, and windows, so you can lie in your sack and watch the blizzard whirl, and feel smug every time the lightning sizzles on the ridge. And the air so thick and fuggy you can't see the other end of the hut." I got so wound up in my auctioneering I almost believed a hut was there.

"Plenty of cups of tea, and some good books?" asked Peter Child from his berth jammed hard against the snowcave wall.

"Yes, the lot. You couldn't get better in a five-star hotel. Now, that's worth more than half-a-crown a minute? Come on then, who'll give me another bid?"

"Four hundred quid," said Child. "Any reduction for members of the Alpine Club?"

"Sorry, not a show. We're all members anyway and we shouldn't have got ourselves nipped off in a clammy hole like this."

"Oh."

We all lapsed into silence with the thought of shelter too vividly painful to joke about. Geoff had said to make the mind a blank, a discipline he'd learned during the grimmest hours of corvette service in the war. If I couldn't do that, I'd purposely fill my brain with impressions of all the huts, the bivvy rocks, the snug tent camps I'd known. I'd transport myself into another world, and backtrack down the years, warming my hands at every refuge on the way. In the beginning the places came sluggishly and then in a flood; the years and people and shelters tumbled in confusion like coals into a dark cellar.

As I sorted them into order I saw shelter as more than a primitive urge, it was the nub of living. In shelter man had first thought and made fire and the wheel. It was refuge that sieved the absorption with existence from the thinking that was living. Speech and music, poetry and art, first grew where men lived together, though apart in thought, where there was fire and habitation. It came to me what this means in the mountains. Huts, tents, shelter rocks, were more than stops along the way; places where men stayed to eat and sleep, leaving to hunt deer, cross passes or cut transient steps up summit ice. Shelter in the hills meant more than cleaning a rifle, mapping the cross-country tramp, or resting for the climb. In huts or under bivvy rocks men were relaxed and talked and sang and felt the wonder of the wild hills. By the fire they bragged like Norsemen, argued like Jesuits, sang like minstrels, and dreamed like poets. This was a fulfilment in itself, a place for the sharpening of the mind in the relaxed comfort of the body. Such hospices were the beginning and end of mountain life with the swift minutes of action sandwiched in between. Here men saw the mountains and their living with them in balance. I saw the shelters I'd used in the Aspiring mountains, the French Bivvy, and the Aspiring Hut, the rock bivvies; the unattainable one below me on Ruth Flat which I'd found in 1947 when three of us had scratched over Wilmot Saddle in a nor'west storm; the Rock of Ages in the Kitchener Cirque; the leaning shelter

above the bushline on the Aeroplane Ridge. The people of those
moments were in my mind, their faces clearer now and the words
and laughter, the fire against the rock and the sharp astringent smell
of scrub smoke.

Our house at Albert Town was only thirty air miles away beside
the Clutha River which came down from Lake Wanaka. Judith and I
had argued about building the house: "It'll be a wonderful place
where Conway and Reda and you and I can be together in the
holidays. The hottest summer climate in New Zealand, and hills
all around."

"You don't fool me even if you're fooling yourself," she'd said.
"You know that really the house will be your hut at the beginning
of the Aspiring hills. You'll be with us, but on the first fine day you'll
be growling about like a bear wishing you were up there in the
mountains."

I shut out the blurred image of my family and thought of the high
huts of the Mt Cook peaks; the Haast Hut from which I'd climbed
Tasman, the Hooker Hut and the Gardiner; the Douglas Rock Hut
and the Welcome Flat Hut west across the Copland Pass. There were
tents and snowcaves among the mountains near Milford Sound, on
Mt Grave and the flanks of Mt Tutoko. I saw again the headwaters
of the Perth where Scotney and Croxton and I had made the first
two ascents of The Great Unknown. I was warm in the mountain
living of the past in the huts of the Rakaia, where the trail led over
Whitcombe Pass to Cave Camp in the Whitcombe River. There were
huts and rocks and shelters all along the way. In my six years of
Tararua days we ran like harriers over the tussocked ridges to Mt
Hector. It was on this windswept five-thousand-foot mountain that
I learned two sharp lessons: the power of mountain storms, and the
need for shelter.

The word went round and round and I came back over the years
to the present; a cold snowcave on the Volta, and the wind howling
just as it did outside Kime Hut that September night in 1937.

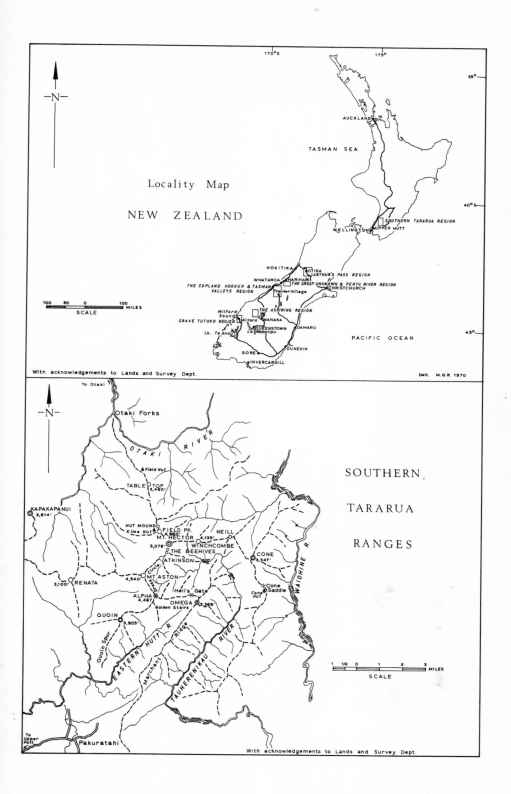

Locality Map

NEW ZEALAND

TASMAN SEA

AUCKLAND

170°E   175°

35°

40°S

WELLINGTON UPPER HUTT

SOUTHERN TARARUA REGION

HOKITIKA

OTIRA
ARTHUR'S PASS REGION

WHATAROA
HARIHARI
THE GREAT UNKNOWN & PERTH RIVER REGION
CHRISTCHURCH

THE COPLAND HOOKER & TASMAN
VALLEYS REGION

The Hermitage

THE ASPIRING REGION

Milford
Sounds
GRAVE TUTOKO REGION

Milford

WANAKA

QUEENSTOWN
Lk. Wakatipu

OAMARU

Lk. Te Anau

PACIFIC OCEAN

45°

GORE

DUNEDIN

INVERCARGILL

100 50 0   100
SCALE   MILES

With acknowledgements to Lands and Survey Dept.

Delt. M.G.R. 1970

To Otaki

Otaki Forks

OTAKI   RIVER

Field Hut

TABLE TOP
3,480'

SOUTHERN

TARARUA

RANGES

KAPAKAPANUI
3,614'

HUT MOUND
Kime Hut
FIELD PK.

MT. HECTOR 4,135'
5,076'

NEILL

WINCHCOMBE
THE BEEHIVES

ATKINSON

CONE
3,547'

3,100' RENATA

Circle
MT ASTON
4,540'

ALPHA
4,467'

Hell's Gate

OMEGA 3,368'
Golden Stairs

Cone
Hut

Cone
Saddle

WAIOHINE R.

QUOIN
3,905'

Quoin Spur

EASTERN HUTT R.

Marchant Ridge

TAUHERENIKAU RIVER

To
Upper
Hutt

Pakuratahi

With acknowledgements to Lands and Survey Dept.

2

Tararua Blizzard

And we that are in the vaward of our youth, I must confess, are
wags too.

—*Henry IV*, Pt 2, Act 1, Sc 2

IT BEGAN WITH a chance meeting when Graham Bagnall stopped me
on the steps of Victoria University on one of those fine light southerly
days when Wellington Harbour sparkled with unruffled blue; the
long humps of the Southern Tararuas rose in the north-east distance,
snowclad, bright and clear.

"How about coming away this weekend?"

"Where, Graham?"

"Up the Winchcombe Ridge. We'll go in from the Hutt Valley
and cross the main range. Over Mt Hector and down to Otaki
Forks. Been wanting to do it for years. Need two full days. Good
thing, the forty-hour week."

I couldn't say yes fast enough. Bagnall had a justifiable reputation as a tramper of the greyhound variety who went places, and he knew his Tararuas. We trusted him and followed. He had a dry and ready wit, eyes that looked shrewdly over the tops of tortoiseshell spectacles, and a wiry frame.

"What about transport?" I queried. Few students had cars, and getting to the hills was a hurdle except for official club trips.

"No trouble," said Bagnall, the words sputtering out in decisive bursts. "Don Viggers is taking a Tararua Tramping Club party into the Tauherenikau Valley. He says there's room for us in the truck."

"Good old Tararua Club."

There was an acknowledged and bantering rivalry between the University Tramping Club and the Tararua Tramping Club, but over the really important things like food or transport we bludged from each other with ribald cheerfulness.

"How do we get from Otaki Forks back to town?"

"Easy. There's another Tararua party going out the same way."

"What's the fare, Graham?"

"The usual. Five bob each way." He paused and then said off-handedly, "If you want a few bob . . . ?"

"That's OK," I interrupted gratefully, "I'll manage all right." In a university where students were broke I was flatter than most. Ten shillings out of a clerk's weekly wage of thirty bob was a fairly good bite; board in Wellington didn't leave much for extravagances such as transport and food for a weekend tramp.

"Count me in, Baggy. Just the two of us?"

"No," he said. "I've asked Norm Dowling as well. Do you know him?"

"I've met him once or twice. Down at the Tararua clubrooms. A quiet bloke isn't he?"

"Yes," laughed Bagnall, rubbing his palms. "A good counter to you. You don't think I could put up with your endless exuberance all alone, do you?"

In the lecture-room my mind was leagues away from British colonial policy in the eighteenth century; I was up on the top of Mt Hector looking across the snow-hazed Tararuas. I was flattered that Bagnall had asked me to join him. The Winchcombe Ridge was regarded as one of *the* expeditions of the Southern Tararuas, and the man who did the crossing acquired the reputation of being a tough tramper; he became one of the elite band who, fit and eager, could look after themselves on the long bush and leatherwood scrub ridges and then cross the exposed high tops like point-to-point huntsmen, wet or fine, and to hell with the fences.

．　　　．　　　．　　　．　　　．

From Pakuratahi, a few miles beyond Upper Hutt, the clay trail led over a breathless hill called The Puffer and down a bush creek known imaginatively as Smith's until it met the Tauherenikau River.

"How about a boil-up, Graham," I asked as we came to the hut where the Tararua Club were engaged in a long campaign to stop the river eating away the manuka flat and the hut.

"No time," said Bagnall. "We've just had breakfast."

"It's a long way up the river to Cone Saddle Hut," said Viggers. "You'd better have a hot drink before you leave." The Tararua Club were famous for their cuppas.

"Thanks all the same, Don." Bagnall was itching to be away. "We'll have a good binder when we get there."

"Weather doesn't look too bright, might get some rain soon." Viggers looked at the sky and shook his head. The sun was as dull as a drunk after a lost weekend.

"Come on," Bagnall flung over his shoulder and he started walking.

"Look after yourselves," said Viggers solicitously; his deeply lined face wore an air of cheerful gloominess. "The Winchcombe Ridge isn't a place to trifle with."

As we dived into the manuka track I took a last glance at the hut and said to Dowling, "Not much of a weekend for them, eh Norman? Stuck down in the valley all the time."

"We'll have to keep going," urged Bagnall as we went up the track at a pace that was more trot than jog. "It *could* rain, so we'd better push on. We cross the river five miles up the flat, just opposite the Cone Hut."

The further we went the worse the weather became, but we waded across the dark water to the far side where the boulders on the sombre green flat were red with lichen and the beech forest bowed up dull and silent to the Cone Saddle.

"Where's the Winchcombe Ridge, Graham?"

"Up there in the cloud," he said, waving briefly at the tops where the mist hung and the high scrub and tussock bent round in a dark circle under Mt Hector and back towards Mt Alpha.

"Gloomy place," muttered Dowling, staring up the river where the trees hung over the lustreless water flowing from the gorge.

"Don't worry, it'll be a fine day tomorrow," said Bagnall. Without bothering to stop or look around he was off up the track at a purposeful pace. There was one thing to be said for his hurry, you didn't get the time to worry much about what the weather was doing; you concentrated on getting there with the least fuss. I had heard a lot about his decisive leadership and his impatience with mucking about. It wasn't that he was dictatorial or without bush manners; he drove himself with a cheery briskness which assumed that you would follow. He went up the dour forest track with the objectivity of a regimental runner and there wasn't any purpose in argument until you covered the distance, and then he would laugh and talk with you about anything from primroses to polygamy.

If Bagnall's idea was to get us to the Cone Saddle Hut in fast time, he achieved it; all Dowling and I saw was mud, a blur of trees, and the continual flapping of our leader's bush singlet over two piston legs held together by a black pair of running shorts. When we staggered into the hut, Bagnall was there waiting for us, throwing broken branches into the grey ashes of the fireplace with such adroitness and energy that I half expected them to burst into flame before he lit the match.

I was tired and hungry, for breakfast had been skimpy and lunch had been just as light, eaten on the run with more urgency than enjoyment. I was already beginning to realise that reputations have to be paid for and that whatever else the weekend might hold for us, it didn't promise the opportunity to gourmandise. Food cost money and we didn't have much to spare for luxuries like eggs, bacon or beef. Bagnall had a hatred of sausages; you only had to mention the things and he did a war-dance while he told you, with a hackling of red hair, of the eighty-seven reasons they were bad for you. Instead we lived sumptuously on tinned beans—"The bits of bacon with them gives you enough protein"—rice and dried apricots. There was tea, thank God, and we drank it hot and stewed black and filled in the voids with bread; we preferred it doughy because it gave you a nice full feeling.

Bagnall made the tea with studied care, the mark of the old hand; the bending over the billy with a torch until the water sang, the nonchalant flinging-in of tealeaves, and then the ritual of beating the sides of the billy until the leaves sank. This was regular ceremony in all Tararua temples; it was the bond which united all trampers in their brotherhood of mist, mud, scrub and sun.

"It's a good hut," said Bagnall, fanning the fire vigorously with a tin plate while the wet wood sizzled and spat and the smoke billowed into the room.

"Any hut is a good hut if it keeps the rain out," replied Dowling, taking up the invitation to argument. "Just a question of degree. Some are better than others."

"Exactly. Comfortable huts are bad. They make you lazy and you don't want to leave them."

"No danger of overstaying ourselves here then, is there?" said Dowling as he dug our staple ration of baked beans out of his pack and opened the top with his bowie knife. "But it has a sort of atmosphere. Damp, smoky, sacking bunks. Typically colonial. Adequate but not palatial."

"We'll be away before dawn," I chipped in, "and I don't care how ramshackle it is. The main thing is that it's a roof and it's quiet. We could be in lots of worse places."

"Such as?" Dowling lifted a serious face.

"Spain. Things aren't going too well with the Republicans. They're going to lose the civil war. Franco's getting too much help from the Germans and the Ities."

"We'll be next. 1914 all over again."

"How long?"

"Within five years. Adolf Hitler and Musso are using Spain for trying out their latest weapons and we sit by and do nothing. And the longer we put it off, the worse it'll be. That's why I'm glad to be here in a dirty old possum-trapper's hut. We haven't much time left so let's make the most of it."

Dowling tipped the beans into a billy and hung it over the sulky fire. He sat there in front of the smouldering wood with his long face resting in both hands and hummed something classical to himself. The turn of the conversation and our tiredness made us quiet. After a half-hearted attempt at starting another discussion we went to bed determined to be up well before light.

But a sewn-up blanket wasn't the warmest covering—I envied the other two with their kapok sleepingbags—and soon after the candles were snuffed the opossums came out and held a groaning nocturnal court on the roof of the hut. I wondered about the day to come and the years beyond. A star peered brightly through a hole in the iron roof above my head and down on the table a mouse fossicked and rattled in its search for food. The wind came and went and the deep watching silence of the hills settled round the hut.

We were up and away by three am after a light meal, with clouds scudding below a covering of over-bright stars.

"Going to be windy," I said, closing the door behind me and wishing we could have sneaked another hour's sleep. A few hours before, the Cone Hut had seemed the last word in gloominess, now I was wondering if there was any sense in mooching on in the coming rain. The climb through the forest with dim torches went on interminably, for we wandered off the track often and stood shivering in the darkness while Bagnall found the way. More in a mood of retaliation than pathfinding we hacked desultory blazes with a slasher. The wind was stronger now and the dwarfing trees grated and moaned in the darkness.

"What's the use of going on?"

"We can't go back. Never get there in time to catch the lorry. And the river's bound to be well up with all this rain. I don't think we'd get back across the river. We're committed."

The dawn came, an insipid washed-out whiteness on a track already running with water.

"A cold good morning to you," muttered Dowling as we hastened head-down for the shelter of the scrub on the far side of the bald top of Cone Summit.

In fine weather the Tararua Ranges can be beautiful, a great pattern of bush ridges and spurs with the deep clefts of river and gorge where the light flashes silver in the early morning sun and the undulating tops run tussocked and clear for sixty miles. They have a tranquillity, a friendliness, that lure you ever back again to wander over their limitless variations. The balance between valley, ridge and summit is quite perfect for there are no grim rock turrets and hanging snowfields to be footstools for ambition. Anyone of commonsense and fitness can go to them; they are to those who love them places of content. But let wind or winter come, they can be as spiteful and as dangerous to fools as higher hills.

That September morning on the Cone at 3,500 feet the flanking rivers, the Waiohine and the Tauherenikau, were choked with stubborn mist and the sun rolled like a dull ball above the grey leather clouds banked along the highest ridges. We went on dourly, climbing over the hummocks of shrubbery, slowly gaining height, ticking off the names of tops on the inventory of our day. Five hours after we'd left the Cone Hut we halted in the doubtful comfort of the last scrub and ate a small packet of biscuits. With food again in our bellies we perked up and cocked a stroppy eye at the long ridge ahead.

"Better put gloves on, and more clothing," advised Bagnall.

"Long trousers too?"

"Not yet, wait until we need them, Paul. No point in getting them wet too early."

Our clothing was about as inadequate as our food, as we never threw away garments unfit for city use but wore them out to the last fibre in the leatherwood scrub.

Bagnall pulled back his parka sleeve and looked at his watch. "Come on," he said, impatiently, "we're twenty minutes behind schedule." He stood above us on the muddy track waving an arm and pointing at the misty redoubts ahead.

As we lumbered glumly to our feet Dowling said quietly, "Our boys about to go over the top at Passchendaele. Remind me not to join the infantry in the next war."

"I suggest we get this one over first," joked Bagnall as he went at the gap in the scrub with hunched shoulders.

"It looks a trifle unpleasant up there," said Dowling, watching the bursts of cloud breaking in the gale and the plunging slivers of rain.

It was more than a trifle unpleasant. As soon as we left the greenery and faced the steep climb up to the bare summit of Winchcombe, the swirling mist wrapped us in and the wind flensed us. I'd been in Tararua storms before, but nothing as bad as this one. The wind blew us off our feet, hail rattled off our parkas and punished our bare legs, rocks the size of walnuts flew from the ridge, but the noise was the worst. The wind was a beast, an invisible dragon that roared and bellowed, and the safety of Kime Hut lay west and north, behind the dragon's teeth. We left the exposed ridge and tried to move on the leeward side, but the gullies were filled with snow and the surface glazed by the cold wind. We had no ice-axes so we hacked our way back to the ridge crest with sheath-knives. We herded behind an outcrop of iced rock.

"For God's sake, let's put longs on."

"Never do it. Wind's too strong."

"What do we do?"

"Keep on going. Try for Kime. Only three and a half miles away."

"Three and a half years in this!"

"Shorter than going back."

We went on. Bagnall was right. The only thing we could do was to go on. And we did. The wind divided us and tried to conquer. We were strung out along the ridge like three beads rattling and dancing in the wind. Now we were no longer a party but three men separated by the blizzard, three small black puppets hanging to frozen tussock, clinging to glazed rock. I lagged, and inevitably Bagnall and Dowling drew away and often I lost sight of them in the mist and the snow flurries.

Then the cramp came on me. I yelled for the others to wait, but the wind killed my shouts and sucked away my breath. I moved jerkily, detached and purple-legged and cut from flying hail. I lay down on the snow and could have slept; it was quieter and warmer and very peaceful and I licked a spear of iced tussock. But it would be warmer at Kime. Just over the top of Hector. The wind dropped long enough for me to recover from its blows. Then I remembered that despite the advice of the leader—"No extras, we'll travel light for speed"—I'd brought a pound of honey in my swag. I scraped at the frozen mass with a tablespoon but the handle bent, so I dug at it with a stone. My sheath-knife had gone, I'd dropped it from numbed fingers back along the ridge.

It was good honey. The will to live returned, so did the wind, but I stopped when the wildest bursts came, and dug out some more honey. The other two men were flagging and I caught them up, and we sat in the saddle under the last snow slope leading to the summit of Mt Hector, sharing the honey and the same stone.

"Funny place for a picnic," mumbled Bagnall, his eyes red and restless.

"I've sunbathed here in the height of summer," said Dowling. "Thirsty day, no water. You could hear it gurgling down in the Waiohine Gorge miles away, it was so still." His lips were unnaturally red; there was ice caked on his balaclava and frozen mucus hung from his nose.

We helped each other into long trousers but couldn't do up the belt buckles as our fingers were too stiff with cold, and crawled the rest of the way to the top of Hector where we flopped to the snow behind the illusory shelter of a few miserable icy sticks that marked the top.

"Got to get to Kime. Got to get to Kime."

That hut had become my final goal. In fine weather on the top of Mt Hector we would have preened ourselves at what we had accomplished and our day would have been over, but in that blizzard where there was no sun, only an undifferentiated whiteness, our journey was yet to begin.

When we staggered to our feet, Bagnall still lay face-down in the snow. We shook and punched him, but he didn't stir. Too weak, too close to collapse, we couldn't carry or even drag him.

"Kime. Got to get to Kime. Bring up the sledge."

"Got to get him to shelter."

The wind wasn't so bad on the northern side of the mountain and the way was downhill. With arms clamped around each other's shoulders, Dowling and I lurched up to Field Peak where we leaned together against the wind, shielding our faces from the pricking hail. The wind suddenly died and the mist moved closer; a white gravecloth and a ringing silence. We teetered about peering for a sign, our sense of direction lost now that the guiding wind had gone. The snow went down persuasively on every side and merged with the waiting mist.

"Which way?" Dowling was confused too.

"Not sure."

A thread of sound came through the mist, a faint whisper of distant running water. "That's the Waiohine."

"Could be the Otaki River. We could've turned in a circle."

"Must keep together."

"Yes."

If the mountain prised us apart we were done; we'd wander utterly confused into the green maze of the headwaters on either side of the divide. Dowling's balaclava was sheathed in ice, his mouth was a dark hole hanging between hollowed cheeks, snow crusted his eyelids. I knew that we were near the end of our strength but we were past pain or fear. Dowling's mouth closed and his lips framed words I couldn't follow. He was outlined against the mist, a lolling gasping head.

"What is it? I can't hear you." I muttered with a last flicker of irritation.

"Praying."

He gave me a lopsided smile and lurched off. I followed, not caring where we went. Not far from the top of the mountain the mist suddenly parted and we saw, hunched in the windswept hollow of the gully, a fortuitous patch of red: the roof of Kime Hut.

We stood unbelieving for a minute and then shambled down to Kime, pushed open the door and fell on to the wooden boards. We didn't revive for some time and when we eventually struggled to our feet our swags were still on our backs as we fumbled about the hut looking for food. We fell over quite often and giggled vacantly, unable to believe that we were free after hours of tyranny from snow and wind. We ate a little sugar and sat wobbling on the form with our backs to the table.

"Where's Graham?"

"Oh Lord." Dowling's eyes were wide. We slowly remembered that Bagnall was still up in the storm on the summit of Mt Hector; too weak and weather-hammered to help him down the hill, we'd left him in the snow. He would not have deserted us.

We gobbled another spoonful of honey, stuffed a few sodden biscuits in our pockets and went out to the wind and the snow. We climbed back to the top of Field Peak, stopping and calling every few yards. There was no reply, only the wind again and the sharp flying snow. Down in the saddle between Field Peak and Mt Hector we halted again, to rest ourselves as well as to call . . . No answer.

I was frightened then, more than I'd been before. We waited until the worst gusts had passed rumbling down toward the Waiohine. I hated the wind and the snow; we'd lost Bagnall, because we hadn't stuck by him, I'd never go near the mountains again.

"We've *got* to find him," yelled Dowling.

We searched towards Mt Hector until we found him, a dazed figure staggering downward but still on course for the hut. A lonely ice-covered man looking for shelter, battered, homing in on will-power. We laughed, shook him and swore at him in our relief. The wind froze our wet cheeks as we led him slowly down the snow.

By the time we reached the hut our last strength had gone. Dowling and I put on a few bits of dry clothing and crawled into our sleepingbags. But Bagnall sat on the form where we'd propped him. "Where am I?"

"Safe in Kime Hut. It's all over now, Graham."

He lolled for a moment and then said, "What day is it?"

"Sunday."

"Why?"

Then the door opened and a man came into the hut, stamping his boots and thumping his hands together. He told us his name but I forgot it immediately. He'd come, he said, to collect his skis at the end of the winter. He was a brisk and fit Tararua Club man, a fellow of practical commonsense who put on the kerosene primus, made a billy of sweet cocoa and held it to our lips while we sipped. Dowling got out and helped him change Bagnall and lift him into his sleeping-bag.

"Where have you blokes sprung from?"

"From Cone Saddle. And we didn't come, we were blown." Dowling's sense of humour was back.

"*What*, along the Winchcombe Ridge and over Hector in *this*? You're lucky you made it. It's a terrible day, the worst I've known. Nearly turned back on the Field Hut side of Table Top." His glance swung from Bagnall to Dowling, then to me. "Baggy's absolutely done in. Exhaustion, and exposure."

"Will he be OK?"

"I hope so. He's a tough rooster." He started getting a meal ready and asked as he peeled the potatoes, "Why didn't you turn back? You've all been round the Tararuas for a while." It was a question, not an indictment.

"We just kept going until it was too late to retreat, and then we were committed."

"And well you ought to be." He gave us a grin and went on peeling. "You blokes get some sleep, and I'll wake you up in a couple of hours when the meal's ready."

I went off to sleep with the burr of the stove, the hut was warm and living; outside hail rattled and the hut staywires thrummed in the wind. Nineteen hours later I awoke stiff and aching, but clear-headed, and with senses sharpened as after fever. The hut was very still and the mountain silent. I had a strong perception of a new dimension, of a limitless freedom and an infinite cleanness. The incidents of the previous day were set in the perspective of balance between men and storm and mountain where many things blended to one harmony. Now we were part of it.

The others awoke. We shared a quiet breakfast of scraps of honey and cheese and hardboiled eggs from the Cone Hut. Our benefactor of the night before had gone. There was a note saying we were so

done in that he hadn't had the heart to wake us, but that he was
going out and would tell the Corrigans, who kept the post office
and taught school down at Otaki Forks, that we were safe and should
be down by midday.

We packed and left. Light snow was falling and a snowlark hopped
before us with fluting cries. The air was soft from the plains and
smelled of spring.

On Hut Mound I stopped and looked back along our trail of
broken snow glittering in the morning sun. Beyond, remote and
calm through the slow mist, rose the outline of Field Peak and Mt
Hector; but it was on Kime Hut where the ice-light flashed on eave
and wind-stay that my last glance rested. . . .

"Next time I want to climb Mt Hector in winter," I said as we went
down the long spiral to the green forest, "I'll do it the easy way;
from the hut on Mt Alpha."

"You can count me in," said Dowling.

3

The Hut on Mt Alpha

Where the clouds can go men can go; but they must be hardy men.

—*Andreas Maurer*

WE DIDN'T WAIT for the winter or the approach from Mt Alpha. In December, Bagnall led Don Viggers, Arthur Thompson, Arthur Oliver, Derek Freeman, Dowling and me on an energetic twenty-hour tramp up the Winchcombe Ridge and over Mt Hector again. We crossed the Southern Tararua Range to Mt Renata and Mt Kapakapanui and out to Waikanae.

It was midsummer, and the hills were friendly.

Norman Dowling didn't come with us on the winter crossing of the Southern Tararuas in August the next year; he had been killed in late December 1937 on the McKenzie Glacier. With Stan Davis and Derek Freeman he had just made the second ascent of Mt Evans in Westland. Dowling's death jolted us, as we were all close friends.

When I was asked to lead a Victoria University College party on the winter crossing of the southern Tararuas I wished he had been alive to keep the compact we had made near Kime Hut the previous year. In 1938, Munich, with its appeasement of Adolf Hitler and the betrayal of Czechoslovakia, was gloomy news. But it was difficult to grieve too long for one man; tomorrow there would be many. Against this background of certain war our near-miss on the Winchcombe seemed a puny affair. I had learned that mountains could strike. I was yet to discover how hard.

Six of us, Barnie Butchers, Roger Steele, Rex Collin, Arthur Fredric, Cedric Wright and I left Wellington on Saturday 13 August 1938 for Pakuratahi, a few miles beyond Upper Hutt. Our idea was to cross the Southern Tararua range from east to west by following along the Marchant Ridge to the Golden Stairs, pass over Omega, drop down sharply to a saddle in the bush, and then climb up to Hell's Gate. A mile due west lay Alpha Hut at a height of 3,600 feet. We'd stay the night there and next morning climb up to the summit of Mt Alpha (4,467 feet). If the weather was fine and the snow conditions good, we'd follow the open tops round the Dress Circle, traverse Mt Atkinson and The Beehives to Mt Hector and Kime Hut, and then drop down to the Otaki Forks. Our hired lorry would come round and take us back to Wellington on Sunday evening.

The trip was a regular winter tramp done by all the local clubs. Though people needed to be fit and experienced it wasn't an alpine crossing in the one-up-manship sense; but bad weather and difficult snow conditions could soon raise it to that peerage. I had been over twice before, in winter as well as in summer and, having already done many of the classic tramps in the Southern Tararuas, I felt able to lead a party. Most of the other old hands of the University Club weren't able to come, but I knew the five men in my team well, and thought I knew the Tararuas. I had experience enough to have a respect as well as a liking for the ranges; there was to be no record-breaking.

The morning was overcast with a promise of rain from the sou'west when we stopped at Dobson's Bivouac, a canvas shelter deep in the beech forest under Mt Marchant. We boiled the billy—an unfailing ritual in the Tararuas—talked and skylarked, and then wandered leisurely along the knotted blazed track to the Golden Stairs and Omega. The weather closed down as we plugged steps up frozen snow to Hell's Gate, and cloud whipped from Mt Alpha across the dark green trench of the upper Tauherenikau to the tiered outline of the Winchcombe-Hector arete.

"I'll bet you're mighty glad you're not on that ridge today, Paul," said Butchers. "It looks really hairy."

"You can say that again, Barney. But it wasn't all that bad," I answered with a deprecative toss of the head. Secretly, I wouldn't have been over on the Winchcombe Ridge for all the beer in Lambton Quay. The angry appearance of the ridge and of the day unsettled me, but I shrugged the feeling off: "Let's press on to Alpha Hut—hot showers and dancing girls."

This was a stock joke, the most you could say for Alpha Hut was that it gave shelter. It was cold, draughty and depressing in bad weather; a corrugated-iron outhouse with a mud floor, stuck among the dwarfed and moss-trunked beech trees close to the forest line. It was extravagantly furnished with a long wooden bush table, two hard forms and wirenetting bunks. There was a hearth for the fire, which always smouldered, a chimney that let in more air than it belched smoke, a wooden cupboard for stores and generations of hardy mice, a door, and two windows. When the wind funnelled up the Eastern Hutt River between the Marchant Ridge and the Quoin spur, the palace shook and the windows clouded with mist. Some wag, tired of the perpetual gloom of the hut, had painted a tangarine sun with garish rays on one pane and underneath the consoling caption, "The sun always shines at Alpha." Though such optimism deceived no one, the hut was a credit to its builders and it came to life and self-respect when crammed with muddy talkative trampers and the table lay heaped with great mounds of potatoes, onions, bread, butter and sausages; then laughter as well as smoke went up to the rafters.

I had been there often before and, for all its faults, I loved the hut as one does an impoverished and shabby relation who is always ready to take you in and share the little that he has. Close on nightfall we came there, glad of the rest, more concerned with food than tomorrow. We demolished a large billy of soup and beef stew, dunked our bread in successive pannikins of tea, and yarned about hill people and the hills, and university life. There was vehement discussion about the shame of Chamberlain's treaty with Hitler, and some realistic reflection on the aftermath. The certainty of war followed us even into the peace of the Tararuas; we heard more than the wind in the rumbling up the dark mountain. Alpha Hut was no escapists' Shangri-La; mountain living gave us the taste for freedom and the determination to keep it.

Tired but excited, I pottered about the hut making sure of an early start the next morning; the bread cut, the wood stacked by the fire, the plates and mugs set for breakfast. I was fussing unnecessarily and I knew it, but couldn't relax or find a satisfactory reason.

About ten I gave up and crawled into my blanket bag, but I didn't sleep. The wirenetting bunk was as pliant as a fakir's bed of nails,

the mice ran squeaking along the rafters and bickered among the
mounds of food, and someone snored across the room. Behind
the socks and shorts and jerseys hanging from a wire above the hearth,
the fire kept up a peevish mutter. The hut was filled with shadows
of yesterday, but I worried about tomorrow. Would it be fine? How
long would the crossing take? What about Arthur Fredric's knee?
He'd cut it back at Dobson's—would it stand up to the long tramp to
Kime? What if the day was stormy? Should we press on, or go back
the way we'd come? I wished I could be stronger; a good leader
wouldn't worry but take all this in his stride. The wind gusted and
then crept away. The fire died and the hut was very dark.

Morning came slowly through the windows and the hut was alive.
It was alert with questions, fragments of conversation and the smell
of cooking. There was an air of purposeful optimism, and the night
was gone.
    "Not too bad a day. I've seen worse."
    "Anyone nabbed my jersey?"
    ". . . modern teaching method is to . . ."
    "This isn't my ice-axe. Mine's a Grivel . . ."
    "Never! The Gresh has the best counter-lunch in town."
    "Better put the snarlers on. Push the billy over . . ."
    ". . . after the Capping Ball we went to a bash-up at Roger's . . ."
    "Last February on Mt Crawford we went down to the Waiohine."
    "Anyone not take milk?"
Movement and noise; people eating, talking, whistling, singing,
pulling on boots, fastening parkas, rolling sleepingbags, tying up
rucsacs. Six men in the morning, and a mountain waiting. The sounds
of a mountain hut brought back my confidence; we were young and
could do anything.
    Half an hour before dawn I went out and looked at the weather. It
wasn't good, but by 7.45 am I decided that conditions had improved
enough to justify our going on. I watched the rest file out of the hut
and heard the hollow thud and the muffled echo of the closed door.
For the instant they stood motionless around the doorway on the
frozen snow. I saw them as a group: five men in black storm
clothing in front of an empty hut, a wisp of smoke whipped from the
corrugated-iron chimney, sombre trees with snowed branches
twitching in the wind, and behind, a grey sky and the sou'west scud.
    Momentarily I felt detached, as if I had turned over a page in an
old album and had come unexpectedly on a long-forgotten photograph. Someone stamped cold feet, another made a last-minute
adjustment to clothing and each became a man I knew: Barnie
Butchers, a teacher, lean and sharpwitted, an aquiline head on thin

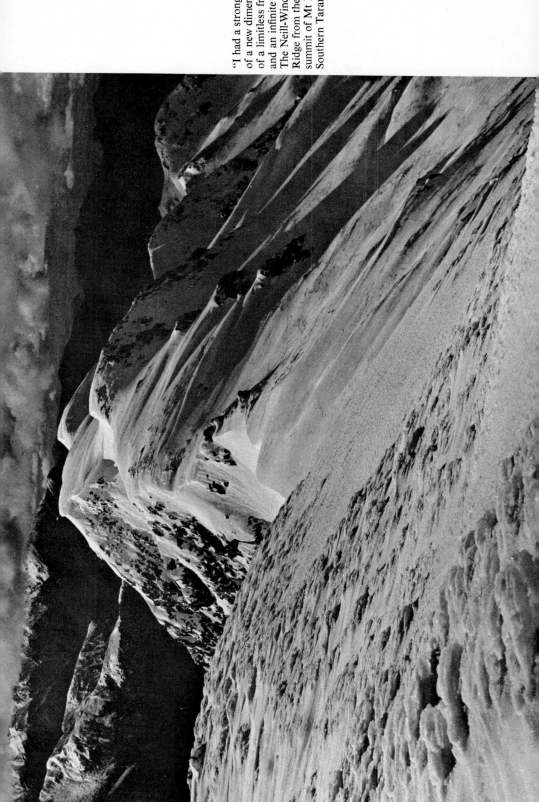

"I had a strong perception of a new dimension, of a limitless freedom and an infinite cleanness." The Neill-Winchcombe Ridge from the winter summit of Mt Hector, Southern Tararua Ranges.

"Just imagine, a roof over your head, a comfortable bunk and a warm sleeping bag. . . ."
A Southern Tararua Hut in winter.

shoulders; Roger Steele, a law student with a stubby bowsprit of a pipe clenched between cragged jaws, a deep rumbling laugh, a trick of staccato speech, blue eyes, fair hair and cheeks as red as summer apples; Arthur Fredric, quiet and dark and never idle, a short fit man who could motorbike from Wellington, kill and carry a stag haunch from the Marchant down to the road and home again the same day; Rex Collin, a friend of Fredric's, who listened and watched and thought before he spoke, small ears and curly dark hair and eyes that crinkled; and Cedric Wright, a soft voice, Celtic, a leonine head, persuasive, argumentative, a culinary Midas who could find gold from dregs of food bags.

As we moved off from the hut and up through the stunted trees, I had the sensation that part of me was left behind between the familiar past and an unknown future. Though the morning was dour and the snow sunless when we plugged over the top of Mt Alpha, the wind, steady and from the west, was reasonable by Tararua standards, and the visibility fair.

"It's going to be a sullen stomp to Kime," said someone.

"Hope they'll have the billy on," from further down the line.

A mile and a half around the Dress Circle we came to Mt Aston, which had the reputation of being one of the windiest spots in the Southern Tararuas.

"Let's keep going," I said hopefully, "the wind's no worse and we're a third of the way to Hector."

But the wind was in ambush, and the driving sleet which stormed out of the Waiotauru in a swirl of fog blew us from our steps on Mt Atkinson. We milled around like troops caught under sudden and unexpected shellfire. Fredric was the only man still in shorts. I'd suggested he put on long trousers before we left Alpha Hut but he had said the wind wasn't as cold as the winter surf at Lyall Bay. But now he decided he'd change. We anchored him while he pulled long storm trousers over his shorts. "I'm fine now," he said.

We pushed on a hundred yards and the mist came thicker and the wind harder. Quick, make a decision. Keep on, or retreat? I jabbed an arm in the direction of an unseen Mt Hector and we staggered in a wind-driven echelon over the next snow hillock. The sleet turned to snow. Somewhere close by, a high spur led off deceptively into the labyrinth of the upper Tauherenikau. Were we on that, or the correct route? Which was the way to Kime Hut? I checked by compass. The bowl was full of water and the compass card waterlogged. There was a sudden flutter in my stomach, like an eggbeater going round and round. "We'll go back to Atkinson and pick up our bearings," I said.

We backtracked wearily. Through a hole in the murk we caught

a fleeting glimpse of The Beehives. Forward again. The wind blew a
full gale now, the snow whirled in our faces, the fog came thicker
than before. Only The Beehives between us and Mt Hector now. We'd
do it yet.

But The Beehives lived up to their winter reputation, they were
iced; in high wind their steep flanks were too dangerous. At ten
past one we turned back for Alpha Hut, four miles away across the
windswept amphitheatre. Ours was no glorious retreat. Wind, fog
and sleety snow harried incessantly and we straggled head-down to
the storm with but one thought—the hut. We had taken five and a
half hours to cover a miserable few miles and this took the stuffing
out of us; in fine weather we'd have pushed on to Kime Hut in little
over an hour.

When Fredric said he wasn't feeling very well no one took much
notice. We were all close to exhaustion, and each man had temporarily reached his limit, storm and retreat dissolving our cohesion.
At the saddle on the north side of Mt Alpha, Fredric was clearly
worse, but our thinking was as sodden as the snow. We tried to
support him as we bumbled along, but couldn't manage even that.
Stops grew longer and more frequent.

Just below the top of Mt Alpha Fredric slumped into the snow.
With an effort he fumbled with the pocket of his rucsac and dragged
out a flask of brandy which he insisted on swigging. We argued with
him but couldn't stop him. We staggered around in the wind vaguely
knowing something was wrong, but were just too done to do anything about it.

Fredric perked up and we went on, Butchers, Collin and I ahead,
Steele and Wright with Fredric following slowly behind. Three men
with open mouths and glazed eyes, we jumbled together in the
vicious wind on the top of Mt Alpha, waiting . . . I was past co-
herence, and had been in front breaking trail all the way back.
Butchers and Collin were no better, but I managed to drag the top off
a tin of snow dye with my teeth and scatter it as a marker in the soggy
snow.

We went on—we were past waiting any longer. When we were
near the bushline and not far from Alpha Hut, we stopped to see
how the others were getting on. In the comparative calm of the
mountain's flank we had recovered a little, and were about to turn
back up the hill to help when we heard voices calling and calling,
urgently. Rex Collin was in a rather bad way so I took Butchers'
pack and went back up to Steele, Fredric and Wright, while he
helped Collin down to the bushline and the hut. I came on Wright
and Steele bending over Arthur Fredric who was lying in the snow,
unconscious and very pale.

"He collapsed. Said he had a terrible pain in his chest."

Steele looked at me. "We dragged him as far as we could. We're completely shot, can't go any further with him."

The parka hood had fallen off Steele's head and his fair hair, crusted with windblown snow and sleet hung over a gaunt face and too-bright eyes. "How can we get him down?"

I looked up the mountainside where the mist blew and the wind keened and the faint snowcrest met the unrelenting sky.

"Get a sheet of roof iron from the hut. Drag him down on that. Can't leave him here," Cedric Wright said.

It was Cedric who found the sheet of iron and with his ice-axe belted the holes through which we threaded the flax climbing-rope. And it was he who rallied us, led us back up the mountainside, and gave us the strength to lift Fredric on to the improvised sledge.

The journey down to Alpha Hut had an impalpable quality as if we moved in a world of blurred shadows; the inert man on the stretcher with the snow sifting into unblinking eyes, the dull grate of the iron over rocks, the white wake of corrugated furrows, the wind-tossed branches at the bushline, and the dreary forest tunnel curving down and down. I had an unreasonable impulse to shake Fredric, to see him move and to hear him speak. One of the men turned and shook a silent fist at the implacable mountain.

When we rounded the last corner in the track and came to the clearing where the hut stood it seemed so undignified to drag a man where he could walk, such an unexpected way to bring him home. But the hut didn't seem to be surprised at all. The two dark windows stared blankly as we plodded up to the door and dragged the sledge slowly inside. The hut was coldly dark, and the ashes were black in the hearth. No one spoke. We stood over Fredric utterly limp, trying to reconcile this terrible return with the verve of our morning departure.

Wright knelt in the dirt beside the sledge and felt Fredric's wrist. Then he got up and looked at us and shook his head: "No pulse, no heartbeat I can feel. I think he's dead."

We were desperate then, and lifting Fredric on to the hut table, we started artificial respiration. We worked in relays in the candlelight and handed over to the next shift only when we couldn't go on any longer. Wright had taken charge from the first. He made us eat—chocolate, sugar, anything that would give us energy—and detailed two of us to get the primus going and boil water—with tea for us, and a hot chest-pack for Fredric.

We toiled for over an hour but the figure on the table didn't respond. He was cold as stone.

"Better stop, boys," said Wright, shaking his head and gasping with fatigue. "We've done all we can, he doesn't need us now. He's dead, God rest his soul."

We flopped on the form beside the body, too unbelieving to be shocked, too worn out to feel anything. But Wright was the first to recover. With a Celtic regard for the decency as well as the awe of the occasion he did the things that death requires: the binding of the ankles, the hands and arms to the sides, the mouth and eyes closed, and other things. He did these with a sorrowful gentleness and all the time singing quietly, just as if he was putting a tired child to sleep. I had sometimes thought Wright rather a blustering man, full of blarney, but that night in Alpha Hut I saw his depth and the mystic qualities the Irish have for life and death. Mountains show men as they really are. We ate a little and went to our bunks and our thoughts. This was the first time I had seen death so bewilderingly close.

Fredric was on the table in the darkness with the wind piping a soft coronach round the creaking hut. He was dead and we were alive. I tried to work out the reason, the logic in the day and death. I had the illusion that when the dawn came and the light filtered slowly through the snow-covered window, Fredric would be waiting for us by the open door with swag on back and ice-axe in his hand. But there was no illusion in the morning, only shock and pain as we left him on the table and walked in silence through the doorway. The padbolt squealed home and we turned our back on Mt Alpha and went slowly along the gloomy forest ridge toward Hell's Gates.

"There'll be the police, and the relatives."

"Yes, of course."

And I thought of Fredric lying on the hut table, and his unknowing family at breakfast; the endless "if onlys" came with every step.

A combined Wellington Tramping Clubs party went in and brought Fredric out. I went and saw his family, whom I had not met before. There was the funeral and a cold grey sky and later the inquest. As leader of the expedition I gave evidence, an ordeal that had to be faced.

That night in Wellington I had a visit from Don Viggers and John Gabites. We talked for a while, and as they rose to go, Viggers said hesitantly, "You're not going to give up the hills, Paul?"

"I don't know, Don. I just don't know." The room was cold and bare, a chair and a table, no covering on the floor. If I gave up the mountains, I gave up my friends and the huts we'd share. "I want to keep on climbing, but . . ."

"Stop blaming yourself," said Gabites perceptively. "It wasn't your fault. The pathologist said at the inquest that Arthur Fredric had a bad heart, he could've dropped at any time."

"He died in the mountains though."

"And that's exactly why you've got to go back, at least once." Then Viggers said quickly, "How about coming south with us at Christmas? Up the Rakaia, over Whitcombe Pass and down to Cave Camp?"

"New country. And a good gang. Bernie Greig, Chas Munro, Arthur Oliver, all people you know," added Gabites.

By the time he'd rattled off the rest of the names I'd decided: "All right. I'll come—and thanks."

As I saw them out I understood what had eluded me for some days: the mountains might take, but they also gave, and friends and shelter were more important than regret.

Early that summer those of us who'd been with Fredric made a trip to Alpha Hut. We toiled up the Quoin Ridge to Mt Alpha in perfect weather when the forest was tinder-dry and the Eastern Hutt River tinkled seductively round the folds of the interlocking spurs. We spent a cheerful, reflective night in the hut and next morning put up a wall plaque we'd brought with us. I recalled then the note that John Pascoe had written me that August: "Before I was in any kind of mountain tragedy I thought that such things could happen only to other people, that I'd be immune to death; just as you can't imagine growing old and completely decrepit."

I had a last look at the plaque and round the hut as I shut the door. Alpha Hut was a good place; people lived there.

4

Cave Camp

I have never let my schooling interfere with my education.
—*Mark Twain*

THE TRIP TO THE RAKAIA grew closer. I managed to rake up enough
for the steamer fare from Wellington to Lyttelton but my boots were
worn out and I didn't fancy the prospect of wandering the Alps in
bare feet. I was due for a rise, but not until after Christmas. A week
before we were due to leave Wellington, I told Don Viggers, the
leader of the trip, that for unforeseen reasons I'd have to pull out.

"That's a pity," he said. "Sorry you can't make it, Paul."

I was more than sorry, I'd set my heart on going. Several days
later the Government messenger came over to my desk behind the
counter in the Magistrate's Court office. "It's for you, Paul," he
said wiping his forehead. "The heaviest delivery I've had for months,
feels like a couple of bricks."

I took the parcel and ripped it open. Judgment summonses and adoption orders flew off the desk in every direction, and when the paper was off I could only stare: there among the dry processes of the law reposed a brand-new pair of climbing boots with clinker nails, the leather gleaming and smelling sharp and biting. From inside the left boot I dug out a brief note, "We *want* you to come. Hope they don't give you blisters." There was no signature. Tararua trampers were like that.

I wore those boots round the office the remainder of the afternoon. When I went clumping into the Clerk of Court's office with an armful of summonses he dropped his pen and looked at me over the top of his desk. "I think you'd better take those hiker's boots off, Paul. You're shaking the building down. Haven't heard a sound like that since the New Zealand Division marched up the line to the Somme," he added with a smile that softened the usual gruffness of his voice and the deep lines around his face.

I went selfconsciously out of his office followed by the incredulous stares of solicitors and their clerks in the hallway, but I didn't care a hoot; I was already swagging up the Rakaia with my cobbers.

December 1938 was the last Christmas of peace, but war was forgotten as fifteen of us, Tararua Tramping Club and Canterbury Mountaineering Club men, passed Lake Heron and headed down the Lake Stream towards the Rakaia River. This wasn't my first climbing trip to the Southern Alps but even the weight of nine days' tucker and camping gear couldn't take the thrill from the day: the rolling foothills of long tussock, the wide river flats where matagouri clumps broke the sweep of sheep-cropped grass, gravel, and the tireless meander of the Rakaia glinting in the sun. Away in the west the high peaks beckoned a white finger and we followed, a gaggle of men and women chattering like parakeets, pointing, watching, listening, feeling the release that entry to the mountains always brings.

At dusk we stopped for the night at Thompson's Hut beside the sheep trail that wound over and down to the Rakaia. People were everywhere, and rucsacs, bits of gear, and mounds of food littered the hut. And the noise ebbed and flowed like the tide of a bright sea as we peeled potatoes, collected water from the soft night stream and hung the billies to boil from blackened hooks. Through this babel darted Viggers, a cheerfully serious hut-master who ruled his pupils with words of consideration, his face under a fawn balaclava always tipped awry. There was a tang of woodsmoke, tobacco, and the soft oily smell of wool. This was what I'd come for: a hut, some food, people, and the promise of tomorrow.

Sleeping was a problem. People lay two and even three to a bunk.

They cluttered the floor and curled up by the fireplace, but we turned inconvenience to cheerfulness and joked in the yellow candlelight. After supper and some songs we settled down and the mountain sounds came back: the sleepy creek beside the hut, night birds calling, the muted roar of the river over shingle, and the frosty creaking of the roof. I stubbed out a last cigarette and watched its red glow die.

We were astir soon after dawn, and outside the ground was hard with frost white on the tussock. Up valley a long white band of fog hid the summits but here and there the early sun came through with bright shafts which lit the riverbed and then moved over the hillsides. As I watched, a tip of snow gleamed through the mist, growing rapidly in outline and substance. Mt Lauper shimmered and swayed like a spiralling genie with two great legs astride the river and a cummerbund of diaphanous vapour at the waist. The appeal of the mountain was more mystic than physical; I could understand why the hill people of the Himalaya worshipped their peaks and had too much veneration for them to want to climb them. And that sight of Lauper was the greatest impression of the day. It was with me while we lazed in the sun round Washbourne Hut a few hours up the valley, and even my first experience of a cold and turbulent crossing of a major Canterbury river didn't subdue it.

Perhaps it might have gone if Viggers hadn't organised a tiffin of hot soup by the time we reached Duncan's Hut. This old ruin had atmosphere: if you were literal in your appreciation of the back country, the holes in the roof and the weathered mossed shingles were a poor jest under an overcast sky and chilling wind. But huts are more than halfway houses on the journey to beyond and I wanted (once I was dry) to prowl round Duncan's and listen while it gave its saga of birth and life and aching old age to the wind.

We camped that night in a patch of scrub by Lauper Stream not far from the point where it debouched into the Rakaia. The blue sky of morning had grown through afternoon to glowering cloud and falling snow, but nothing could subdue the energy of Viggers. He soon had fires going and Mavis Davidson and her cooks bending over the Christmas dinner pots. We dined well on hot mutton, green peas and plum pudding with real snow on it. Someone produced a bottle of cheap wine and long after dark there were amicable voices arguing, Watson-Munro prophesying that his breed of physicists would harness a new and revolutionary form of energy, and Stan Davis and Derek Freeman haggling in a tent across the way about the calorie and vitamin content of their favourite foods. Others played cards—bridge fiends are ubiquitous—and made their bids as matter of factly as if they were comfortably seated in a suburban sitting room. When the candles were doused and the last persistent singer had given up there was only the sound of wind in the scrub and the fresh clatter of Lauper Stream shivering its way down from Whitcombe Pass.

The morning was bright with new snow giving the peaks a dancing brilliance. The party split up, one team going over to try their luck with the Three Sisters on the Jollie Range, while the rest of us went round the bottom of the Lauper Ridge and wandered up the Ramsay Glacier. The east face of Mt Whitcombe impressed us with its ferocity, and at the head of the Ramsay neve Erewhon Col was an inviting curve leading to the Bracken ice plateau and the stronghold of Mt Evans. North of Erewhon Col the Amazon's Breasts burgeoned rounded and virginal white. Ruapehu apart, this was my first essay on glacier ice. I cut tentative steps, prodded hairline cracks in the flaky ice and gawked at the crenellated towers on the soaring Main Divide.

Breaking camp the next morning, always a time of mixed reactions, we left the few cut sticks of tentpoles as the only evidence of our passage and walked up toward Whitcombe Pass. With the imprint of Samuel Butler's *Erewhon* still sharp I almost hoped that we'd come to the Pass on a day of mist and wind and see the monolith rocks like graven statues. But the day was clear and sunny and the rocks on the summit of the Pass neither held any mystery nor gave any fugal recital. We climbed Mt Martius to the north of the Pass. Martius was a delightful adventure, snow all the way and a widening panorama of Mt Evans and the lush greens of Westland rolling to the sea. The day was very hot, and on the way down to the Pass someone easily persuaded me to plunge into a glacial pool where the melt ran fresh from the ice. The shock was unexpected—a long drawing-in of breath and a vow never to do it again, but I sat while shutters clacked and the cold bit like a vice. The shadows of late afternoon crept over the Pass as we ambled leisurely down the Whitcombe River toward Cave Camp. The headwaters of Westland rivers are deceptively gentle places and that somnolent afternoon the upper park of the Whitcombe was a demesne for lotus eaters: high tussock, bronze-red scrub and white mountain flowers in long green collars. In Canterbury the air was sharp and dry and clear, but here there was a conspiracy among the hills, the slow drift of flat-based cumulus and the softly purpling haze working a languid magic. There was no compulsion to hurry and we forgot objectives, timetables, and the logistics of the march; life was for sitting and talking, for watching and for silence.

The delusion that travel in Westland was all flowers and fleecy clouds soon ended when the Whitcombe River became a water-misted gouge twisting down between thick rainforest and glaciated bluffs.

My euphoric daydreams left me and I was captive to a new sensation, that of power. The Canterbury hills strolled to the sea with easy courtesy, with a wellbred affectation of boredom, but the Whitcombe was blunt, it knew it was strong and it told you so. The ridges, the ice, and the crags of Westland weighted you with their power, and the river, shouldering them aside in its hurry for the sea, was their mouthpiece. The Whitcombe didn't talk, it trumpeted. The wildness of the country and its river gave me their mood and I hurried down the winding track in the forest in a flare of excitement. We came to Cave Camp at dusk just as the last sun tipped the summit of Mt Evans and the first moreporks were *quor-cooing* from lofty perches in the forest. An exploratory star peered over the shoulder of Park Dome and the warm night air rattled with the noisy flight of beetles. Many places may in realisation, be poor reflections of imagination, but my preview of Mt Evans so excited me that I could hardly wait for morning.

Nor was I disappointed with Cave Camp. There was room enough for only a few of us on the sandy floor and the overflow were banished to tents, one on each side of the cave entrance. But I was in the Cave with the sandflies, the mosquitoes, and the occasional longlegged weta. I'd known tent camps, I'd dossed under logs in pouring rain, but I'd never spent a night under a bivvy rock before. That night in Cave Camp was for me a zenith of contentment, all the romantic elements were there: the candled shadows curving and bobbing on the rock wall, the hollow reverberating note of the river and the warm foetal comfort of darkness. My passion for shelter rocks was formed that night as I lay with a good meal under my belt, a pipe in hand, and an ear to the hill talk of the old hands. There was woodsmoke too, the sharper, more acrid smell of Westland timber. I ran my fingertips along the gritty cave wall; it felt good.

I was awake at dawn. Mt Evans was an angry impasto of dull red rock, hanging ice and cloud serpents framed in the scrub spurs of the Jourdain Cone, Park Dome and Mt Thorndike. The river was black, veined with running streaks of white, roaring in anticipation of rain. In spite of the gloomy morning we were cheerful with the predatory urge that a good night's shelter gives to mountaineers.

Four of us, Bernie Greig, me, John Gabites and Chas Watson-Munro, thought we'd attempt Mt Thorndike. We were away early up the Wilkinson River. Travelling was typically Westland, rough, scrubby and high with boulders. A side creek led up to the tussock line where grey bands of mist were waiting to meet us on a ridge that led easily enough by lustreless snow and wet rock to a virgin summit at six and a half thousand feet. A second party led by Stan

Davis and Derek Freeman joined us on the top. In our descent we followed Stan Davis plunging down a long snow couloir, singing and yodelling to an easy run-out in a rocky valley.

The following day brought rain, a flooded river, and a wind which worried the bush edge scrub. The sandflies and the mosquitoes counterattacked us and we lay swollen-eyed in our bags. I smeared myself with a paste of kerosene and cooking fat, and was relatively immune to the beasties but shunned by my fellows. The seasoned men in the party spent the day in smoking, argument and pleasant reminiscence but I made several impatient trips outside the cave to see what the weather was doing.

After I had crawled my way over them at least half a dozen times, Stan Davis protested: "Why don't you relax, Paul? You're in and out of your bag like an old man with the skitters."

"Blasted rain," I grumbled. "What a waste of a good climbing day."

"You'd better resign yourself to a day in the sack," said Viggers. "If you're going to become a good mountaineer you'll have to learn to take the wet with the fine."

"It might clear up soon," I replied stubbornly.

"Look, son," Davis wagged a finger at me, "when you've been around the Alps a bit more, you'll learn that bad weather and mountain men don't mix. This rain's set in for the day. Make the best of it. You could be up there in the storm."

"OK Stan," his logic was undeniable, "but isn't there something we can do?"

"Well, as a matter of fact, there is," he drawled. "You can help Derek Freeman and me. We've got a little job to do. But lord love a duck, let's have breakfast first. It's only half past six."

After the meal, Davis called me over. "Here's the plate Derek and I are going to fix to the side of the cave. It's in memory of Norm Dowling. We were with him when he died on the McKenzie Glacier after we'd climbed Evans last year. On a fine day you can see the glacier from here quite plainly."

When we'd drilled the holes in the rock and set the bronze tablet Davis stood back and admired the result. "Not too bad considering the few tools we had to work with."

The sound of the wind and the river in spate came strongly through the momentary silence. "He was a hell of a good bloke, old Norm. One of the best . . . And I'm glad you're here, Paul. You were with him on the Winchcombe Ridge on Mt Hector, weren't you?"

"Yes, in September last year. Three months before he came down here." I was back in the Tararuas struggling over to Mt Hector and down to the shelter of Kime Hut, but I could live with the images of

Dowling and of Fredric now. The mountains had given me back far more than I had thought they had taken.

The following day we packed up and headed down the Whitcombe. As we climbed into harness and faced toward the track that led out to the West Coast I was more settled than I'd been the evening we came to Cave Camp. Peaks were incidental, cover and companionship came first.

"Had any thoughts on where you're going next Christmas?" asked Davis as we swung along the trail with the receding symmetry of Mt Evans framed in the descending bush ridges.

"Anywhere there are mountains, Stan," I answered vaguely. "Up another West Coast river perhaps. I like this country."

"Why not the Perth then? It's a branch of the Whataroa. And there's an unclimbed peak in there, a beauty. It's called The Great Unknown."

5

The Great Unknown

I cannot rest from travel: I will drink Life to the lees.
—Ulysses, *Lord Tennyson*

I DIDN'T REALLY CARE what sort of a mountain The Great Unknown might turn out to be, it was the name that attracted. There was also the added bonus that the mountain hadn't been climbed. Then I found out that "Bonk" (A. H.) Scotney, who had been over Perth Col from the Rangitata the previous year, was also harbouring thoughts about the mountain. We joined forces and Jim (J. H.) Croxton agreed to make up a third. But the man in Wellington who knew most about the Great Unknown was John Pascoe, who had done much original and enterprising climbing exploration in what was known as "The Garden of Eden", and Pascoe was its geographer as well as its hovering angel. The Great Unknown was the sou' western cornerpost of his country; how would he react if he knew we were contemplating trespass, the unforgiveable alpine crime?

"Go and see him," said Scotney. "He won't eat you."

So off I went to Johnny for information. This took some courage and a fair amount of cheek, for Pascoe had already attempted the mountain under adverse conditions and had given it a bad fright. I needn't have worried. When I rather diffidently broached the subject he said, generously, "Help yourself to The Great Unknown. I don't own it."

But his attitude went further than that. He gave us firsthand information, lent us his photo album, and passed on all the tips he'd garnered from his Perth-Adams explorations. He also gave his pontifical blessing: "Wish I was coming with you," he added when I saw him again just before Christmas.

There still remained one major problem, how were we going to get from Christchurch to Whataroa in South Westland? There was a war on, and bus services were cut down.

"Don't worry," said Scotney, "we'll find a way. Let's get to Christchurch first. Something will turn up."

When we got to Christchurch it seemed that nothing had turned up but obstacles. There wouldn't be transport south along the West Coast from Hokitika to Whataroa for two days.

"That's torn it," said Croxton, pulling a long face.

"We can always alter our plans, go up to Arthurs Pass. And there's the Waimak," I offered with a small show of optimism. We sat morbidly on the hard wooden seat of the railway station watching the Christmas crowds hurrying to their carriages.

Suddenly Scotney got up. "Well," he said briskly, "I'll see you blokes later. Just remembered I've got some business to do."

"How long are you going to be?" said Croxton suspiciously.

"Meet you back here in an hour. Outside the main entrance to the station." And he was gone, shouldering his way through the throng.

Croxton and I went and had a cup of tea and a pie. The tea was like something that had come out of a ship's side, and the pie had a crust that a gorilla would break its teeth on. The meat inside was as tough as chopped-up violin strings. But we were hungry. Sharp on time we went to the front of the station. Taxis and cars came and went, but no sign of Scotney.

"I reckon he's done a bunk."

"He wouldn't do that," I said incredulously. "Bonk doesn't do things like that."

Croxton was about to launch into a really lurid fantasy on Scotney's whereabouts when a Chrysler tourer with gleaming brown paintwork pulled in with a flourish of turning wheels and Scotney thrust his head out from under the canvas hood. "Don't stand there gawking, hop in and let's get down the road."

Croxton and I threw our gear into the back seat and wedged ourselves alongside Scotney. No one spoke until we'd passed the city limits and were burring along the main road west. Scotney reclined against the leather upholstery with the incidental aplomb of a magnate who, having given the chauffeur the day off, was enjoying a quiet spin by himself in the Rolls. With an easy elbow resting over the door and a cigarette cocked elegantly from the angle of his mouth, he whistled softly and beat time with three fingers of his left hand on the steering wheel. A sporty tweed hat set racily over definite eyebrows, a patrician nose, high cheekbones and a strong-angled jaw complemented the picture.

Puzzled, elated, but infuriated by his careless assurance, I couldn't be silent. "Nice car, Bonk."

"Yes, not bad."

The speedometer drum hovered round the fifty mark.

Croxton put the question that was worrying me, "Did you hire it, Bonk?"

"No."

The telephone posts at the verge of the road flicked by. The car sang as sweetly as a skylark.

"You didn't pinch it?" I ventured.

"Don't be daft." Scotney took the butt from his mouth and flicked it out of the car in an extravagant arc. "Waal," he drawled, "if you bums *must* know, I bought it."

"You what?"

"That's right. I drove a hard bargain with a secondhand car shark. Cost me a hundred bucks."

We goggled at him; this was mountaineering in the grand manner.

"Well," said Scotney with incontrovertible logic, "you want to get to Whataroa, don't you?"

"Of course, but what about the money? I haven't got enough to buy the back wheel."

"Chickenfeed, think nothing of it," said Scotney expansively. "It's just that I've got a weakness for Chryslers. And so, I hope, have lots of other people. I'll sell it again when we get back to Christchurch."

We had a breakdown at Hokitika but Scotney dragooned a sleepy mechanic into reluctant repairs. On the winding road near Hari Hari we nearly hit a logging truck and only avoided collision by running off the road and careering up a mossy bank.

"Friendly people, these West Coasters," said Bonk. "That guy was so close I could have shaken hands with him."

About 10 am on a warm but cloudy West Coast morning we rolled into Eric Berry's homestead near Whataroa. Scotney had met the Berrys on his way out from the Perth the year before. The family welcomed us with the easy and genuine hospitality of their province, fed us with hot scones and great cups of tea, and pressed us to stay for lunch. Would we stay for the evening meal? There was wild pork on the menu. In a country where time is second to friendship we tactfully explained that we wanted to cross the Whataroa footbridge and make Hughes Creek Hut by nightfall.

"Sorry you can't stay," said Mrs Berry, puzzled at our obvious impatience to be off. "One night wouldn't delay you too much. The weather's not settled and the hills will still be there tomorrow."

Our mouths watered at the vision of roast wild pork and golden crackling, but we left; we were city folk, and time was our burden, not a means to living.

We had scarcely walked a mile before I was regretting Mrs Berry's roast pork spluttering inside the kitchen oven; rain was falling, and seventy pounds of swag cut into my shoulders and chafed my waist. At the Whataroa-Perth junction we clomped over the swing bridge, missed the track and wasted two hours' sweat trying to barge through the luxuriant shrubbery of the lower Perth. The track to Hughes Creek Hut, when we found it, led up a steep zigzag to a dismal swampy plateau in the dense rainforest where we wandered like water hens. When Hughes Creek hove in sight we were a silent trio too tired to find the hut, and we camped by the creek side. After a meal of sausages and soya beans we went early to bed to the accompaniment of rain drumming on the roof and the thin *coo-eet* of night raiding wekas prowling round the tent.

Next morning after a four-hour tramp we reached the Bluff Camp beside the Perth River.

"We'll camp here," said Scotney, pointing to a soggy clearing just above the Perth. "It's nice and close to water."

I guffawed. Croxton looked at the dripping foliage and remarked that water was the one thing we didn't need to worry about as there was plenty of the stuff all around us. But when the site was cleared and the fly stretched taut over the tent we became more companionable; we had a home again, a place for shelter, and maybe afterdinner controversy. With Bonk in the party there was always plenty of that, and we all thrived on it. (I think we went into the Perth because of it.)

Bonk came back from the river and stood with arms akimbo where Jim and I were struggling with the fire. "Our worries are over, men. There's a deerculler's cage across the river."

"Goodoh. Now I won't get my feet wet," I said. I was secretly relieved.

"When the site was cleared and the fly stretched taut over the tent, we had a home again, a place for shelter. . . ."
The Bluff Camp beside the Perth River.

"We sat in the cage and pulled on the hemp rope until we reached the far side. . . ."
Bonk Scotney crossing flooded Scone Creek.

"There she is," said Bruce, "Mount Tasman, the Queen of the Alps. . . ."
From left: Silberhorn, Tasman, and Syme's Ridge. From the Malte Brun Range.

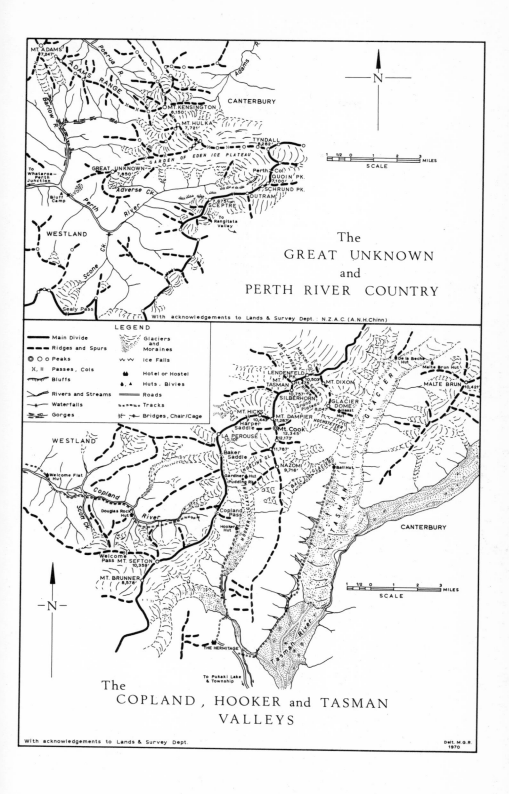

The
GREAT UNKNOWN
and
PERTH RIVER COUNTRY

With acknowledgements to Lands & Survey Dept.: N.Z.A.C. (A.N.H.Chinn)

LEGEND

Main Divide	Glaciers and Moraines
Ridges and Spurs	
Peaks	Ice Falls
Passes, Cols	Hotel or Hostel
Bluffs	Huts, Bivies
Rivers and Streams	Roads
Waterfalls	Tracks
Gorges	Bridges, Chair/Cage

The
COPLAND, HOOKER and TASMAN
VALLEYS

With acknowledgements to Lands & Survey Dept.

Delt. M.G.R.
1970

All the way up from Berrys' we had talked of how we were going to climb The Great Unknown but no one ever mentioned how we were going to get across the Perth. It wasn't a river to trifle with. Swift and deep and authoritative, it was the main barrier to the mountain; like the sandflies which continually plagued us, it was always there, an obstacle cutting us off from our peak. John Pascoe had told me that he thought the best approach to the peak was his route from Adverse Creek in the upper headwaters of the Perth Valley, but I was keen to try from lower down the river. For one thing, from photographs our side looked as if it might be easier, and for another, it could save days of unnecessary walking. I was never keen on excessive swagging as a means to alpine virtue.

"It's all decided then," said Bonk after we'd argued for a whole hour after the evening hoosh. "Let's be sissies and try the easy way. Tomorrow we cross the river by the cage and head up the bush to the scrubline. From there on it's anybody's guess."

"Worth a go."

"I think so too," said Jim scratching at the red sandfly mounds on his forearm. "We've got a clear fortnight. At the worst we'll only waste two days."

The next morning we climbed into the cage and ferried ourselves over to the north bank of the Perth. The journey was exhilarating. The cage, a wooden tray with steel brackets, hung from two rusted wheels which ran on a wire cable stretched across the river. We sat in the box with legs dangling high above the foaming river and pulled on the hemp rope until we reached the far side. This was the theory, but the practice was rather more exciting. Bonk was the first to try. He gave a heave and the cage ran down the incline of the sagging wire rope, but halfway across the river, when he was starting the long uphill haul to the far side, the cage began swaying from side to side. The amount of swing was small at first but increased rapidly and alarmingly. We watched Scotney with a mixture of amusement and concern as he fought to keep control; he looked like a black parrot swinging on a wildly gyrating perch. Then Croxton and I went through the same ridiculous performance while Bonk yelled advice and laughed at us as we each came over.

We scouted around and eventually picked up a light blaze which led up in a north-easterly direction through forest, and near the bushline, through a belt of horizontal scrub. Three hours after leaving the cage we came to tussock, thick mist and light but penetrating rain. The purpose of the day was to find a reasonable place to pitch our high camp. For two and a half hours we stumbled around in the mist but found nothing feasible. The ridge was too exposed and devoid of shelter and the snowgrass basin no more than a weeping sewer. We slid down the hill to our camp across the river and our glumness went with food and shelter. We held our carol service by candlelight and hoped that Christmas would bring us the one present we wanted above all others: a clear and sunny day. It didn't.

By 2 pm on Boxing Day we were back above the scrub in clear weather. It was a different mountainside. The sun was warm and our spirits high as we dug out a platform in the snowgrass at 4,500 feet. Blackbirds whistled from the scrub, and far below the Perth went shining down to the coast, winding through the green forest, red with pockets of flaming rata. But by late afternoon the mist was back and with it rain which seeped into the tent and made a quagmire of our diminutive perch.

During the night the wind grew stronger and about 2 am I awoke with a slap of cold wet canvas in the face. The tent had blown down. Though we cursed the weather, the wet boggy hillside, and the idiot urge which had brought us in search of The Great Unknown, we crawled out and made repairs to chafed guy ropes and a disintegrating tent platform. Bonk sang and Jim whistled while I bailed out the accumulated water. When they came dripping back inside the tent I was intrigued not only by their cheerfulness but also by the reason for it. Why should men be cheerful and helpful to each other in circumstances which by city standards were ludicrous? After that night, more unpleasantly inconvenient than dangerous, we were a team.

"You know Bonk, I've discovered something?" I said as I tied the tapes that secured the doorway.

"And what's that, Paul?"

"I've just realised we're not mad to be up here."

"Is that so?" replied Scotney with a satirical lift to his eyebrows.

"No, the trouble with us, and all the other blokes who knock around the hills, is exactly the opposite. We're horribly, horribly sane."

"With emphasis on the horribly," came the muffled comment from Croxton as he burrowed deeper into his bag.

"Mr Powell," Bonk shook his head in ponderous amazement, "I think you've got something there. You're showing signs of at last beginning to grow up . . . Put the billy on, and we'll have a toddy of cocoa to celebrate."

Just after eight that morning Croxton pushed through the tent flap. "If you want to climb the mountain today, you'd better do something about it."

"What?"

"Is it fine?"

"Not exactly," Croxton replied with the understandable caution of all meteorologists, "but it looks as if it could be. The rain's stopped and the mist is clearing."

Nothing rouses turbid mountaineers more than the cry of "The weather's clearing." Meals are thrown together and eaten with impatient scraping of plates, boots materialise over socked feet, food, gear, and storm clothing are thrown into swags, and the surprised inmates erupt on to the mountainside.

The higher we climbed the more the day improved. The snow-grass basin where we'd camped, with the tent a vanishing white jot in a sea of yellow and green, changed to a very dismantled and serrated rock ridge going up to the north-east. We went at the first hurdles that the mountain set up against us like colts entered in a steeplechase and then, winded and hungry, we stopped and ate.

"Good place for a picnic," said Bonk, opening a tin of sardines with his ice-axe. "Now, I'm all for home rule for Scotland but I reckon the capitalists ought at least to provide sardine tins that will open. Why do the keys always break?"

Jim cut slices of Bell's Brick, the standard wholemeal loaf of Canterbury's mountaineering 1930s, wonderful stuff with a nutty flavour which gave a satisfying full feeling. You couldn't bolt that bread, you developed the jaw muscles of an adventure-strip hero. I topdressed the slices with honey and thin slices of raw onion, a favourite tribute to the art of gastronomy taught me by Bonk. We loitered as long as we could until we remembered that we were supposed to be climbing a mountain.

Grovelling our way up a chimney in the rock ridge, we came to a snowfield which dipped down to a saddle and then gained a fair measure of alpine respectability by transforming itself into a steepish snow ledge leading to the summit. Crevasses and rockfalls enough to make us cautious, and hard granular snow dusted with the recent south-west storm, made us work for our mid-afternoon success. A cold southerly mist blew across the final ridge, which resolved itself not into one summit, but three, each with overhanging cornices jutting over the clouded anonymity of the upper Perth Valley. It wasn't a day for arguing which snow dome was higher, but we stood in the passing murk and quibbled while the pebbles of ice rattled against us. We observed the laws as well as the spirit of gentlemanly debate with no voices raised, no personalities. We might have been at a university open forum.

"Sense as well as dialectics tells me the nearest cornice is the highest point," said Scotney.

"As a scientist," objected Croxton, "my observation tells me the farthermost point's the highest."

"It's too cold for casuistry," I insisted. "If you blokes had an atom of commonsense, you'd agree with me. The middle bump is the true summit."

But we didn't fight on such an important point of honour, we traversed each summit in turn, built a cairn on each of the northern tops, and left a note of our tenuous occupation.

I refused to leave until I'd lit my pipe, sucked down a few conquering puffs, and defaced the unfortunate mountain with a litter of matches and blown wisps of tobacco. We didn't have our national flag to plant triumphantly on the summit, no one said anything pompous about conquest, but we smiled as much as you can with hail driving in the face, and shook numbed hands. A fleeting hole opened in the mist and far below we caught a short glimpse of The Garden of Eden Ice Plateau. If the name of our mountain sounded grandiloquent at sea level, at the aneroid reading of 8,300 feet it was apt. The Great Unknown was the mystery that we felt on this cornerpost of wild and rugged country. Out of the summit cloud, we slid yodelling down to the saddle and sat drowsing in the sun.

Scotney was indefatigable around the camp. He made our celebration feast of pemmican stew, tinned peaches, and chocolate sauce. Then we sat in the dry tussock as the moon swelled as full and rounded as an apple behind the Godley peaks; they were golden spires and the valleys were a sheeny soft black. The bite of frost sent us to bed to smoke cigars and talk reminiscently of the eventful day. The night was very still and the sleepy murmur of the distant creeks came clearly through the night. This was the Westland I'd come to find, and to enjoy.

The reason for our interest in The Great Unknown was more than the climb as we had hoped to clear up some points about the topography. Four years before, A. F. Pearson, H. A. McDowall, H. M. Sweeny and John Pascoe had accomplished an epic transalpine crossing from the Rangitata River headwaters to the upper basin of the Adams River in Westland. For the first time many of the features of The Garden of Eden Ice Plateau were explored and named. Curiosity about the unmapped country at the head of the Poerua and Barlow River systems led them to the virgin summits of Mt Kensington (8,150 feet) and Mt Hulka (7,721 feet), but heavy mist shrouded the mountains and they saw nothing of the headwaters of the Poerua River. When we left Wellington we were as eager to do something to unravel the mystery as we were to make the first ascent of The Great Unknown. Pascoe's last words to us were,

"Hope you boys get the peak, but even more I hope you sort out the country west of Kensington and The Great Unknown."

The morning after our successful climb we slept in until eight; the sun was already high, the day perfect, and my inclinations were for a day of ease in the tussock.

But Jim Croxton thought otherwise: "We ought to go up again," he said, "and take some photos. We didn't see a thing yesterday."

"What? Climb the same virgin twice in twenty-four hours?" Scotney said in mock horror. "Can't do that. Ain't ethical."

"Oh no!" I chipped in. The thought of those thousands of feet to climb again was too much.

"All the same," Croxton persisted with an earnest furrowing of his forehead, "we should. It's a wonderful chance to clear up all the uncertainty about whether the western end of The Garden of Eden drains into the Poerua or the Barlow."

In my laziness I couldn't have cared for an instant where that ice ran to—I wanted to potter around for the day. Croxton had his way. Shortly after 1 pm we were back on a summit that repaid our reluctant sweat a hundredfold. For some time we didn't speak, but just sat on the high rocks and watched.

"Now I know why this peak's called The Great Unknown," said Scotney, shielding his eyes against the sharp clear light. "Just look at it. Miles and miles of new country, icefields and summits everywhere. Bush, rivers, sun."

"There's so much to see, Bonk. I don't know where to look first."

We sat there in the sun with a hint of south-easterly breeze. Everywhere mountains slashed the blue sky in effortless symmetry, Evans across in the Whitcombe country, D'Archiac overlord of the Rangitata, Elie de Beaumont and Cook haze-softened and inviting in the south. There was an order in the balance between earth and sky that spoke of more than chance: this was creation.

Croxton was the first to shake off the spell. "We'd better record all this," he said, taking out his camera and shooting a continuous panorama. I took compass bearings and drew a sketch map of the jumbled country to the west and north. Scotney copied down the bearings as I called them out, arbitrated our wrangles over which peak was what, and pointed out the long trench of the upper Perth River running back to the glistening ice of the Main Divide. Then he stopped as if words alone could not describe the scene.

"Tennyson's *Ulysses* was made for this country. 'I cannot rest from travel: I will drink Life to the lees.' . . . Good stuff."

"Go on, Bonk."

"Enough for now. We're here to survey."

We gave ourselves to photography and amateur mapmaking. When two hours later we regretfully left and wandered down the snow of lengthening shadows we still carried the summit mood with us, a satisfaction that came from more than a victory confirmed. We'd proved that the whole of the heavily-glaciated western end of the Garden of Eden fell sharply not into the Poerua but into the North Barlow River. Don Viggers's party came over Perth Col and down one of the Barlow tributaries that month and confirmed what we had seen.

By late afternoon we were back at our high camp in the tussock. The forest below rang with bird sounds, the mellow repetitive tinkling of bellbirds, kakas with peculiarly grating calls, and the rapid *zipt-zipt* of the riflemen. When evening came the vesper flutings of blackbirds rose from the last reaches of alpine scrub and then died away as darkness and the moon rose from the black shadows of the hills.

"It's been a great day," said Jim. "Even better than yesterday."

It had always been part of the plan to go into the upper Perth Valley. Bonk spoke of this secluded glacial basin hard under the main range in such enthusiastic terms that he continually stirred our curiosity. The afternoon that we came down from The Great Unknown for the second time I suggested that instead of returning to the valley floor and swagging a laborious way up the Perth River we ought to try and find a high-level route to the headwaters: "It seems a bit goofy to waste all our lovely height. Here we are camped at over four thousand feet. All we've got to do is to keep on walking round the shoulder of The Great Unknown and we're there."

The afternoon was one of those peerless Westland days when the benignity of sun and rolling hills made anything appear a certainty.

The next day we went down to our base camp in the Perth and carried up enough food for a week. Thick mist hung motionless over the mountain the following morning, excuse enough to enjoy a leisurely breakfast and three hours of indolence while we argued with Bonk about the ethics of the Russo-Finnish war. By 11 am the debate tailed off and reminded us that we really ought to be up and away. Breaking camp, we fumbled off into the mist, building rock cairns as we went. Our pace was that of happy potterers without a hounding timetable. We blamed the whiteout for the delays, but the frequency with which we stopped to talk or to fossick in the tussocked creek basins proved that our mood was one of enjoyment rather than set-jawed discovery. We were men wandering with their home on their backs, gipsies of the alpine meadow. There was no complaint about our tardy progress, nothing of the intensity of the military campaign that turns so many mountaineers into slaves of the clock.

Even when the mist broke to blue islands we kept the same intermittent and unhurried pace, Scotney a few yards above me up the hill leaning on his axe and his strong baritone rolling back from the encircling rocks, Croxton fifty yards below picking over the rocks and whistling quietly to himself. We floated rather than walked around the mountainside, each of us responding to the hill in his own way. Often we were silent, sometimes we sang together; usually we walked spread in a straggling line like careful skirmishers, and fresh surprises awaited us in every hidden gully.

We went far enough to see that my high-level route was a summer's day illusion and that the ridge on to The Great Unknown from Adverse Creek barred our easy way with rock towers and steep ice gullies. We'd have to follow the conventional river way into the Perth park. Before we turned back to our high camp-site in the lower Perth we had a last scan around and ate our cheese and bread and drank cool snow water from the unnamed creek.

"Doesn't look far," said Croxton wistfully. "Only spitting-distance from here to the park at the head of the Perth."

"Sorry about the route, bit of a fizzer," I said apologetically.

"Nonsense!" from Bonk. "We didn't come here to survey a damned road, but to enjoy ourselves, and we have. We've had a day to mull over for the rest of our lives. When we're toothless and bald and shaky and even the grandkids are bored with us, there'll still be this day to come back to."

As we passed through the hanging valley where the high snow melt from The Great Unknown ran flashing over the cirque walls and slipped quietly between the profusion of alpine buttercups, I knew Scotney was right. Next morning we folded the tent and went slowly down the hill. Just as we entered the scrub, brigand keas started plundering our old camp-site. I looked up and saw them outlined against the cold ridge and the whipping cloud and heard their long nostalgic calling from the hill.

"It was a good camp," said Jim.

There were compensations as we swagged up the Perth. We had a memorable New Year's night at Scone Creek where the lightning flared and the thunder came rolling down from Sealy Pass. Close to the roaring water we found a cave with a sandy floor and drew lots who should first eat from an ancient tin of bully beef. Was it a relic of Teichelmann's 1924 expedition to the Perth?

"Tonight," said Bonk, stirring the meat into the evening stew, "we'll be eating alpine history."

"Let's hope there's enough of it," I said.

The rain kept on all New Year's Day and wet us from scalp to toenail. There was flickering candlelight and the high thin whine of predatory mosquitoes by night, and hot springs by day. Then we pushed on, clambering beside the foaming river or searching for the elusive smear of track in filthy scrub and vine-tangled forest. But our tent home came with us and eventually we came to the promised land, a little thinner and hungrier, but satisfied. In all the trip, the camps were the stay of our nomad life, and the camp in the upper Perth was the best of them all. We set up house on a mossy flat among the tussock and the wilderness. It was an elysium of giant white buttercups—the leaves were so huge we used them as cups—celmisias, and slender gentians. The Perth Glacier moaned and groaned at night, and petulant rocks fell down the shattered ribs from The Garden of Eden ice. By day clouds drifted slowly and sent their broken patterns across the grey shards of the moraine. Avalanches plumed and rattled off the hanging ice of the Main Divide. There was a purple haze over the inner cirque where we'd camped, and in noonday a drowsy deep stillness, a Xanadu atmosphere which made us forget we'd come to climb. The mountains were very old and infinitely wiser than we: they had time, but ours was almost gone.

We were a quiet crew on the morning that we packed to leave. When you've camped and climbed together long enough you know what other men feel and think without words.

"I wonder where we'll be in a year's time," I said. But I took the smoky taste of bush tea, the blood-red rata, the green forest, the mountains, and the nights of camps and friends with me to war. They were my citadel.

6

Hills of War

No more shall I see on a day of still weather
Far range upon range to infinity dwindle,
Snow crowned and ice-girdled, all slumbering together,
Erebus and Arrowsmith and D'Archiac and Tyndall.

—Arnold Wall
The Old Botanist's Farewell to the Southern Alps

I VOLUNTEERED FOR NAVY SERVICE overseas in April 1940, but didn't leave New Zealand until that December. The last few months were precious and I was away in the Tararuas almost every weekend. But if the ranges were the same, the huts were different. One weekend you tramped with a man as if you and he still had the years together in the hills, the next weekend he was gone. The war didn't take friends, it spirited them away. The effect was bewildering. The huts were filled with ghost faces and voices, tricks of speech and idiosyncracies of manner. I enjoyed the hills and the huts with a greater intensity and was loth to give them up, yet I couldn't escape the restlessness that followed us on every tramp and came into every hut at dusk. The shadows were peopled when the candles were lit. We laughed and sang and tramped with great vigour, but the wistfulness was inescapable.

Easter came nearer. I had a last fling with Tararua and Canterbury Mountaineering Club friends. We slogged up the stony Waimakariri and camped on Harman Pass in cold driving hail. At midnight the storm lifted and the stars were ice chips. The frost burned on the snowgrass and the moon came rounded over the dark mountain ridges. The night was full of the challenged roaring of mating stags, and the fathomless Westland creeks were whispering with invitation. We shivered underneath the frost-stiffening canvas and talked until dawn. In the early morning we crossed back into Canterbury over the Whitehorn Pass and ambled down to the Park-Morpeth Hut for a luncheon snack. The dry scrub crackled under the billy and our offering of blue smoke rose lazily into the windless mountain sky. The tea was tinged with the taste and smell of the hill. Then up to Browning Pass, where the small iron-roofed hut was monopolised by a dusty relic of the Westland goldrush days: a miner's bellows as tall as a shoulder. The leather windbag was as dry and wrinkled as an old musterer's weathered skin and as wheezy as his tobacco cough. In the Westland evening we went down the Styx where the air was clear with the foretaste of winter and the hut tucked itself under the forest fringe. The lush grass of the flat and the hiphigh fern were beaded with whitening dew. There were the same hut sounds and smells and laughter until John Gabites said, "How many more Easters must pass until we're all in the hills again?"

A year to the day after Scotney, Croxton and I had arrived in the Chrysler at Whataroa, I left New Zealand in the *Rimutaka*. Our small convoy was escorted by HMNZS *Monowai*. Even at sea there was a link to the hill life now fast receding: Roger Steele, who had been with me on the unhappy Mt Alpha trip, was a signalman aboard the *Monowai*. When several days out from Auckland the *Monowai* left us with a flickering of signal lamps—a brief "Good luck" winking from her bridge—I thought my last tie with the hills of home had gone. But the mountains of the future were closer than I knew, for it was aboard *Rimutaka* that I first met Geoff Baylis who was after the war to share so many Aspiring adventures with me.

The navy kept us busy while we did our preliminary training at HMS *Ganges* near Ipswich. There were forty-five of us, and there wasn't too much time for thinking about hills or home as we were caught up in the excitement of war and the expected invasion of Britain.

When in early April 1941 we went down to Chatham Naval Barracks to await drafting to ships, the cold facts of living in a strange country at war came home to us. We were split into small groups and dispersed to destroyers, minesweepers, motor torpedo boats, or light cruisers. I went, with two other New Zealanders, to Liverpool on draft to HMS *Harvester*, a destroyer of the polyglot and strenuously overworked Liverpool Escort Force. There were times when I hated the sea and times when I loved it, and there were fleeting moments when the destroyer messdeck had the same hubbub as a crowded hut, and the disciplines of the sea and the mountains were fundamentally similar. Both could be dangerous, wet and stormy places. Though I settled down to sea life fairly quickly I was never able entirely to get over my hankering for the hills. Other men had their pin-ups, girlfriends, wives, seductive popsies on the grey steel bulkheads; I had mine, a photograph of Mt Tasman.

"Queer taste you've got, chum," said an English rating, peering up at the long ice ridge of New Zealand's second-highest mountain. "Too frigid for me, any road." He laughed. "Can't take her to the Palais de Danse."

"Maybe not, but she's got one great advantage, Nobby."

"Eh, and what's that?"

"I can be sure she won't have run off with some great bone-headed soldier while I'm away at sea."

I must have caught him on the raw, for he never poked fun at my pin-up again.

When leave came round, a week, or even a few hours, I headed for the country. The towns were drab, dark and dirty and on two bob a day I didn't have either the inclination or the resources for the more usual and sophisticated enjoyments. Even beer was scarce and watery.

On my first boiler-clean leave I left blitzed Liverpool and headed for Wastwater in the Lake District. If the train was dreadfully slow, the trip up to Drigg was beautiful. The countryside of the early English summer was at its best with rolling hills of green fields and stone fences and clusters of leafy trees. Even the railway embankments and the bordering woods were massed with bluebells and wild flowers.

At Drigg I cadged a ride up to Wasdale Head in a security police van for twenty Capstan cigarettes. As we went further into the hills the old feeling of lightness returned and for the first time since I'd arrived in Britain I was happy. Here was real hill country at last. The road wound round the edge of Wastwater, a placid stretch with just enough shimmer on the lake to give it life and reality. From the hills across the water, *The Screes* ran down to the scalloped shore in wide fans of sunlit rock. There was a nostalgic twinge when I remembered the foothills of the Rakaia, or the evening wavelets breaking on the tussock fringes of Lake Lyndon. I was a long way from Arthurs Pass.

"Been here before?" queried the driver.

"No. I'm from New Zealand. Done a bit of climbing though."

"You've come to the right place then. Before Adolf got nasty you couldn't move around these parts for climbers with their ropes and things. If you ask me," he said tapping the side of his temple and giving a tolerant waggle of the head, "you're all a mad breed."

My homesickness vanished; I was used to these remarks back in New Zealand. To be classed with the insane gave me a feeling of stability. When I'd finished my enthusiastic attempts to convert a friendly policeman who was more interested in pints than peaks, the crags were there, purpled, shadowed and exciting: Great Gable, Pillar and Scafell. These were the hills I'd read about. Mallory, Winthrop Young, Odell and Smythe had scrambled here before they climbed in the European Alps or the Himalaya. H. E. L. Porter, who had climbed extensively in the Mt Cook district and on Aspiring, was sure to have climbed here too. As I stepped out of the van, an incongruous figure in naval rating's rig with a swag on my back, I wasn't a stranger; I was back in an atmosphere I knew. Befriended by an elderly couple at dinner in the Wasdale Hotel, I talked and listened about the hills. The man had climbed in his younger days. Though the diningroom was deserted, I was no longer lonely. Lord knows what I burbled about, or what New Zealand adventures I exaggerated under the relaxing influence of understanding company and after-dinner port; I didn't care. My hosts received the broadside of six months' accumulated nostalgia.

"We have a son at sea. He's an engineer officer in a tanker," the woman said quietly. "He's a climber too."

I was whistling as I walked along the road between the neat stone fences and under the warm stars. The gravel crunched underfoot and the beck flowed softly over the flinty stones and under the mossy rocks of the arcing bridge. Owls hooted sleepily from the beech trees and the cries of sheep came distantly from the fields. The night air was busy with the droning of beetles and the slow beat of water on lakeside shingle. I walked into the Fell and Rockclimbing Club's hut rather uncertainly. I'd heard so much about English reserve. Naval ratings, even climbing ones, might be politely shown the door after an embarrassed silence.

"May I come in? I'm from New Zealand . . ." My voice trailed away after the inadequate introduction. The faces round the table lifted more in surprise than annoyance at my interruption. There were hemp ropes coiled and pieces of climbing gear neatly stowed against the walls. Photographs of mountains stared down. I had come too far to back out: "I've done a bit of climbing," I said.

"Have you now? Well, come and join us."

A tall blonde man with a smile as bright as the sun on the Main

Divide came over and took my outstretched hand. I'd debated with myself all the way from the hotel whether the English shook hands on meeting strangers. Within a few minutes I was as much at ease as if I'd known them for days. After a dish of tea I left for the hotel with an invitation to come and scramble with them on Scafell the next day. The accents might have been different, the hill names strange, but the talk, the atmosphere was the same as that in any New Zealand hut.

I climbed with one of the men the next day. We had an afternoon on Scafell which was close to perfection: a day of rock chimneys, sun, and the argot which all hill people have in common. When we'd emerged from the gullies of Moss Ghyll we lay on the summit like indolent grass snakes; the crags were softened with haze and cuckoos called and answered across the valley. Away to the south, beyond the folded hills, Liverpool lay smoking and rubbled. The sea and the war were westward, but pocketed in the hills, I was free.

"Do these mountains," asked my companion with English directness, "seem small to you compared with those in New Zealand? No ice here, no glaciers. No forests as you know them."

"Not really. I'm enjoying myself too much to think about comparisons. Our hill country may be higher, but the light's harder; the peaks younger and sharper. Yours are older but gentler in outline and their colours softer. They've reached a balance between summit and valley, between man and mountain, which ours lack. Your mountains have a tradition in history and a literature which goes back for centuries. Our recorded history's only a century old. The New Zealand hills are wild, some would say uncouth. Perhaps," I added mischievously, "they're like all Antipodeans—rough and colonial?"

"The thought never entered my head," laughed my companion. "And please," he was serious now, "don't equate all Englishmen with condescension."

We sat on the grassy ledge, and far below the beck twisted and shone down to Wastwater. We took off the rope at the foot of the crag.

"Do you come here often, John?"

"Every leave that I can." He went on coiling the rope and then said casually. "You do miss them, don't you?"

"Yes," I answered.

The outing had done more than stretch my legs and clear my head; the touch of rock, height and depth, clouds and wind had brought me back to living. And life to me was friends, people in huts as much as on the hill. I rejoined the ship at Gladstone Dock. As we steamed down the Mersey to the Bar Light and headed into the fresh slap of the open sea I was no longer homesick. Every landfall was a homecoming; Loch Ewe and the stern Hebrides, the white cone of Hekla above the winter Iceland sea, Greenland's Cape Farewell glimpsed from the crest of a Denmark Strait greybeard, the hills of Newfoundland and Nova Scotia taking slow shape through the fog.

I hiked down through the Cairngorms as the moon climbed over the frosty roofs of Kingussie. The hill people took a stranger in, gave food and warmth and shared their fires. Hills might be high or low, but only people and shelter gave them meaning.

7
Arthurs Pass

An adventure is only an inconvenience rightly considered.
—*G. K. Chesterton*

I NEVER GOT THE CHANCE to return to the Lake District or to wander among the hills and huts of Wales. As for the Isle of Skye, I saw no more of its people and crags—the rock climbs of the Cuillins were legendary—than could be glimpsed from the after-deck of the *Harvester* as she cruised slowly down the Minches. Skye was dark, historic and mystic but, for me, always over the water. I planned to spend my next long leave first in Wasdale and then nose my way

"Ede went to the front again and after a quick search of both sides of the 'schrund he cut up the Lendenfeld side. . . ."
Jack Ede in action on the upper section of Syme's Ridge, Mount Tasman.

"We stumbled down to the hut quite done in . . . we had been on the mountain for twenty-seven hours. . . ."
Bruce Gillies and Jack Ede the morning after Tasman.

"I hunted about . . . and eventually found a large overhanging rock close to the dried-up creekbed."
Bruce Gillies and Paul Powell under the bivvy rock in Scott's Creek, Copland Valley.

over to Skye, but when I left *Harvester* and returned to Chatham, the Navy had doubts about my health. My lungs, they insisted, were spotted. My next rail warrant was made out not for Wasdale Hotel but for a sanatorium in Hampshire. A year later I was back in New Zealand at Otago University.

"Make sure you get plenty of rest, moderate exercise and lots of fresh air," the naval people had told me. I had been in the service long enough to know where obedience to orders started and ended; the injunction about getting lots of fresh air seemed commonsense, and eminently convenient. I obeyed orders and went back to the mountains.

One day, not long after I'd started at the Otago Dental School, I met Barrie Jones.

"Hullo," he said with his dormouse smile, "I thought I'd got rid of you the day in 1940 when you left Wellington with a mob of rough naval types. Where have you sprung from? Staying long?"

"Hope so, Barrie," I replied and launching into my saga I told him about my need for rest and fresh air.

"Hmmmm." His face registered concern. "Serious case all right."

"Bosh!" I was annoyed. "I'm as fit as a flea. I tramped over to Silver Peaks and back yesterday. Ran like a ferret most of the way."

"Ah," said Barrie waving a cautioning finger under my nose. "You'll have to stop that, my lad. Bad for your windbags."

"Blast you medicals," I growled. "You're all the same. What d'you expect me to do? Live in a glass case?"

"There's only one solution," said Jones. "You can keep on going to the hills on one condition . . ."

"OK Doc," I interrupted impatiently. "And what's that?"

"You must always have a doctor with you."

"And where do I dig up an itinerant medic? What about his fees?"

"No trouble at all, old chap. You've got one right here. Dr Barrie Jones."

"But the last I saw of you in Wellington, you were a science student."

"I wangled my BSc and I'm doing med now."

"Gawd help New Zealand."

"What's more," Barrie ignored my taunt, "I'll call in another opinion as well, Po Chambers. He's keen to get in to the hills."

"But you're both only fourth-years," I protested.

"Don't worry," Jones reassured, "we know all about the *bot*. Just finished pathology lectures on it. And what's more," he added, "don't forget you're getting a total of eight years medical enlightenment if Po comes too."

"What about the fee?" The Navy had taught me to bargain.

"The odd beer will do," he said, walking off towards the Medical
School.

That August Barrie, Po and I went up to Arthurs Pass with a
University Ski Club party. Barrie was in charge. His quiet manner
gave little sign of his ability, but he could concentrate on problems
and pursue them to success. The greater the obstacles, the better
Barrie worked. There were no skis in Dunedin, so Barrie made
them, blades, bindings and sticks. He ordered the Southland beech,
designed the metal and leather bindings, and had a whole gang of
us slaving night after night until the whole party were equipped. He
achieved this with an unobtrusive leadership which compelled us
to follow.

My return to Arthurs Pass was as pleasant as it had been unexpected—a year before I'd been flat on my back in bed—but I soon
discovered that I would never make a ski champion.

"I don't think you'll ever learn to do a decent christie, Paul,"
said Barrie, shaking his head despairingly.

"I'm inclined to agree with you," I said, rubbing my battered
stern. A long line of holes in the snow marked my not-so-elegant
descent down Temple Basin.

"It's not that you're not trying. But I don't think your heart's in
it. I've been watching you, your mind's away up there on Rolleston."
And he pointed to the peak across the valley where the long curve
of the Goldney Ridge flashed in the sun. Behind it rose the top of
Rolleston, a meeting place for sun and snow and sky.

The old itch was back, I wanted to climb that mountain again. But
my ambition was more than climbing; I wanted to carry on where
the war had stopped me. It would be a new beginning, a remembered
baseline from which to reach out and make new friends, see new
country, and find shelter in new huts.

"What about my chest?"

"Oh *that*," laughed Barrie. "There's nothing wrong with it. And I
doubt if there ever was."

"You medicals are the limit." There was the long clean hiss of
other skis over snow and the voices floating down the snowy basin.
"That's exactly what I've been trying to get into your thick skulls
ever since I left my ship in England, two years and twelve thousand
miles ago."

"Diagnosis is an art, and the patient the eternal mystery." His
mind was far away too. "If you ever had the *bot*, Paul, you cured
yourself."

As we walked the snow-packed road, crossed the red bridge and sauntered down the long incline between the beech trees to Arthurs Pass township we talked of Tararua days, of huts and hills and friends.

Just before we went into the cottage where the party camped in cheerful crowdedness, I said, "Why don't you come too? Let's climb Rolleston together."

He thought a little and then said slowly, "Thanks, there's nothing I'd like more. But I can't run out on the others. I'm supposed to be their leader."

As I collected my bits and pieces and walked out the door, Barrie was waxing his skis. He stuffed the stick of wax in his pocket and took some of my gear. We didn't say much. A goods train rumbled out of the tunnel and the wail of the engine siren went echoing back and forth across the valley. The tunnel was dark but the snow above the bushline still held light. We walked together up the crunchy path to the Canterbury Mountaineering Club's hut. The railway lines down in the yard gleamed coldly.

"It's going to be a hard frost."

"Yes."

He was well down the path when I called out, "How about you and Po Chambers coming up the Matukituki next vac, up to French Ridge Hut? We can climb something together. It's new country."

He was just a darkness moving across a patch of snow. "I'll hold you to that promise, you old hump."

The hut, a gable-ended affair, sat on a hillock overlooking the rest of the settlement with an air of male superiority which came as much from the accident of its position as from the earnestness of its misogynists. It was said to be the Club's proud boast that no female had ever entered the place. I walked on to the verandah like a neophyte taking eager steps into a monastery. It wasn't that I didn't like women, rather that I had grown used to the company of men. The mystery of mountains absorbed all my time and money. I was still the young hunter; bills, babies and bailiffs would have to wait. But when I went in the hut doorway I wasn't sure that I was happy with my move. The thought of climbing Rolleston was one thing, but I didn't know any of the men in the hut. I'd forgotten that the CMC men I'd known were still at the war.

A hand clapped my shoulder and a voice—I'd heard that eager voice before—said, "Hullo, squire. Come over to join the he-men?"

Always bad at remembering names, I waited embarrassed for a clue to his identity. I flicked the beads of a mental abacus: Tararua huts, faces, voices, bush tracks, sun, rain and snow on the rolling tops. "Bruce Gillies," I said, with relief as well as pleasure. "Boy, am I glad to see you!"

As we fell to swopping mountain yarns, he said: "What are your plans?"

"Anything that's on, Bruce."

"How about joining Jack Ede and me?" he said quickly, saving me from the admission that I was a stray lone wolf on the fringes of the pack. "Tomorrow. Rolleston. Away at dawn and back before dark." He called across the hut to a shortish man who came out of the bunkroom. "Hey, Jack. Come over and meet another candidate for the Rolleston Stakes. An old and unsavoury sailor friend of mine."

I liked Ede at once; he was a nuggety man with sandy hair, a pointed chin always waggling in conversation, and hands that waved in the air. Ede didn't make points, he painted them. The eyes were bright and there were lines of humour as well as concentration at the corners. Gillies and he made a good pair, a complementary portrait in restlessness. Bruce was taller, both hands in pockets or arms folded with the knuckles bunched under his armpits, a slight stoop of the shoulders. There was a peculiar intensity in his voice that combined a trace of nasal overtones with a rise and fall, but the accent was good New Zealand. The words came with a drawl that gathered to a rush and finished way up in the air with a penetrating chortle or an expressive shrug of the shoulders and a palmed lifting of the hands. Bruce couldn't be uninteresting if he tried; he either raced along the crest of exuberance or worried to the hollows. When the next wave came he was off again.

"Well," he drawled after we had spent an hour making ready for the early morning start, "everything's set. Now, who's going to sleep with the alarm clock?" A lock of straight brown hair fell over his forehead, and the eyes sparkled behind the spectacles hanging on the end of the long nose. "What about you, Paul?"

"No thanks, Bruce, I hate the things." I'd had enough of alarm bells that rang in the night.

"Give it to me then," Ede said. Jack had a strong sense of duty and he enjoyed every minute of it.

About midnight the hut filled with noise, people clumping around with nailed boots, swags dumped on the wooden floor and another bucket of coal thrown on the fire. There was a squeal of a vigorously-pumped primus and a clatter of mugs on the wooden table.

Curiosity called me from my bag. I walked into the living room.

"Powell!" yelled a figure in blue air force uniform.

"Banfield," I returned. "Bruce Banfield! Haven't seen you since that day we climbed Rolleston together six years ago."

Two hours later we were still talking by the greying ashes; the unexpected meeting was a reef too rich to be ignored. The hut creaked and the fire died lower and our shadows faded on the shiplap walls.

That day six of us climbed Rolleston and crowded together on the summit. Winter, for all its dangers of avalanche and exposure, was the most revealing time to climb a mountain. The air was clear of haze and we could see for miles. Everywhere there were mountains sharp and white, and the deep thrust of valleys. Someone started an argument whether the high and graceful peak far away to the south might be Mt Tasman.

"Well, squire," said Gillies with finality, "there's only one way to settle this discussion. Go and climb it."

"Can you come, Banfield?" asked Ede. "Make a foursome in the Haast Hut?"

"Not a show, Jack. I'll probably be overseas by Christmas. Rolleston's my last flutter in the Alps."

"It'll have to be the old salt then."

"What, me? Tasman? You must be joking? I'm not in that class yet." But secretly I was flattered. Vanity waited on every mountain top.

We left the summit as shadows were fingering the ridges and spreading down to meet the forest. The sun went down leaving the mountain gaunt and pallid white against a pea-green sky.

"Something brewing," muttered Gillies. "I don't like it, squire. It's too quiet. Let's get down to the hut, there's a storm coming." And he loped off down the winding road from the Pass with the rest of us straggling out behind. An hour and a half later we climbed up the steep path to the welcoming lights of the hut. The kitchen was full of people, the noise of their talking and cooking activity hitting us in the face as soon as we went in the door. The smell was that rare compound of sweat, wet boot-leather and frying bacon.

"Whew!" said Gillies clapping both hands to his head. "What a fug. Oh, my sinuses. Can't we have a window open?"

"Stop your moaning, Gillies," said a voice from the scrum around the primuses, "and have a cup of tea."

We were loafing around the fire in the main room indulging in a session of alpine lineshooting when the hut started to shake.

"Wind's come up very suddenly," said Ede.

"That's no wind." Gillies was well on his way to the front door when the rumbling swelled to a sustained roar. The hut creaked and groaned like an old tramp in a mid-Tasman storm. Pictures flew from the walls, tables, chairs, food, plates and mugs jigged and fell to the bucketing floor in a mishmash of confusion.

"Avalanche!" yelled a voice. "The whole hillside's coming down."

"Earthquake!"

"The hut's caving in!"

Then the power failed. The night was full of roaring. I made a bolt for the door. Unfortunately nine other men had the same idea and we all jammed in the opening like insects waving agitated arms and legs on a flypaper. Gillies was outside doing his own little war dance and dodging the chimney pot and flying bricks that hurtled down the roof. When the worst jolts were over we retreated shame-faced into the room and started clearing up the mess. But one intrepid mountaineer came to the front door with a sheepish expression.

"Come in," we called, "and help us to clean up the mess."

"I donʼt think Iʼd better. Iʼm in trouble myself."

"I see what you mean," said Gillies wrinkling his nose.

"There I was," moaned the unfortunate, "sitting all by myself and enjoying the peace of the everlasting hills, when that damn shake started . . ."

"Go on," we urged, crowding to the doorway, but keeping an olfactory distance.

"Well," he explained, "I thought at first it was some of you chaps up to your usual practical jokes, so I just stayed put. When I realised it was a dinkum shake, I tried to make a run for it, but—you see—"

"Go on. Donʼt stop," we roared.

"It was too late. I got sort of tangled up with my braces." He stopped and looked at us beseechingly, but we were without mercy, we wanted the whole story. "And I fell." He lifted two imploring hands. "Now, canʼt you pass me out a bucket of hot water and some soap?"

While he washed his sins away we kept up a running commentary well laced with earthy observations.

"You ought to know better, a climber of your experience going down to a dangerous place like that without a rope on," said Ede.

Rain fell monotonously and insistently for the next few days. One by one the men packed and went down to catch the train.

Gillies was among the first. "No good hanginʼ around," he growled. "When it gets like this, itʼs set in. Going to come down for days."

Jack Ede and I hung on, waiting for the break that would give us another climb. When our last day was up and Jack and I went down the path to the station we were talking of the future.

"Now, Paul, make sure you get out for plenty of training runs," admonished Ede. "Tasmanʼs not a mountain to be trifled with. And sharpen those crampon points of yours. Theyʼre as blunt as tree trunks."

8

Haast Hut and Mt Tasman

O monstrous! but one half-pennyworth of bread to this in-
tolerable deal of sack!

—*Henry IV*, Pt 1, Act 2, Sc 4

"THERE SHE IS," said Bruce. "Mount Tasman, the queen of the Alps.
Second only to Mount Cook. What do you think of her, Paul?" He
didn't wait for my answer but rattled on: "Tasman, eleven thousand
four hundred and seventy-five feet of the steepest snow and ice in
New Zealand. Just wait until you're standing on top, squire. Then
you'll know you've climbed a *real* mountain."

When you were with Gillies you didn't get time to ponder too
much, he bore you along on the tide of his enthusiasm. His zest for
living, his verve, had an infectiousness that made it as natural and
exciting to want to climb Mt Tasman as it would have been to go
down to a shipping office and talk your way into an ocean cruise

with only a ten-cent bit in your pocket. He didn't fret over obstacles
though he could appraise them pretty soberly. His continuing theme
was, "Try something new, squire, try something new." And the
Cook district was new to me.

I wasn't too sure how I'd cope with hours of difficult snow and
ice climbing, how my ankles would stand twelve hours walking
with crampon frames on my feet. "It can be tough, Paul," Bruce
had warned me. After six hours of flexed muscles, you can feel them
wanting to scream." And he'd clapped both hands to his head and
given such an agonised expression that I hadn't known whether to
laugh or to say straight out, "Bruce, you and Jack had better count
me out. Tasman sounds beyond me—far too hairy." And I still
wasn't sure about my lungs.

Gillies came out of the Hermitage just as Ede tumbled out of the
bus from Christchurch. My doubts were lost in the excitement as
we stowed Jack's gear in the diminutive Morris Eight and clanked
up to Ball Hut about fifteen miles away up the side of the lateral
moraine of the Tasman Glacier. We stayed the night at Ball Hut, a
rambling corrugated-iron affair which smelled of dieseline, ski-wax,
and the wetness of a winter not long passed. We had the place all to
ourselves and I prowled around getting the feel of the hut, glad of
the warmth, the smell of food cooking, and the last sunlight fading
to early stars above the peaks across the tumbled ice and grey rock
of the glacier. William Spotswood Green had passed here with his
guides, Emil Boss and Ulrich Kaufmann, in 1882 after a stormy
night-out and near success on the first attempt on Mt Cook. Edward
Fitzgerald and Mattias Zurbriggen had come and gone this way in
the eighteen-nineties. For Fitzgerald, Tasman was a consolation
prize; he lost the first ascent of Mt Cook to Tom Fyfe, George
Graham and Jack Clarke.

I went for a stroll in the dark but though I didn't meet any of the
oldtimers, I went back into the Ball Hut with a sense of atmosphere
that I would have missed had we arrived early in the day and then
pushed on up the glacier.

"Where have you been?" asked Ede as I came blinking into the
hut light. "We were thinking about coming out to look for you.
Thought you might have fallen down the rubbish shute on to the
Ball Glacier."

"As a matter of fact," I said, "I've been having a long chinwag
with old W. S. Green, all about his night-out on Mt Cook, and he's
given me quite a few useful tips. You never know," I added as I
poured myself out a cup of tea from the enormous brown enamel
teapot, "they might come in very handy if we have one on Tasman."

"Better get to bed," growled the practical Gillies, "and save your energy for the gutsbust up to the Haast Hut tomorrow."

The blankets were clean and warm and the uncased pillows soft. For a while I lay in the darkness listening to the wind soughing round the hut. Through the window I could see the dark outline of the eastern peaks and one bright star. The Ball Hut was a snug place.

I awoke to the rattle of dishes about 3.30 am. Jack was up and cooking breakfast. Outside it was still dark with the intensity of the last hour before dawn. It was cold and the sounds of our preparations echoed hollowly through the empty rooms of the hut. As we packed our gear after breakfast I was aware of a change in our attitudes to each other. I had sensed this growing on the way up from the Hermitage the night before. We were still individuals with our own distinctive personalities but the mountains were bringing us mentally closer.

After a four-hour rock climb from the glacier we were getting near the Haast Hut. The snow was well down the Haast Ridge that year and at 7,000 feet the hut was almost covered. A party had been up the ridge about a fortnight before and had dug their way down to the door, but fresh and heavy snowfalls had piled to the level of the eaves. This was a shock to me. All the way across the glacier and up to the Haast Ridge I had built up in my mind one comfortable picture: a hut perched invitingly on warm red rocks, the song of the primus, and endless cups of tea.

Ede pulled down the long-handled shovel fixed to the outside of the hut, and was soon busy digging down to the door. After twenty minutes' hard work we had cleared the last of the snow away from the entrance, but the roof and the sides were still completely covered. I walked down the snow steps to the door. The wood was weathered by many seasons of rain and wind and frost to the smoothness of old bone. Slowly the ice packing around the jamb gave, the door yawned back and shafts of light flooded in.

Every hut has an atmosphere, a character of its own. Some are new and fresh with the smell of paint and good repair, others are older but welcome with light on clean scrubbed benches and shining metal pots. But this place was like a vault. The air was damp and fusty with the smell of mildewed kapok, wet blankets, last season's cooking and the stink of kerosene. When you trod on the floor the boards were toneless and dull hollow. Nothing in the building sang. When my eyes focused to the darkness—the windows were still underneath the snow—I saw a long trestle table against the wall, a chipped and battered form, a cupboard or two with broken latches

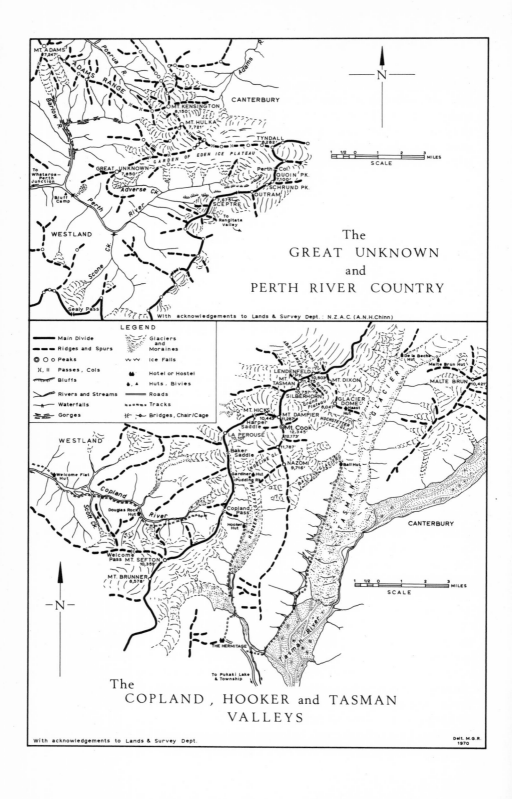

The
GREAT UNKNOWN
and
PERTH RIVER COUNTRY

With acknowledgements to Lands & Survey Dept.: N.Z.A.C. (A.N.H.Chinn)

LEGEND

—— Main Divide	Glaciers and Moraines
– – – Ridges and Spurs	
◎ ○ o Peaks	Ice Falls
)(, ‖ Passes, Cols	Hotel or Hostel
Bluffs	Huts, Bivies
Rivers and Streams	Roads
Waterfalls	Tracks
Gorges	Bridges, Chair/Cage

The
COPLAND, HOOKER and TASMAN
VALLEYS

With acknowledgements to Lands & Survey Dept.

Delt. M.G.R.
1970

on the end wall. Against the other wall stood a kerosene stove with curved black iron legs supporting a rusty cooking-plate. Two faded blue chimneys with funny little mica windows sat primly over the sooty wicks. There were gobs of congealed fat and dirt and kerosene crusted down the sides of the framework. I walked back quickly to the door and climbed the snow steps. Away across the valley, Malte Brun rose a great sharp hump of red rock and clean sky.

"Don't stand there gaping, m'boy," said Gillies, pushing past me and dumping his swag with a businesslike clatter on the dirty floor, "we've work to do."

I didn't move. The hut wasn't what I had expected. "Don't you like the old dump?" asked Ede as he carved the hardened snow away from the window pane with a table knife.

"It does pong a bit, doesn't it? Like a Chinese brothel after the fleet's left Hong Kong."

"Come on, admiral, you'll get used to it. It's not the Waldorf-Astoria I know, but you can't expect red carpet and dancing girls for five bob a night." Gillies hunched his shoulders and blew into his hands. "But just you wait until it starts to blizz; you wouldn't swop it for the People's Palace then." He pushed a smoke-blackened pot into my hands: "See if you can find some water in the tank at the end there."

While I dug down through the snow and hacked through the ice in the tank in search of water, I heard the muffled sounds of housework. Gillies laughed at something Ede said and came out and stood on the snow. He scratched the side of his head like a gopher, expanded his chest with the mountain air already tinged with early frost, and said briskly as he looked at the peaks, "This is real, man. This is *real*."

When I went into the hut again there was a different quality about the place. In a few moments the atmosphere had changed from dinginess to light even though the main room was as musty as when we'd first arrived, and the one candle that spluttered in the neck of an empty whisky bottle accentuated rather than relieved the gloom. The stench of kerosene, dampness, sweat, and old cooking was as overpowering as before, yet the hut suddenly felt like home.

"It's not so bad after all," I conceded, sitting down to puzzle out the reason for the change.

"The Haast Hotel grows on you," said Ede, as he stirred a mixture of cocoa and dried milk with an elegance that fascinated me. He held the spoon pinched between thumb and forefinger with the other three fingers spread, half bent, and opened from the palm. It was a trick of his I'd never noticed before.

Bruce came prowling back through the door to the bunkroom with

his nose twitching. "Bit high in there all right. As soon as we can
we'll have to shovel the snow away from the other window and let
the fug out. It's mighty powerful. Snow's been getting in along the
back wall where it's against the rock." He changed the subject
rapidly and said with characteristic directness, "Let's take our ice-
axes for a walk and wander up the ridge to the top of Glacier Dome
to see what Tasman's like. It's only a quarter to three. Plenty of time
for it. What do you say?" He looked sharply at Ede and then at me.

"You've already made up your mind, Bruce."

"Well," he gave the word a slight drawl, "no sense in hanging
around the hut all the afternoon. Wastin' good daylight."

"I'd like to go," I volunteered.

"What about the hut though?" said Jack sniffing the air and looking round with obvious distaste. "Hadn't we better debrothelise
first?"

"Forget it," said Bruce decisively. "Let it wait for the first wet
day. We came up here to climb Tasman, not to do housework."

"You and Paul go," said Ede, still stirring the cocoa with meticulous
concentration. "I'll stay, clean up the hut a bit and get the meal
ready. Besides, I want to sort over the gear. It might be fine tomorrow,
so we'd better get set for a midnight start."

"Done," said Bruce as he went over to his pack and took out a
manilla rope. "Come on, admiral, let's go."

As Gillies and I went up the steps, our boots scrunching in the
snow and the rope around our middles, Jack followed us to the doorway: "What time do I expect you back? I'll be mad if you're late
and the stew's spoiled."

"Oh, any old time, Jack," I said. "By dark. But if the snow's in
good nick and the night looks fine, why, we might just carry on to
the summit."

"If you do that," riposted Ede, "I'll beat you both up with the
shovel when you get back."

We were pushing up the snow and almost out of sight of the hut
when we heard Ede call, "And don't make those steps too far apart,
I don't want to do the splits every time I lift my feet in the morning."

The snow was soft and our steps ankle-deep, but we took our time
as we skirted the outcrops of red greywacke and moved slowly up
past the Lady's Slipper. We stopped just below the last snow curving
toward the rock top of Glacier Dome, but we talked rather of people
than of mountains as the sun flashed over the broken ice towers of
the Hochstetter Icefall and the rolling snow buttresses and spires
of the Minarets. There was a wonderful feeling of peace, of sense and
order, in the day of brightness and mountains.

"Old Jacko's a good bloke," I said, following the sweep of the

Tasman Glacier to the unclouded saddle at its head.

"One of the best. Takes life very seriously. It's the war."

"He's a sergeant in the Army Ordnance isn't he?"

"Yes, been busting his neck to get overseas, but they won't let him go."

"There are enough of the boys away, poor bastards."

"Yes, we used to moan about the huts being too full at Christmas. Now they're empty all the climbing season. It's not the same."

"Or for them, either, the blokes in the Forces I mean." I thought of friends far away.

"What was it like?" asked Bruce.

"Like most wars, I suppose. There were good times as well as bad. But the worst thing was being away from the hills. That's when I really felt homesick. I used to carry a photo I'd ripped out of an *Auckland Weekly News* with me. A picture of Tasman. Most blokes had photos of their girlfriends, or their families, to moon over. I got to believing that as long as I kept that picture of Mt Tasman with me, I'd be OK, that I'd get back to climb. It became a sort of mascot."

"It did the trick, eh?"

"Yes. And now I'm back, I can't believe it. And after Tasman too."

"Well, squire," said Gillies, coiling up the rope and getting ready to move off, "we'll never get the mountain if we don't go up and have a look at her."

As we clambered up the rock to the top of Glacier Dome, and I came so unexpectedly upon the shining amphitheatre of Cook and Silberhorn and Tasman soaring four thousand feet above the mile-wide snow hollow of the Grand Plateau, I knew I was home. And if we were lucky enough to climb Tasman during the next week, that would be an added prize.

Bruce's remark that "It looks a tough proposition. The approach up the lower icefall's wide open for so early in the season," brought me sharply to the present. We hadn't come up to sit on our backsides for the next few days, to see beauty from a safe and pleasant alpine grandstand, or to go into an esoteric trance whenever storm or sunlight fell upon the mountain. We had come to climb.

I looked again and saw another Tasman, a four-thousand-foot face of ice hanging over the Grand Plateau like a curling wave always on the point of breaking. I saw a fleeting picture of a North Atlantic roller, wintry and white. Sea and war and mountain.

"Isn't she terrific?" said Bruce seeing only the challenge. "What about plugging on for another half hour? I'd like to see if the icefall's as broken as it looks." His tone was speculative, but the tilt of the head with the long nose and the prominent cheekbones was eager.

"Bit late, isn't it Bruce?" I ventured.

"Ye . . ss." He rubbed his long fingers on the sharp angle of his jaw.

I thought of food and warmth. "Jack will be expecting us soon," I said, "and if we want to have a crack at the mountain tomorrow, we'd better get back pronto, have a quick meal and turn in early."

"Guess you're right, squire. We'll get up at midnight." He spoke as if night and warmth were over and we were already closing the hut door behind us and starting on the next day's climb. Suddenly he turned and led off down the hill, chatting all the way. Would we be able to get through the maze of broken country to the foot of Syme's Ridge? What was the snow like on the ridge? Was it hard ice, or good crampon stuff that we could make fast time on? How wide was the 'schrund, would it stop us getting on to the North Shoulder where the Main Divide ran south to the summit of Tasman?

Not far above the hut Bruce stopped as if he'd thrown all his anchors overboard at once, and searched the sky. "What's the weather going to do tomorrow?" he asked, pointing to the thin streaks of feathered cloud. "Mare's tails. Blast, it's going to blow."

Then he shrugged his shoulders and started off again, running down the hardening snow beside our uphill tracks and singing in his exuberant and harshly pleasant baritone:

> *"I can roam where I please,*
> *Open road, open sky . . ."*

I envied his unencumbered vitality; Bruce had his values sorted out. He seldom allowed his unspoken sensitivity to intrude upon the joy of adventure.

Jack had the candles burning. The hut was warm and the food smelled good. The two wicks under the blue stove chimneys burned with a serrated flame and the table and form shone clean in the candlelight.

"You've been busy, Jack."

"Wouldn't know the old shack. You've certainly cleaned the Augean stable, m'boy." Gillies went quickly over to the pot bubbling on the cooker. "Umm," he said appreciatively, as he lifted the lid. "Smells good. Nothing like a thick stew to put lead in your pencil. Two plates of that each, and we'll be able to traverse all the way from Tasman to Cook and back in the same day."

"Aw, shucks, I just threw it together at the last minute. Nothing special," said Ede casually, but his face lit up with pleasure. "And there's rice and apricots for the second course."

We talked and clattered our way through the meal and when we were washing up Jack said to me, "From what Bruce has to say, it sounds as if Tasman won't be easy. The ice must be broken up early, worse than it was last time I tried. It was the weather that beat us then." He stopped and gave me a keen glance. "What did you think of the mountain, Paul?"

"A long way. But they always look worse when you see them from the bottom they say." I looked round at the hut. "I'm quite happy to stay behind. You and Bruce go. Three on a rope is always slower than two. I don't want to hold you up."

Bruce came over to the sink. "We three made a bargain in August on the top of Rolleston, remember? And we're keeping it, aren't we Jack?"

"Of course. You're coming with us on Tasman, Paul. It's all of us or none."

With full darkness came mist and a tribe of lost keas who called mournfully from the rocks just below the hut. Their chant had a melancholy quality, an eerie long drawn out repetitive *keee-aa-aa. Keee-aa-aa.* The wreathing mist, the soft whiffle of wind over snow, the dull rumble of an avalanche under Mt Haidinger, and the interminable cries of the birds made a forbidding atmosphere. I hurried in and shut the door. The hut was substantial and the atmosphere normal: Ede writing up his diary and Gillies checking the wiring in his headlamp.

"Bad weather coming," said Jack matter-of-factly. "They always make that racket when the weather's turning for the worse."

"I don't believe it," said Bruce, "they're just swearing at us because we haven't thrown them enough scraps." He went to the door and roared out, "Buzz off. Go down to the Hermitage if you want a feed. We want to go to sleep."

The screeching stopped and they went with a flutter of wings like the shuffle of a fan.

I climbed into my bunk, wrote up my diary and then blew out the candle. The hut creaked and the climbers of its pre-war past drifted about. I thought of them. How many of the men who had lain in my bunk were dead now? Through the clammy blankets I felt the coldness of the plaque against my back. I had read the words on the dull brass when Bruce and I came down from Glacier Dome:

This hut was erected by fellow Mountaineers and Friends in Memory of Sydney Locke King, of Rickmansworth, England, Member of The Alpine Club, and Guides David Thompson, of Okarito, and John Richmond, of Fairlie, who were overwhelmed by an avalanche on the Upper Linda Glacier on February 22nd 1914, after ascending Mt Cook.

The ice slopes under Mt Dixon sent intermittent cannonades

thumping and clattering, growling discontentedly in the night. I thought of the route we'd have to take from the top of Glacier Dome to the foot of Syme's Ridge, a mad mile of heavily-crevassed country exposed through most of its length to the threat of ice avalanches which fell from the bossed east face of Mt Tasman. Crevasses didn't worry me particularly, neither did the image of the long white knife-edge leading up to the Main Divide; survival there was subjective, it depended on our skill and care. But there was no telling when those cliffs of hanging ice and huge triangular cornices pouting from the summit ridge might sweep down.

I tried to work out the problem as if it was an alpine equation but I couldn't get the two sides to balance. Had other men lain restlessly in this same bunk, feeling the plaque, and thinking? I gave up with only the first line of the equation solved. I was in the Haast Hut, safe if not snug, between damp blankets. Tomorrow was another day. The answer waited somewhere between the hut and the summit of the mountain.

Dawn brought a dirty nor' wester which shook the hut with bursts of wind and pitted the snow with flurries of continual rain. We spent the day cleaning up and arguing, mostly about the war.

"It can't go on after 1947," said Bruce.

"Nonsense," I said. "What about the war between France and England in the fourteenth and fifteenth centuries? That dragged on for a hundred years."

"This one had better not." Ede made a wry face, "We'll run out of food, and it's too far to be trotting up and down to the Hermitage once a fortnight, especially when it's raining."

The war had followed us up to the hut, and though we joked about it, our talk of climbing friends was a constant reminder.

Each of us found different ways of patience. Ede checked and re-checked his gear. He had a fascination for needle-sharp crampon points, all twenty of them, and honed them to infinity with a rusty file he'd unearthed from the hut toolbox.

Gillies prowled restlessly between the bunkroom window and the hut door in a pair of outlandish tennis shoes. Sometimes he'd settle at the table with a tattered Western until a lull in the storm brought him hopefully to the door. He'd look out briefly and then shut the door with a snort. "Hosing down. Can't see across the valley. This could go on for days."

I discovered that I'd left most of my tobacco down at Ball Hut.

"Lord, now we *have* got trouble," said Gillies, "you ought to give it up, Paul. It's a rotten habit."

"I happen to like it," I returned.

"Here's to Mount Grave," said Rodda, "the best virgin."
Mt Grave towers above Grave Creek and the Harrison River. The climb was made up the right-hand skyline ridge.

"Tomorrow," said Faigan, "it's back to the cove. I wonder what's on the breakfast menu at Milford Hostel?"
Base camp at Harrison Cove. *From left:* Leo Faigan, Paul Powell, Roland Rodda.

"This hollow in the scrub, beside water, with wood for a fire, was greater than the highest summit rock, and conquest."
High camp under Mt Grave. *From left:* Paul Powell, Jack Ede, Roland Rodda, Leo Faigan.

"Bad for your wind," said Ede earnestly.

"Smoking hasn't done Mick Bowie any harm," I said triumphantly. Guide Bowie was as famous for his pipe as he was for his climbs. There was a legend that you could find your way up to the summit of Mt Malte Brun by following the trail of his spent matches. I took the rest of the day reclaiming wisps of stale tobacco from a heap of dross I'd collected in the bunkroom. When I lit the first cigarette it tasted like a mixture of old socks, linoleum and blasting powder.

"Phew," said Ede, fanning the air violently, "you must have cast-iron lungs."

"I've got to hand it to you, m'boy," said Gillies admiringly, "it's certainly a ripe brew."

The weather lifted rapidly early next morning and Gillies came rushing into the hut in high excitement: "Come on you lazy bums, it's time we were away."

We ate hurriedly and scurried out of the hut and up the snow. From the top of Glacier Dome, Tasman was a wonder of sparkling ice. I wanted to climb that peak.

An hour later we were deep in a maze of crevasses. The walls shone green and blue and their depths fell to purple darkness. Every lead we tried petered out.

We stopped to talk it over. We were right under the hanging ice of the east face.

"Looks as if we're stymied."

"Don't you believe it, squire," said Bruce. "Let's go down a bit. I think there's a chance we may get through with a bit of ice work."

When we came to the place, Ede and Gillies looked at it and discussed the pros and cons with clinical detachment. But it seemed a pretty forlorn hope as we stood on that small island of ice in the labyrinth of crevasses. The sun came over the Dixon Ridge behind us with a rainbowed halo and sent a wave of light running up Syme's Ridge.

Miles away down-valley, Lake Pukaki was green and peaceful. I wondered momentarily whether I wouldn't be happier watching the sunrise over the Alps from the assured safety of the front porch of the Pukaki pub. They gave you a good breakfast down there.

"It's our only chance," said Ede. "Let's give it a go."

It was a rather awkward place, but it had the great advantage that once across we wouldn't have too much trouble in covering the remaining four hundred yards to the foot of Syme's Ridge. The way led along the top edge of a great splinter of leaning ice which spanned the crevasse. It was hard green ice and dropped dramatically into blueness on both sides. But there was one very good thing about that ice-flake; it stopped me worrying about the thousands of feet of muck hanging between us and the summit ridge of Tasman.

Ede was all action and energy. He swung his axe like a Viking as he cut the first steps in the side of the splinter. I had a ridiculous urge to yell out, "Fore" or "Timber", but I merely said quietly, "Hey, Jack. Hang on a minute will you, I've forgotten to take my anti-vertigo pills."

Ede just bared his teeth in a funny little grin and kept on cutting a line of bucket steps on either side of the green flake. His axe didn't ring, but met the ice with a dull whump. His face was beaded with sweat. The sun rose higher, throwing a grotesque pattern of shadows across our causeway.

"It's going to take a long time," said Gillies.

"We've got all day," I replied. "Just as long as we get back to that hut before dark . . . I'd give my eye teeth for a nice cup of tea."

"Stop talking and keep your eye on Jacko," warned Gillies.

Ede had covered twenty feet. With one leg dangling on each side of the splinter, and the sharp crest bisecting his crutch, he'd bash out another two steps and then shuffle forward. It all appeared very precarious and even more uncomfortable.

"That's all the rope I can give you," I yelled to him.

"Come on then."

"Have you got me?" to Gillies behind.

"Sure thing, Paul. Like the Rock of Gibraltar."

I wished I really was as nimble as a Barbary ape when my turn came to slither down on to the ice ridge. But you learn fast in hard places. I soon discovered that the easiest way was to lean forward with legs at full stretch and swing into the next steps with a bounding action.

"Good for you, Hopalong," laughed Bruce. "Give her the whip."

The splinter gave a gentle shiver and funny noises came up from the depths.

"Don't worry," said Ede. "They often do that. It's just settling."

Then Gillies was working across as nonchalantly as if he were out for a Sunday walk. When we were together on the other side, he asked me, "Well, squire? What did you think of it? Sporting, eh?"

"Nothing to it, Bruce. But I'll tell you one thing."

"Oh, yes?"

"I understand, now, what you mean by *real*."

"Come on," said Bruce. "The rest is catsmeat, we start running now."

In a few minutes we were at the lower end of Syme's Ridge. The way to Tasman was before us. But I was loth to turn back. "Can't we go on, just a few hundred feet up the ridge? Now I'm here I want to feel we've at least set foot on it, and a line of steps would be handy when we come back tomorrow. Save a lot of time."

"Too late, Paul," said Gillies. "It's two o'clock now and at least three hours back to the hut. That means we won't have tea and get to bed until six at the earliest. Only give us five hours' sleep if we get up at 11.30 pm."

I appealed to Ede.

"Bruce is right, Paul. There isn't time."

Gillies clapped me on the shoulder. "Cheer up, admiral, it won't run away."

We turned down hill. The horse ride across the ice-flake seemed nothing now. Woolly cumulus drifted lazily over the Malte Brun range, and the afternoon sun gave mountain and snowfield a disarming benignity; the brittle early morning light with its sharpness of ice crystal and thin angular shadow had worn to smoothness. The curving shadows and crevasse furrows were as contemplative as the forehead of an old man, serene and without malice. Even the east face of Tasman was quiet. In spite of our fears, nothing substantial had fallen all day. Our soft trail rose and fell behind us in flowing parabolas among the folds of the glacier. This was the best part of the mountain day. We were homeward bound to a hut and thought pleasantly of food and candlelight and sleep.

"We'll be home in not much after an hour," said Jack, when we had reached the Silberhorn corner and were among the last of the large crevasses. Below, running out from the bulge in the icefall, the hollow of the Grand Plateau lay unbroken and welcoming.

We were heading down a snow lead with a huge crevasse on each flank when we heard the hiss. Three heads swivelled round. There was noise and wind and fear. Then Ede and I were off our feet and under the hissing snow. The rope between us was bar-taut and the pressure unrelenting. I didn't feel any fear now—that had passed; only a vast annoyance, merging into resignation. Then the pressure eased and everything sang, the air was filled with the ringing of bells and the sun was far away.

Gillies was beside me. "You all right?"

"Yes."

"Let's get Jack."

We pulled the rope free and saw a head come from the snow, and then Ede's face. We helped him to his feet.

"Blast, I've got snow down my neck."

"Never mind that," said Gillies, "let's get out of here."

We scampered through the last crevasses to the safety of the Grand Plateau. My knees were shaking now and my chest was full of hammerbeats.

An hour later I let my axe fall with a thump against the corrugated iron hut and walked into the bunkroom. The sun came through the window and fell brightly on the memorial plaque so that the brass shone.

We had an early tea and went to bed while it was still faintly light. The weather had deteriorated again, the mist was back, and with it came the keas. I climbed grumbling from my bunk and drove them off. At midnight the alarm rattled off but heavy rain was falling; there'd be no climb that day. I squiggled down happily in my bag and slept.

The next day was one of blue sky for the mountains, and calm for me. About noon the sun came through the clouds and the peaks were clean and beckoning in the gentlest of southerly breezes. We sat on the rock wall outside the hut chatting or drowsing in the sun; the mountains were no longer grim. I had reached that balance with my surroundings and myself that brought a relaxed sense of enjoyment. I was free to listen and feel, to taste the mountains. Tomorrow was there, but only as an accident of time. Today I could swing my feet against the rock wall, drink innumerable cups of tea and let my mind drift. And the hut was there too, a place of morning departure and a landfall for evening return. The corrugated-iron roof and walls, the open doorway and the two windows with their quartered panes were more than convenience and refuge from storm: they were the nub of mountain life. The climbing day came in between.

We went in and made our final preparations. We were sure that the next day would be fine, hopeful that during some point of it we would reach the finality of snow and ice that was Mt Tasman. After tea we ran a last check over our team gear for the climb. While we were doing this I sensed the explanation of the same scene the morning we'd packed before we left Ball Hut. Gillies' rope was no longer *my* rope but *our* rope. The primus ceased to be *Ede's*, it was *ours*. When the trip was over and we returned to compartment existence in the city, we'd slip back to the habit of *mine* and *yours*. We'd be different people again. But tomorrow the mountain would bind us into a unity of individuals. We'd find the summit of our thought and living upon Mt Tasman. And the tug of the Haast Hut would be our link with true balance.

At 1.30 in the morning we pulled the hut door behind us and walked up to the rocks just above the hut and strapped on crampons. Ede had insisted that we didn't do this inside the hut. "If every party walked about the place with their crampons on, the floor would soon be shot."

After an early start you're seldom in a reflective mood, sleep is close behind and breakfast sits heavy on the stomach. But my attachment for the hut and the cover it had given me made me wonder when we'd be back.

The crevassed area gave us little trouble and we passed the avalanche rubble by torchlight with no more than a mumbled comment. Even the ice-flake elicited nothing but alpine jargon:

"Give me a tight rope."

"Watch this next bit."

"Have you got me held OK?"

"Yes, on you go."

"That's the end of your rope, I'm coming over."

In the half light the pit was just another degree of blackness. Until full day came with its contrast of shape and depth and distance we seemed safe in a fold of greyness. But when we came to the foot of Syme's Ridge we really woke up as the prisms of ice began to flash and the mountains grew to their full dimensions. We were small men on a very big mountain. It seemed that one minute we'd been talking in the Haast Hut and had in the next instant run slap bang into Tasman.

Ede bent his head back and scanned the buttress, a bulbous toe of ice stuck impudently over encircling crevasses. He peered left, then right. "No show of getting around it."

He scratched his temple slowly then walked up and took an exploratory peck with his iceaxe. He had the puzzled expression of a master builder who, suddenly faced with an awkward construction problem, doesn't know quite where to start. "It's ice all right," he said apologetically, as if he alone was responsible for the obstacle.

"Of course it's ice," said Gillies impatiently. "Let's get on with it."

Jack made no comment but went for the wall. Slowly he chopped a long staircase while I fed out his rope. I couldn't look up, for the ice chips fell in a continual stream, but I judged his progress from the duet between him and Gillies: Bruce spurring him on with terse directions in a drawling growl, and Ede's higher sharper voice floating down the buttress.

"We can't take all day, Jack. This is only the beginning. Make the steps smaller. Save time."

"You won't despise my steps when we come down. Might be dark by then."

"Oh Lord," Gillies gave a long sigh. "I want to be *off* the damn peak long before dark."

"Who's cutting these steps?" said Ede between breaths. "Better to arrive late than not at all."

"I'm with you all the way on that one, Jack," I yelled.

"And what's more," said Ede warming to his theme, "I always take a girl with me on the rope, and her name's Prudence."

"Oh, well—" I heard Gillies say in resignation, "you're doing fine. Just hurry a little if you can."

Ede scratched like a tiger and the ice chips flew and hissed and bounded. Gillies stamped his feet and hummed, *The Man on the Flying Trapeze*. Bruce had a flair for the moment.

"Up you come, Paul," Ede sang down. It was easy with the help of the rope from above and the wide steps under my crampons.

"Tough going, eh Jack?"

"Yes, like trying to bash holes in a billiard ball with a wooden toothpick."

The ridge was still rather steep, a thin ice line that curled toward the Main Divide. With three on the one rope we made slow progress and the state of the ridge didn't help. The surface was icy, too hard for crampons, and the snow beneath was treacherous incohesive stuff that ran out from the cut steps in streams of small white marbles. We flogged the top off the ridge and moved one at a time. The serried crevasses far below waited as patiently as crocodiles.

"Here I am," I thought, "on one of the famous climbs in the Alps and I'm so busy pumping an ice-axe up and down into the mountain, so engrossed with taking in and letting out the rope between Ede at the front, and Gillies at the rear, that I haven't got the chance to look around me. For all I can see I might as well be in an ice-cream factory, shoving bits of wood into eskimo pies. I'd see more down at the Haast Hut sitting on the rock wall and talking to the keas."

We went dibbling up shaft by shaft, shuffling from step to step with bent backs. I had expected to be stimulated by the climb, scared even, but I hadn't foreseen the unending labour, the nagging tiredness in arms and ankles. We were more old men with walking sticks than all-conquering supermen.

"Aw, to hell with it," I called out. "How about a spell for the galley slaves?"

We stopped, drove in our shafts and belayed the rope round each axe-head. The ridge was too steep to sit down on, so we clung to our axes like coolies to their leaning staves.

"What a mountain! Can't even sit down on the bloody thing."

"You'll get used to it, Paul," offered Gillies.

"You're lucky to be here," from Ede.

I was. The relief from head-down drudgery was wonderful. Our ridge was a flying buttress set against the mountain wall like the open blade of a white knife. The cutting edge had been fretted by innumerable days and nights of sun and storm to a scalloped fragility of overhanging cornices and flutings. From Mt Lendenfeld in the north the Main Divide dipped twisting down to Marcel Col and then curved like a scimitar to the glinting North Shoulder of Mt

Tasman. But it was the sun that gave the mountains life and movement, transforming them to white spears and giving the illusion that they moved and breathed. Shadows were born and grew and died where ice gargoyles jutted from the sweeping flanks. Every crystal was a sorcerer's apprentice to the shifting light; and there was great silence.

We clung to our axes for a little while and watched.

A snow pipit came, a cheery bundle of tawny feathers and a bright eye, a fragile jot which flew off with thin reedy cries that were soon lost to the mountain. We got up and went on, and in that space between thought and action I had remembered the valley whence we'd come; the yellow tussock and green grass, the undertones of running water, the feel and smell of earth. I risked a glance to the brown hills of the Mackenzie plains. They were still there.

"I'm ready, Jack." And my hand felt the snow cold on the manila rope.

Our crampons grated as we scrabbled over the black rocks until we faced the next section of the importunate ice crest. It was here that Gillies gave a humorous proportion to the morning and helped me forget temporarily the sensation of exposure and the waiting rectangle of the Grand Plateau now far below. He had taken over the lead and was slaving on our passage when he suddenly lifted both his hands from his axe—a most immoral thing to do on a steep climb—and yelled exuberantly, "L'Amour . . . She is W-O-N-D-E-R-F-U-L."

"For God's sake, Bruce!"

With outstretched arms and a rapturous smile he shouted again, "L'Amour . . . She is W-O-N-D-E-R-F-U-L."

"Take it easy, Bruce, we're not on the summit yet."

"To hell with the summit. I'm in love, you idiots."

It was a bizarre but appropriate place for such an expression of devotion. Bruce told us he was engaged to Shirley Grave, of Oamaru, the youngest daughter of the late W. G. Grave, mountaineer-explorer of Fiordland.

"Coming up here for your honeymoon, Bruce?"

"Don't be daft," he said.

Just after midday, when the peaks were shadowless with soot-black rocks and dull-whitewash snow, we reached the 'schrund that slashes through the ridge not far beneath the North Shoulder. There was enough room to sit down on the lower lip of the crevasse and eat, our first rest in any pretence of comfort for over eight hours. We were well above the level of Marcel Col now, and our height and closeness gave the impression that we belonged more to the mountain tops than to the valley. We had sweated hard and wanted liquid more than food, but we ate a rusk or two with butter and half-frozen honey. And the closer we came to Tasman, the less we talked of her.

"You're a dark horse, Gillies. Fancy keeping such a nice juicy piece of gossip from us all this time."

"How long have you been engaged?"

"Oh, long enough, too long—and yet too short," he smiled and the strained, concentrating look had gone.

"All the same, you might have told us."

"Sorry, I forgot," he answered quietly, and then, "What? Confide the secrets of my life to you two unsavoury types? You and Powell are the roughest pair of brigands this side of Westland." He rose suddenly and said with businesslike crispness, "Well, can't talk of love, there's work to be done." Bruce was back on the mountain.

Ede went to the front again and after a quick search of both sides of the 'schrund he cut up the Lendenfeld side. The wall was steep but its habitual hard green ice was overlaid with two or three inches of snow, enough to jab crampons in and take thrusting picks. After toiling all day, nose to the mountain, I felt a terrific sensation of release as we came slowly out of the white pit and walked on to the ample summit of the shoulder at 2 pm. At eleven thousand feet we were at last on level terms with the surrounding peaks. Our horizon was no longer vertical but horizontal; the beach fringe of Westland could be seen through a gap in the woolly clouds, the peaks of the Malte Brun Range and the escapement down the Tasman Glacier and moraine. The windshield of a car winked from the Hermitage road. But the invention that we had done with height and depth disappeared when I looked down the east face of Tasman to the shrunken Plateau or over the tumblehome of ice flutings falling to the Westland forest. The last part of the ridge leading up to the summit of Tasman was a thin wafer rising in ice towers where the vertical and the horizontal blended and then went abruptly about their separate business. I felt many things—detachment, exhilaration, concern at the late hour and the infallibility of a night-out if we continued. I wished we hadn't stopped. While you're on the move the mind shuts out impressions from inside as well as from without.

"It's worth a go," said Ede as casually as if he was buying a cake of soap from the corner dairy. "The weather's settled." But there was a thoughtful wrinkle on his forehead.

"What's it going to be? Up or down?" But Gillies was itching to go.

"A pity to chuck it in when we're so close. Might never get the chance again."

Ede looked at the summit and then at me. "What do you think, Paul?"

"I'm not sure," I replied, juggling the hot potato of decision. "I want to climb Tasman, but I also want to get back."

"No question about that," said Ede with a grin, "our skins mean something to us too, y'know."

"It looks darned hairy to me," I said watching the sunfire on the ice and the undulating cornice line to the summit.

"Come on, squire. It's not as bad as it looks," humoured Gillies.

"All right then, Bruce, what are we waiting for?"

We spent the next hour picking a careful way along the ridge and below the wedges that hung delicately over Canterbury. The gap between the North Shoulder and the summit had a last defence: two steep hummocks of ice set like cupolas before a final minaret. When the ridging was knocked away there was room enough for two boot-widths and an abundance of thin air. And so we mounted the switchback until at precisely 4 pm the summit of Mt Tasman was under our feet. Our jubilation on the summit lasted a short seven minutes, a solemn yet ludicrous round of handshaking, a few hurried photographs and a cursory glance at the mountains, and the depths. I had three impressions: relief that we'd at last arrived—the pleasure and the pride came later; admiration for Gillies and Ede; and annoyance that at this intersect with space, we had eyes but so little time to see. Daylight was a ruthless banker and our account was already heavily in overdraft.

I detest hurrying on mountains. To me they're thinking places more than iced poles, but that afternoon as the shadows of Tasman lengthened across the Grand Plateau, I was in the van. We pigeonholed backwards off the top and over the hummocks like three tired courtiers bowing their way from the haughty presence of a throne. After an hour of this we came back to the North Shoulder, picked up our swags and, facing out, cramponned down the hard steep snow to the 'schrund. Time was getting the better of the alpine bargain. The few words we spoke were related strictly to the necessities of the descent. We were ridiculously eager to get down as far as we could before night caught us, yet painfully restrained by the need to take full care. There was no yodelling, no laughing, no philosophy. The peaks grew cold with a creeping white. This was the most dangerous time of a mountain day. We were tired with the continual concentration, and mind and body wanted rest.

The stars came out while we were still on Syme's Ridge but were soon swallowed by bad-weather cloud. We switched on torches and went down into an endless world of the immediate minute where our ambition was no more than the next half-seen step. About 10 pm as we came to the final steep pinch at the end of the ridge and to the top of Ede's morning staircase, my torch dimmed and

went out. Our pace slowed to a fumbling crawl. We were down the
last of the ridge at 10.45 pm but still a long way from home. There
was the mile-long crevasse field under the hanging ice of the east
face and the climb over Glacier Dome still ahead. We shared a
last small cake of frozen chocolate, sucking it slowly with dry
mouths and scummy lips. The rain came, and with it the wind. When
we came to a large avalanche fan newly scuffed across our morning
tracks we debated tiredly whether we should sit the night out, but
Gillies, with his long nose pointed for home, ferreted a way through
the debris and lured us on with mirages of warm blankets and hot
tea. The rising wind hustled us through unending zigzags of a knee-
deep track. The ice-flake came and went. In the foggy darkness we
crossed it *a cheval* with hardly a care for the pit on either side. Another two hours later the worst was over as we plodded wearily
as draught horses out of the snow basin of the Grand Plateau to the
top of Glacier Dome.

But trouble badgered us all the way home to the hut. We doddered
over the rocks of Glacier Dome and wandered in thick mist which hid
the landmark of the Lady's Slipper. Even the irrepressible Gillies
was ready to give up and sit the rest of the night out within reach of
the Haast Hut. Just as we were getting ready to huddle the remaining
night hours out, the mist swirled dramatically aside and through the
wispy gap, we saw an angry green-yellow dawn come up against the
black crags of Malte Brun. We stumbled down to the hut quite done
in. It was 4.35 am and we had been on the mountain for twenty-
seven hours.

We awoke still craving sleep, but Gillies was due in Oamaru that
night. As we sorted out our belongings, the subtle change from hill
to city had begun. But when we bolted the door and turned our
backs to go down to the valley, the Haast Hut was still there, a link
between the mountain and ourselves.

We stopped once on the Tasman Glacier and looked back. The
long rock spine of the Haast Ridge ran up to Glacier Dome. Behind,
Tasman was a fleeting vision in the nor'-west scud.

"Do you realise," said Jack, "that we spent a week-end climbing
Mt Tasman?"

"Yes, I suppose we did." I traced the ridge from the valley moraine
to where the Haast Refuge nestled against the rock with the door
waiting to be opened and the two windowed eyes staring at Malte
Brun.

9

"Heath" in the West Matukituki

Let us be Diana's foresters, gentlemen of the shade, minions of
the moon.

—Henry IV, Pt 1, Act 1, Sc 2

"COME CLIMBING," said Barrie Jones the morning we met in the
Medical School canteen in Dunedin. "You haven't forgotten your
promise, surely?"

"Of course not," I parried as I scratched my head. I'd make lots
of promises, the trouble was to keep track of them.

"Remember?" said Po Chambers, lumbering up like a great blonde
bear with a spreading smile and a cup of tea. "Last year you said
we'd all go to the French Ridge, up the old Matuk."

"Sure, sure. But do you think May's the month to go gallivanting
around the mountains? Days are short, frosty if it's fine and snowing
if it's not."

"No excuses, Powell," said Barrie. "It's all arranged, you can't
wriggle out."

"What about transport? How do we get there?"

"How else but in old faithful, in *Heath*? She's all ready and purrin'
to go," said Barrie.

"Hurrah for the *real* mountains." Po shook a great ham fist. "I'm
fed up with ski-fields and moronic women."

"Oh, well," I replied slowly, as if faced by an insuperable problem, "but we'll need a fourth. I'll see if I can talk Colin Marshall and Bill Hockin into joining our push. They've been up to French Hut before."

"How far's the French Hut? How many hours from the end of the road?" asked Po.

"If, and it's a big if, *Heath* gets us up the road to Wanaka, it's the best part of thirty miles up to Cameron Flat. The last fifteen miles is pretty rough as much of the road's no more than a dray-track and the open fords just love cars that get stuck in them."

"No trouble to *Heath*." Barry had faith in the old bus. "She'll eat them without pepper or salt."

"I hope so. We'll leave her at Hell's Gates."

"OK, but how far do we have to walk?" inquired Po with a serious frown. "I don't fancy being a human packhorse."

"Four easy hours to Cascade Hut, two hours up the west branch to Pearl Flat. Cross the river and up the French Ridge, another three or four hours."

"Phew!" said Po, wiping his forehead. "Six hours up the valley with a four-hour climb at the end of it." He looked at Barrie. "That's not what you told me yesterday, Jones."

"Don't worry." Barrie's face was as bland and innocent as a sweet old lady's. "We'll just stooge along, taking our time."

When the great moment of departure came, we piled in, Po taking the wheel with Barrie sitting beside him. Marshall and I clambered into the back among the char sacks and sieve. This wasn't my first trip in *Heath*. I knew her all too well. She was a black 1927 Buick with the constitution of an ostrich and the cunning of an anaconda. After nights of work and ingenuity we had converted her to a gas-producer, and we fed her on a diet of charcoal. Her tyres were threadbare, her brakes untrustworthy—she'd once run out of control down one of the steepest streets in Dunedin—and when she was in one of her stubborn moods she knew how far to drive us to the brink of foaming frustration. I don't know whether *Heath* had a soul, but she certainly had a mind and was an expert in brink-manship.

So when we sailed out of Dunedin and tackled the first hill I was sitting pretty close to the edge of the seat, just waiting for her to exhibit some new aspect of her never-ending crankiness. All went well until we were some ten miles along the main north road and struggling to crawl over the final pinch of a hill with the cheerful name of the Kilmog. I suddenly got that feeling that came when you suspected *Heath* was thinking up some annoying ploy. The old girl gave a few coughs and slowed to a crawl.

"All out and push," yelled Barrie. But as soon as we jumped out to shove, she picked up revs and started hurtling along the flat stretch with a full-throated roar from the exhaust.

"Satisfying sound, ain't it?" Po yelled at me as I jumped on the running board and crawled over the char sacks.

"Sounds louder than last time I was in the old bus. What have you done to her? Fitted another carburettor?"

"Nothing as complicated or as expensive as that, Paul. The muffler fell off, it was all burned out. Didn't bother to fit another. Makes her sound pretty powerful though, don't you think?"

"It's a state of mind. As far as I'm concerned, she's still the same lovable, stubborn old witch."

The other side of the Kilmog twisted down between hills where the smell of the sea came in tangy from the headlands. The bitumen stretched ahead in a flicker of lights. The engine hummed and the tyres sang as the canvas slapped the wet road.

"At this rate, we'll be at Cameron Flat before dawn," said Barrie.

"I'll believe that when we get there. She's running too well. Makes me suspicious. Bet she's cooking up something really good." *Heath* did that to you. She never gave you the chance to relax. I suddenly appreciated the valour of men who first flew long distances across wild oceans. We were lucky—there was always the consolation of solid ground under our wheels.

"Can't you smell something hot?"

"Bearings?"

"No. It's somewhere in the back."

"That's only Paul's cheap tobacco."

"No, it's worse than that."

The car started to swerve, and Po, wrestling with the great wooden steering wheel, struggled to keep her on the road.

"The brakes have gone." Po sounded really alarmed. We shot down the road, while he swore and tried to crash the lever into a lower gear. The car lurched from side to side flinging Marshall and me into a heap among the char.

We made it, and eventually freewheeled to a stop beside an embankment.

"That was close," said Jones.

"Too hot for my liking," I said.

"Hot's not the word. Flaming," interrupted Marshall, running round from the rear of the car. "The ruddy brakes are on fire."

We scurried round searching for water in the ditches, but they were as dry as a North Otago summer.

"There's only one thing for it," said Barrie.

In the full glare of the traffic we followed his resourceful example.

"Lucky thing there were four of us," grinned Marshall.

When Barrie, who had a penchant for rapid diagnosis, found that we'd been driving with the handbrake partly on, there were moments of slight friction in our camp. After that things went pretty smoothly. The radiator hose sprang a leak and somewhere near Omakau we carried water from irrigation ditches. Two days later we crawled up the last bulge in the track leading through the high bracken near Cameron Flat.

"Not a bad trip," said Po as we went to earth among the wool bales in Jerry Aspinall's shed.

"Depends what you mean by bad," rejoined Marshall. "I'd say that we've left a trail of damage behind us in Central Otago that would make the Goths and Huns go bilious with envy. Quite a catalogue—burnt-out brakes on the Kilmog, one roadside fire where we declinkered near Alexandra, one cocky's field of uncut hay partly burned—that's at least two indictable offences."

"Certainly enough to give us each a six-month stretch in the cooler," I added.

"They say the food's pretty good though." Po was a realist.

"Offence number three," continued Marshall. "Disturbance of the peace, roaring through sundry towns in the middle of the night and waking the slumbering inhabitants."

"Good for the population increase," said Po seriously. "Otago can do with it. Reckon we should get a medal for that."

"What about general nuisance?" I chipped in. "Garage men dragged out of bed at midnight, and unpaid."

"That's no crime," said Barrie. "Everyone knows students are always broke."

"There's more yet." Marshall took a mournful pleasure in listing our misdeeds. "Taking one only length of fencing wire to lash on a disintegrating gas-producer unit."

"We'll be lucky if we get off with a life sentence."

"And further, damage to stock. Sundry animals hit on the way up from Wanaka. We'll have the SPCA, the Federated Farmers, the Agriculture Department and the Police after us, the lot." Barrie gave Po an accusing look.

"You blokes are always against me," moaned Po. "It wasn't my fault the blasted brakes kept on failing."

"You were driving at the time. Funny coincidence isn't it, that as soon as you get behind the wheel, we land in trouble?"

"True enough, Po," I couldn't resist a final twist of the screw. "They'll log you for dangerous driving too. At least a fifty quid fine."

"That's worse than prison." Po was the picture of dejection. He raked his thick blond thatch with a worried hand. "That settles it then. It's full speed ahead up the old Matuk to the French Hut.

Sounds a perfect hide-out, we'll be safe up there, eh?" And he grinned.

Rain came lashing down the valley in the early morning but by dawn it eased off. The paddocks smelled fresh and the river sounds came clear from the mountains.

"I wonder—" were Po's first words.

"Oh Lord, here he goes again."

"I was wondering," speculated Po in a voice that always harbinged trouble, "if we can't coax *Heath* on a bit further. I see the road goes up to those bluffs. What do you call them?"

"Hell's Gates," I prompted.

"Strikes me it's silly to walk if we can ride. What say we stoke up the old fire in the gas producer and hurtle up to the Gates?"

"The only place you'll hurtle us into is the river," commented Marshall with early morning acidity.

"And what's more," said Po, dropping his voice to a whisper, "it'll be a wonderful place to hide the Old Bomb, tucked out of sight from prying eyes behind those big boulders."

We lit the fire in the producer drum and waited until there was enough gas pressure to drive the battered black Juggernaut up the grassy flat with a pall of evil smoke hanging over the road behind us. "Looks like the oil fires after the evacuation of Dunkirk," commented Barrie.

About three-quarters of a mile on, the road petered out by the river. A deserted rabbiter's camp huddled against a large boulder and a handful of sorry beech trees clung to the riverbank.

"Can't leave her here," muttered Po, "too populated. If that rabbiter bloke comes back he's bound to give the show away."

"You're exaggerating as usual," said Marshall. But Po took no notice as he took a rapid appraisal of the green water skipping and bobbing between the shingly banks and set *Heath's* nose dead on course for the river.

"Stop, you dolt!" from Barrie.

"Stand by to abandon ship," I said, fighting my way over Marshall and the char bags until I stood on the running board.

"She'll never make it, it's far too deep," lamented Colin Marshall.

"Won't she?" said Po, fending off Barrie's hand and gripping the steering wheel with the grim determination of a clipper helmsman in a China Sea typhoon. "She'll waltz across, you see." And he thumped the outer panel-work of the car door with his fist.

Committed to the river, there was no turning back now so we hopped out and gave Po steering directions. With the water foaming over the running boards and a heaped-up pile of river at her stern, *Heath* slogged her way over. Once, her square bonnet dipped into a hole in the river bottom and the water rose, lapping the air intake for the gas-producer drum.

"For gawd's sake watch your steering," yelled Barrie, dancing up and down in the river. "If you do that again you'll put the fire out."

I had been in ships negotiating the approaches to the Mersey where the magnetic mines waited among the litter of sunken ships, but this was the zaniest piece of pilotage I had ever experienced. When *Heath* clanked cascading from the river with a wild arm waving at the wheel, we jumped on the running board and thumped Po on the back until he called for mercy.

"Chambers, you're a blooming marvel."

"I knew the old bitch could do it," he grinned modestly.

We conned our panting monster across the hummocked flat and finally docked her in the seclusion of a grove of beech trees. Po climbed out of the driver's seat like a triumphant winner of a Grand Prix. He gave the bonnet a friendly slap and then turned to us and said nonchanantly, "When do we eat? We haven't had breakfast yet, and I could eat the hind quarters off a dead donkey."

There wasn't much food, as we'd spent our combined savings on char and other necessities for the road; *Heath* always came first. But Barrie dug out some bacon, and Marshall and I produced the last of the butter and bread from the rear seat of the car.

"I'll get the wood for the fire," I volunteered.

"No need for that," said Barrie, not to be outdone in ingenuity by Chambers. "*Heath* has everything," and he opened the cleaning door of the gas unit. A stream of glowing molten char fell sizzling on the wet grass. "Here, put your frying-pan on that. It'll cook the bacon before you can say Aspinall. Boil the billy for tea too."

As we squatted on the grass chewing bacon and dry bread with the sun throwing a mottled pattern of light and shadows through the canopy of beech trees, Marshall caught my eye. "This is the life, eh, Paul?"

The river bent shining from the mountains, slow cloud drifted across the Shark's Tooth, and Mt Tyndall was a snow-barred pyramid above the red rock of its attendant saddle. A high-flying kea crossed the valley with wild cries echoing among the bluffs.

"Come on," I said with that blend of restlessness and ease that mountains inspire, "let's get up the valley, and no stopping until Cascade Hut."

We boiled the billy there and then set off again, Marshall leading the van, I just looking at the mountains, and Po and Barrie arguing in the rear. This was my first trip into the head of the west branch of the Matukituki, though I'd been with Jerry Aspinall the previous summer as far as Cascade, mustering sheep.

"What is man, that Thou
art mindful of him?"
A storm-misted
Mt Tutoko seen from
Ngapunatoru Pass.

"After four hours ha
digging the cave was
ready. . . ."
Graham Ellis watche
Roland Rodda work
on the snow cave on
Tutoko Saddle. In th
background rises the
snow-plastered west
of Mt Tutoko.

"When dawn came we were the most bedraggled crew the Harrison had ever
seen. . . ."
From left: Roland Rodda, Paul Powell, Graham Ellis under the mai-mai in the
lower Harrison Valley.

When we came out of the bush at Shovel Flat and saw the dull green of the French Ridge forest rising beyond the tawny pasture, Po threw a suggestion that it seemed one heck of a long way to French Hut.

"And it is," Colin assured him. "All of four hours from here. It's further than it looks. The tussock ridge runs back a long way."

"Hmmm," said Po. "They are *real* mountains all right, aren't they? Lots of snow, too."

"Yes," replied Colin, with an edge to his voice that boded of a grim struggle ahead. "There's lots of snow."

Half an hour later we forded the river at Pearl Flat and started up the track, a very determinate track which wasted no time in letting us know that the hardest part of the day still lay ahead. By the time we had dragged ourselves up the slabby watercourses and the scrubby steeps to the big rock which marks the beginning of the alpine meadow, none of us felt very frisky. The weather had taken a turn for the worse, the upper part of the ridge lay under surly cloud and light snow came with the sou'-west wind.

"How are you going, Po?" I asked.

"I'll manage. One foot in front of the other, but I'll get there."

A few hundred feet above the tarns we ran into the first snowdrifts, and soon we were up to our knees in the stuff. The light started to fade and the wind became stronger; it stormed out of the dreary cirque at the head of the valley with an edge as keen as a scythe. We all took turns at breaking trail, and the jauntiness of the earlier hours was gone. Even Barrie was silent as he leaned into the wind as he pushed uphill.

But Po was as jolly as a friar on a feast day after Lent. His exuberance was without end. "Wish I had my boards with me. Marvellous snow for skiing. Lovely dry powder snow."

But I thought that the windblown snow which had found its way through my parka was terrible and all too wet as it ran melting down my back.

Night had come, a dark night of driving snow that built long icicles on the rocks where our torches shone, but this didn't seem to worry Po at all and he started to sing a long wobbling song that went on and on just like the ridge and the snow.

Even when we couldn't find the hut, Po was still annoyingly cheerful. "It must be round here somewhere, in one of these hollows. It's quite simple. We just keep on searching until we find it."

In a mood approaching frustration we went back to the ridge and started again. For another twenty minutes we beat over every hollow on the miserable hillside, but no hut.

"If we can't find it after another go, I think we'll have to down and shelter for the night on Pearl Flat or at least down to the scrub line. We'll freeze to death out here."

"Like hell we will," growled Po. "I haven't dragged myself all this way up here just for nothing. I want that warm bunk and I want it bad."

When I was on the point of giving up, a torch waved in the darkness and a shout came faintly against the wind. When we reached Po he was busy digging the snow away from the hut door.

"How did you find it," I asked.

"I didn't find it, I walked into the blasted thing. Thought it was a snow covered rock. I was looking for something a lot bigger."

"What a pack of dolts," laughed Barrie, coming up to the door and knocking the ice off his parka. "We've been walking all round the place in the dark."

"Stupid site for a hut," said Colin. "Why on earth didn't they build it out on the crest of the ridge where you couldn't miss it?"

Whatever our comments outside, when we got in through the small door, we were loud in praise of the hut. No more than ten by eight, it was snug and well designed. A continuous bunk large enough for six people stretched the full width of the back wall. There were mattresses, six down sleepingbags, cooking utensils and a two-burner petrol stove on the small bench to one side of the door. A diminutive window above the bench gave promise of a spectacular view of Gloomy Gorge. The pitch of the roof was enough to allow head room if you stood in the centre of the wooden floor, and the walls lined with wood panels gave more than a pretence of insulation. A hut book with a hard leather cover and a first-aid kit were stowed neatly on the cross members of the roof. I'd been in plenty of huts before, but for its size, this was the best I'd seen yet; it had an air of compact security that made you glad to hear the wind and the blown ice spicules rattling against the corrugated iron exterior.

"She's a little beauty," said Po enthusiastically. "Worth every bit of push getting up here."

"There was a lot more sweat used getting it all up here," said Colin as he peeled off his storm clothing and hung it to drain on the coat-hook behind the door.

"Every bit of the hut was lugged up on climbers' backs. A pretty good effort when you realise that we're at 5,000 feet."

The release from the storm, the sound of the two burners licking merrily under the pots, and the thought of a snug night while the hail flew was heaven. We were as chirpy as cicadas, as nothing in our whole world of experience could compare with this small kernel of safety. We had a hasty supper and went to bed, an island of conviviality in a howling, hostile environment. I lay exulting in the comfort, listening to the wind trumpeting away on the ridge and watching the slow burning of the solitary candle beside me. Life was light and warmth and companionship and all were best when you had to labour for them.

"What do we climb tomorrow?" asked the insatiable Po. "Mt French?"

"The way the weather sounds, Po Chambers, the only climbing you'll be doing will be in and out of your bunk."

"Oh well," murmured Po from the depths of his sleepingbag, "a day's spine-bashing will suit me just fine. Life's been rather hectic lately."

Morning when it came with a gradual filtering of light through the iced-up window was no more than a fulfilment of the overnight promise. The wind blew and the hail kept up its savage rattle. But there was plenty to do. We ate with the slow relish of hungry men who could eat more. The miscellany of tins lining the shelves above the cooking bench furnished some rice and oatmeal extra to our rations. Hungry mountaineers are never too proud to pounce on the leftovers of other parties, and scavenging among mysterious tins is a challenge as well as a joy. I made a concoction of rice, oatmeal, a few slices of onion and some finely chopped-up bacon rind which I called chupatties. The others complained that they were just what you'd expect a budding dentist to compound. They called them jawbreakers, but they ate them and then berated me because there weren't more.

After lunch—a cup of tea and a scraping of fat from the pan spread over a piece of bread the size of a small water biscuit—Barrie went outside to research.

"You're mad, Jones," we told him. "Why go outside on a day like this?"

"Someone's got to carry on the scientific work of the expedition," he said waving a maximum-minimum thermometer under our noses. "I'm going to cut snow sections and measure temperatures. And it's a pity that you morons," he went on as he pulled on his parka, "don't find something better to do than to lie like a lot of overfed cattle in your sleepingbags."

"Good on him," said Po after Barrie had closed the hut door behind him. "Saves me going out. No sense in us all being martyrs. I'm all for enjoying the blessings of science in comfort. Anyway, it gives the eager beavers a sense of superiority."

"That's rather tough on Barrie, isn't it? You couldn't get a more modest bloke."

"Sure," said Po. "But Barrie's all do and no talk. Most of them are the reverse."

An hour later I crawled out of my bag. "Can't hold off any longer," I announced amid the ironic cheers of Marshall and Chambers. "Your turn's coming," I retorted as I went out into the whiplash.

"We'll send a search party out for you tomorrow," I heard Colin yell through the closing door.

I didn't waste any time, it wasn't exactly the day for enthusing over the glories of Nature. On the way back I called on Professor Jones. With the hut shovel he'd dug himself a snow cave—the first experimental model in the Mt Aspiring country—and was absorbed in studying different bands of snow and ice in its chilly interior. He was not concerned with the snow that blew around his uncovered ears. "Come and join me," he invited.

I clambered in and he gave me a discourse on the physical properties of snow and ice crystals while I shivered and thought longingly of my cosy bag. When I couldn't stand the cold any longer I rushed over to the hut.

"You look cold," said Marshall, with an irritating statement of the obvious.

"You can say that again. There's only one thing wrong with this hut, there's no privy. The proverbial monkey wouldn't last long out there."

"How's Barrie getting on?" asked Po, lifting his eyes from a well-thumbed Penguin book.

"Fine. Don't know how he does it. He's completely happy out there working away with his snow tests."

When Jones came back into the hut he brought news that the wind had dropped and patches of blue sky were breaking through to windward. This had an instantaneous effect on Chambers. With one bound he was out of his sack and peering through the hut window. "Goodoh, eh? Climb tomorrow," he said with a face alight with expectation.

"I hope you'll be as eager as that when the alarm goes off in the morning, Po. It's your turn to cook the breakfast."

His face dropped a bit when I said that, and I followed up with, "Ever cooked breakfast in a high hut before, Po?"

"Well, no," he admitted cautiously.

"It's the experience of a lifetime, isn't it Colin?"

"That's right," said Marshall, with a disarming innocence. "And it's an established and time-honoured custom that the sprog climber in the party always cooks the first early morning brekker."

"Well in that case," agreed Chambers, "I'll hash you up something that will stick to your ribs all day, provided you'll take me up Mt French."

"We absolutely guarantee it," I told him.

When it was Po's turn to go out into the cold, Barrie turned to Colin and me. "Trust you two for a couple of old shysters. Fancy working a fast one like that on poor old Chambers."

"A pretty harmless initiation for a new chum, really," I said defensively.

"Fair enough." Colin came to my rescue. "We old hands deserve an extra lie-in on a cold morning. That means you too, Barrie."

"You've talked me into it," said Jones.

Po came back, "Going to be a beaut day tomorrow. What say we have a crack at Aspiring instead?"

"I think," I said soberly as I leant over and snuffed out the candle, "that we'll see first how we get on with our campaign against General French."

It had been a good day, we had a haven and the hope of a mountain with tomorrow's sun. But most of all, we'd had fun, and that's what huts and mountains were for.

The burr of the primus woke me.

"Tea's ready," said Po. "Don't get up yet, I'll bring it over to you."

"What's the time?"

"A quarter to four on a fine frosty morning. I've been out to the ridge and had a wander around. It's terrific. Not a cloud anywhere and no wind either, and the snow's good and hard where there aren't any drifts. Breakfast'll be ready in a few minutes."

"Much too early, it's still dark. What time did you get up, Po?"

"Oh, about three."

"You're crazy. This is winter. It won't be dawn until half past six."

"I couldn't sleep. Too excited," said Po, scratching the spoon against the sides of the porridge pot until my teeth were on edge.

"You could have let us sleep for at least another hour," grunted Barrie. "If we get up now we'll only have to hang around in the cold until it gets light enough to move."

Chambers faced the grumpy faces: "Sorry about that," he said contritely. "I thought you'd all be pleased to get a really early alpine start." He went on stirring the porridge. "But I don't know what you blokes are grizzling about, it was damned cold when I got up. There was ice on the floor, and the water was frozen."

"Serves you right," I said. "We distinctly told you to set the alarm for half past six."

"All right." Chambers thumped the pot on the stove so hard that the plates jumped on the cooking bench. A tin fell to the floor and rolled under the bunk. Po glared at us: "You're a pack of ungrateful hounds. Next time you get the breakfast." And he gave the cooker a vicious pump.

"It was a nice cup of tea, Po," offered Barrie.

"Huh!" Po kept his back to us.

"You've offended him, Paul."

"Sorry I was bitchy, Po," I called. "I'm always like that first thing in the morning."

"You'd better not get married. If you wake up like that on your bridal morning, your wife'll knock your head in."

"We shouldn't have any trouble in getting to the top of French today." Barrie was a born diplomat.

"Well, what are we waiting for?" grinned Po. "But let's have breakfast first."

We emerged into a dawn of incredible space and colour. Riffled snow caught the first glimmer of light but the dark valleys were still heavy with sleep. The bite of the air, the crunch of crampons and the curve of ridge against the sky soon burnished away our earlier moodiness.

From the top of the nearest snow dome I saw the hut, almost invisible in the vast dimension of the morning. An hour before it had been the centre of our existence. Now it had shrunk to a small pip in the white pith of the mountains, but it had been a citadel, a mental balance-point between the mountain and ourselves. The day before we'd struggled up the hill and, completely absorbed in our need for cover, had seen nothing of the peaks. Now we moved in a world of light.

The others had moved ahead—we hadn't yet put the rope on—and they stood hallooing and waving their arms, urging me not to muck about any longer but to come up and climb the mountain. I waited until the echoes had drifted across the glowing fire of the awakening icefield and blended into the contrapuntal silence of the running summits. All too soon we'd be caught up in the climbing technicalities which would demand unwavering concentration.

"Come on, Paul. We're getting cold."

"Pull your finger out, you silly hump."

"You're like a pregnant old penguin with morning sickness."

I took a last glance at the valley. "Keep your wool on, I'm coming."

"Arrurra-uh!" I saw Po cup his hands as he lifted his head and gave the grunting roar of a mating stag. This was his signal, his call to be up and doing.

The ridge narrowed and the overhanging ice cornices leaned like effulgent eaves over the dark pit of Gloomy Gorge shining through the gauzy mist as so many daggers of bright light. I walked slowly up the curving trail of flashing crystals, toward the others waiting impatiently on the steep threshold of the Quarter Deck.

"Sorry I've kept you all waiting," I said. "My crampon bindings came undone. Had to stop and fix them up."

"We'd better hurry." Barrie pointed to the feathered clouds high above the rim of Mt French. "Take a gander at the sky. There's wind coming."

Po stood like an uncertain St Bernard in the centre, looking at us and then toward the mountain like an impatient hound waiting to be off. "We're not going to turn back now?" he asked. "Can't we sneak up before the weather breaks?"

"Don't fret yourself, Chambers. We'll keep our promise."

"Ever been on a rope before?" queried Marshall, busily uncoiling the line and measuring it out in four equal lengths.

"Not that I remember," replied Po. "But I've read all about it. That should help shouldn't it?"

"In a *Teach Yourself to Climb* paperback, I suppose," said Marshall with a snort as he tied a loop with an overhand knot and tossed it casually over to Chambers.

"That's yours," he said.

"Thanks," said Po. "I'd like something to hang on to, it looks rather steep up there."

"You don't hang on to it, you get into it. Look, like this. You pull the loop over your head, and then tighten the knot at your waist."

"I'd rather hang on to it," said Po. "It's darned uncomfortable like this." He looked reflectively down at the rope around his waist and then up the mountainside. "And dangerous. If one of you blokes fell and pulled me off, the strain would cut me in half."

"You don't need to worry about any of *us* falling," said Colin pointedly.

"That's reassuring," said Po seriously. "I've got a good head for heights myself."

We put him in the middle of the rope, the safest place for a new chum. Colin and I were at either end. While Barrie and Colin made a final check, I gave Po a quick course on how to climb with axe in one hand and the rope in the other. "You carry the rope in coils like this, Po, see?"

He nodded his head in rapid understanding. "Looks simple enough," he said confidently. He waved his axe in the air and growled from his hunched shoulders, "What are we waiting for? Let's go up and climb ol' man French."

"He's going to be a menace," whispered Colin.

"Aw, give him a fair go. He's a good bloke, he'll soon pick it up.

I've seen first-timers go green at the thought of a rope, but he's so wonderfully cheerful."

"That's what I mean. He's got the heartiness of the ignorant."

"Nonsense," I said. "He's just Po."

"Just the same," said Colin, "I'd keep a wary eye on him. God knows what he'll do when we come to the crevasses."

We soon found out.

"I suppose you've read about these too?" said Colin as we stood on the lower lip of the first crevasse.

"A bit." Po nodded modestly while he worried away with his axe spike at the edge of the crevasse.

"I wouldn't do that, Po," I said. "They're temperamental brutes, they've been known to collapse."

"Oh," replied Po taking two or three skips to safety.

We picked out a zigzag line of least resistance and started through the maze.

"And make sure you follow exactly in my steps," Colin sang out over his shoulder. "If you feel a snowbridge breaking, for the love of Christopher Columbus, yell out. Like this." Colin gave a yell of "tight rope" that made the rocks of Mt French twang like a jew's harp; the echoes seemed to vibrate against the mountain wall for minutes. When silence had once more settled across the startled glacier, Colin led off. With his prodding axe and head cocked listening to one side, he looked like a hungry blackbird on an early-morning lawn.

Over the first few crevasse bridges Po followed with surprising obedience. With unconscious mimicry he copied Colin's every move; the sounding ice-axe, the carefully-planted foot, the ear waiting for the first creak of a protesting bridge. "Attaboy, Po," I yelled. "You're going like a bomb."

He gave me a beaming smile and shook both gloved hands in the air like a victorious heavyweight champion at the triumphant end of the tenth round. "A piece of cheese, eh, Paul? We'll climb the old cow yet."

"Just watch that rope, though. You've got it wrapped round your fist like a ball of wool. Carry it in coils in your left hand as I showed you."

Po waved a brief acknowledgment with his axe and then applied himself to the struggle of *Chambers* v *Mt French*. But I noticed that he no longer trod assiduously in Colin's steps. He started cutting the corners. And the rope, instead of hanging in swinging coils from a hand ready for his leader's slip, was wound in a tangle over his hand and halfway up his forearm.

"The latest technique in rope-handling," chortled Barrie. "Imagine what Mick Bowie would say!"

And in such fashion we climbed over the steep snow shoulder of
Mt French and saw the Bonar Glacier falling in a concave westward
sweep around the jutting base of Mt Aspiring. The view was in-
credibly beautiful. For months I'd wondered about it, but now, in
what should have been a rapt moment of alpine revelation, I could
do nothing but laugh. Barrie laughed and even Colin, who took his
technique earnestly, relented with a spreading grin. And Po, the
unconscious hero of the ascent, the potential hub of all our danger,
beamed with such transparent warmth and good humour that we
clapped him on the back with as much respect as if he'd led us
unscathed up the north wall of the Eiger.

"Thanks Po, for the most hilarious climb I've ever had."

"Glad you enjoyed it, Paul," he said, "but for heaven's sake let's
get along the summit ridge to French. If you dolts don't stop laughing, you'll drag me down to Gloomy Gorge. This mountaineering's
a serious business."

We guffawed our way along the easy snow ridge. If there were
tears in our eyes they didn't come from the wind which bowed the
rope and rattled our parkas as we crowded together on the topmost
snow.

"How does it feel, Po, to have a real mountain under your feet?"

Chambers took a quick swing around the horizon at Aspiring, the
Haast Range, the far Tasman Sea coppered with approaching nor'-
west storm: "Marvellous, just marvellous. Like a bridegroom the
morning after his first night."

"Chambers," I said, "if you're always as honest as that, you'll
make a damn fine mountaineer."

The storm chased us home. We went back down the Quarter Deck
with sober speed, Po still insistent on his unorthodox technique. On
the edge of the crevassed country I had a quick word with Barrie
and Colin. Po couldn't hear us as he was away open-mouthed in an
incredulous world of mountains.

"Now this time we'll really have to watch him. The snow's softened
in the nor'-wester and if he tries any more of his short cuts across
the crevasses, he'll go in like an oyster down an alderman's gullet.
And he could stay down."

We were ready when it happened. Po had just said with the right
inflexion of gratitude in his voice, "I'll never forget this day," when
his conversational snowbridge collapsed, and down he went, right
to the neck. We held him easily enough, a surprised white face
hardly distinguishable from the ruff of snow under his chin: "And
here's another thing you'll never forget," we lectured him without
malice while he swung airily from the middle of the taut rope, "Do

what you're told. We don't like inquests, they muck up our climbing plans."

We let him hang there for a second or two just to let the lesson sink home, but when we hauled him out like a seal from its breathing hole, all he said was, "Certainly a novel experience, I wouldn't have missed it for quids."

What can you do with a man like that? There was only one solution; we marched hilariously down to the French Hut, put on the primus and brewed up a toddy of hot cocoa laced with medicinal rum.

"Here's to General French and his hut," said Po, raising his mug to the rafters.

"And to Po Chambers, the almost invisible snowman," I added with a wink across the steamy billy.

We really lived those few days in the French Hut.

The next day was dour with rain and sleet as we pushed down the soggy snow, through the dripping bush to Pearl Flat and headed for Hell's Gates. We were hungry and we were wet. At nightfall when the grove of trees where *Heath* lay concealed came in sight over the rock jumble of Old Homestead Creek we were silent and dispirited; our reluctance to leave the mountains came from more than a nostalgia for our high days in the French Hut.

Barrie put it succinctly when he came up to *Heath*. Giving her rear left-hand tyre a hefty boot, he growled: "I wonder what particular unpleasantness the old girl has been thinking up while we were away?"

But our spirits recovered when the fire roared in her steel belly and she chugged stolidly down to the river. We found an easier ford this time and crossed with little difficulty. As we bumped down the tussock track to Cameron Flat I couldn't resist one last look up-valley. A faint wisp of smoke still hovered over the sombre trees where we'd parked *Heath* and the river sounds came dully through the rain. Two oystercatchers flew with thin querulous cries toward the home paddocks of the Aspinall homestead. There was warmth and comfort over there where the forest ran down from the slopes of Homestead Peak. But we had to go.

"Where are you off to in the hills next, Paul?"

"Some place where there's forest and good wood to burn—back to Westland. Bruce Gillies and Rol Rodda are after Mt Sefton. They've asked me to join them."

10

Adventure in the Hooker

Go, madman, and traverse the rugged Alps, that you may please
the boys and become a subject for recitation.

—Juvenal

MOUNTAINEERS aren't always open about their plans, especially when
unclimbed peaks beckon. This is normal rather than unusual or
sinister; it's part of the game, perhaps the reason for it. Even in the
1940s there weren't many plums left in the Mt Cook orchard. After
sixty years the mountaineering wind had shaken most of the fruit
down. But there were a few choice specimens left, and Mt Brunner
was one of them. Mt Brunner lay at the far end of one of the branches
of the alpine tree and we could see it every time we walked outside
the Hermitage bar and stared up at Mt Sefton, but for all its tantalis-
ing closeness it was not easily reached—there was no chance of
knocking it off with a stick. We'd have to climb right over the other
side of the tree to get at it, and Mt Sefton and the Main Divide were
in the way.

Roland Rodda had been a climbing friend of mine since Wellington days and when he set his eyes on a plum he usually got it. Being as healthily acquisitive as the next man, where mountains were concerned, I was rather pleased when he confided in me one day that we should go and do something about Mt Brunner; and when we found out that Bruce Gillies was interested too, what could be more natural than that we should consider Brunner our inalienable property?

We met at the Hermitage a few days before Christmas 1944 and to conceal our real objective, mentioned carelessly that we were bound for a fortnight's climbing in the upper Hooker Valley. There was a secondary plum up there called Mt Cook, and though that mountain had been climbed many times before, this Christmas Day would be the fiftieth anniversary of the first ascent in 1894. So our motive was more historical than criminal, and Mt Cook would make a fine Christmas present.

We three conspirators met at the Hermitage. Up to this stage all had gone well. No word of our design on Mt Brunner had leaked out —we were forbidden to mention the name in the marketplaces of the alpine world—and it seemed that all we needed to pop the mountain in the bag was a little luck and a large slice of good weather. But the weather part of our staffwork seemed to have slipped up and the peaks were heavily coated with new snow.

"I don't like it at all, squire," said Gillies, pushing his ski cap over one ear and scratching his temple reflectively. "Too much snow. More like skiing conditions than climbing."

"We'll leave for Brunner just the same," said Rol with an extra clench on his pipe. "It's bound to improve sometime."

By late that afternoon we were comfortably sitting in the lower Hooker Hut, counting our jam tins and ready for the first phase of the offensive, the push over the Copland Saddle down to Welcome Flat Hut.

We were up at dawn the next morning, hopeful and full of élan, but the Copland Ridge was uninvitingly beset with blizzard and even the Hooker Hut shook as the sou'-west gusts rumbled up the valley.

"Give it until after breakfast, it won't look so bad then." Rodda stuffed another palm of tobacco into his pipe and went back inside the hut. He inspired confidence. He was so matter of fact, and never gave the slightest taint of drama to any mountain situation. But I thought of the wind and the blowing snow, a heavy swag and a wet hide. I would have been happy to have settled for another day and a night in the Hooker Hut. In daylight, the previous night's noises of the hut's resident ghost alarmed me far less than an alpine storm: as far as I knew ghosts didn't give you frostbite but blizzards did.

We hung around for a few hours waiting for a lull in the weather. The term hanging around was only figurative. Gillies prowled restlessly between the hut table and the door, watching the ridge to the pass, Rodda checked and re-checked his gear with infinite pleasure, and I ate. Nervous men, they say, always eat continually before action. I must have been very nervous.

"Lay off the tucker, boy, we need that for Brunner."

"It's an hour since we had breakfast, Rol. I'm doing us a good turn, getting rid of some weight. Anyway," I said, looking at a swag large enough for one of Hannibal's transalpine elephants, "there's plenty of food. We could have a lovely fortnight sitting in the sun, when it comes. Those tarns back along the Hermitage track would be fine swimming holes."

"The trouble with people these days," said Gillies, making his tenth trek between the table and the door, "is that they don't know how to relax," and he flung himself on to the nearest bunk like a piece of coiled-up clockspring.

We were so busy thinking of the weather that we didn't hear the wind drop. But Rol soon realised that the awaited lull had come. "Come on, let's get weaving and get over the pass." He was as eager to meet the enemy as a subaltern with a swagger stick and a whistle.

We were well up the ridge when the barrage came down, a gale force wind driving bursts of whirling snow.

"I knew it would be like this," I shouted at Rodda who was hanging on like the rest of us to the handiest outcrop of snow-covered rock. Our cursed swags had one advantage—they stopped us being blown away.

"Know-all!" yelled Rol.

I didn't reply. Perhaps he was right.

"It's got to get worse before it gets better," said Gillies with the fatalistic humour of the hills.

It did get worse. I caught a quick flash of the roof of the Hooker Hut before the storm shutters clamped down. I didn't regret that extra egg for breakfast. "You told me this was an easy day for a lady," I said to Gillies.

"So it is. They race over here on a fine day." There was snow on his face and a grin underneath it; things couldn't be so bad if we could still joke about them.

We didn't walk through the gap between the ice-crusted rocks that marked the way down to the upper basin of the Copland Valley, we flew through like wraiths. But when we reached the lower moraine basin and the whole bowl of the valley was there with that peculiar green softness under the scudding cloud, I wouldn't have been back in the Hooker Hut for all the hot tea in Moscow. The old Westland feeling came at me again. It was wonderful to be back. Even the rainy sleet of the zigzag down to the river was good. It had that real Westland taste, the promise of wood smoke, wekas and hot springs. In Westland to be wet was unpleasant, but it didn't bite into you with the melancholy of Canterbury with its long, drab, windswept screes and grey moraines.

"Thanks, you blokes. Maybe it was crazy, but it was fun."

The Douglas Rock Hut, when we came to it in a bush clearing a few minutes below the last of the alpine scrub, was in a filthy state showing dirty billies and pots with the mildewed scum of someone's stew, a table littered with empty tins, and dirt as thick as a carpet pile on the wooden floor. But it was home. While Gillies prepared the meal by candlelight, Rodda and I assaulted the accumulated rubbish. Rodda had a *thing* about uncleanliness in the hills, and I owed the Navy at least one debt for it taught me that to be tough, you didn't need to be scruffy. But the wekas that lived under the floor of the hut more than compensated for the untidiness of its previous human occupants. Friendly, insatiably inquisitive, they walked around with tails flicking and a tolerant but proprietary air that made them as indispensable to my pleasure at returning to Westland as the wild river, the forest, or the bluffs that fell from the heights of Mt Sefton.

The next morning in better weather, shafts of sunlight bringing the trees to iridescent life, we wandered with frequent stops down to Welcome Flat, the hut and its hot springs.

While we were still some distance from the hut, sounds of yelling, screams and revelry came to us over the springy grass.

"A bit early in the day for a party, isn't it?" said Bruce.

"They don't believe in wasting time on the Coast."

"Gimme the Westlanders every time," I enthused. "No puritan stuff over here. They know how to live—and the food!" Visions of venison in a camp oven on the ashes, of thick fresh white bread, the yellow butter and tea so strong and sweet that you could walk on it, were too enticing. I broke into a run.

"Watch it, squire," cautioned Bruce, "if you get in there and fall into your sailoring habits again, you can say goodbye to Brunner."

"I'll risk it." I was nearly up to the door.

"What are you waiting for?" said Rodda as he came round the corner of the hut. "Open the door and let's see what's going on."

When I pushed open the door I saw that there was a party on, one of the wildest I'd ever seen. The din and disorder were terrific. The long room was full of kapok, floating like curdled milk, and through the turbulence a bevy of keas flew with shrieks that made the windows rattle. The birds were so preoccupied that they didn't realise their revels were being spied on. We watched the fandangle for some time. There was a pattern to their mischief. The ringleader, an old bird with wrinkled grey feet and an eye that shone with delight and devilment, was busy slicing his curved brown beak along the greasy ticking of the pillows that hung from a length of fencing wire. When he'd made the long incision, he crawled inside and emptied the kapok in a stream which slowly settled on the floor. The younger birds sitting in obedient line on the table at the far end of the hut waited until the old reprobate signalled with a low whistle for the attack to commence, then took off in line ahead and shot through the clouds of kapok with competing yells and screams, banking sharply and flying back through the agitated mess. It was a most impressive piece of well-organised ground strafing.

"The flak's pretty heavy today, but the boys are really on the job. Look at the empty pillowcases on the floor," said Rodda.

We gave the squadron a few more circuits during which they beat up the hut like vengeful Spitfires. One bird pressed home his attack with such determination that he flew straight into the wire, hit the deck out of control and groundlooped into the rubbish-tin. This unintentional piece of buffoonery produced a paroxysm of ribald screeching from his mates who were still airborne.

"We'd better close the fun down now," I said. "The party's beginning to get a bit rough, even for keas."

But the keas thought our entrance on the scene was an added and unexpected attraction. When we'd eventually chased the last bird out the open hut door, Rodda, Gillies and I were inordinately covered in kapok. The keas had had the best of the bargain. By the time we'd cleaned up the hut, barred the broken window through which they'd pushed in, and cleaned ourselves in the hot spring nearby, it was too late to move up Scott's Creek, the next obstacle in our offensive against Mt Brunner. And I was more than content, I'd had a free show, as well as the unexpected pleasure of another night in hut shelter.

But the next morning Rol had us up, fed, and away before the sun had reached the valley floor. There was an air of determination abroad, of purposeful words, and a tightening of equipment straps when with flashing ice-axes at the high port we stormed across the river and advanced up the rock jumble of Scott's Creek. Believing that the prime maxim of all warfare was swift and resolute mobility, we hadn't brought any tent. We wouldn't need one, I had been constantly assured. "We'll make the actual climb from the West Sefton Bivvy," both Rodda and Gillies had told me. It wasn't until we were forcing our way through the tangled undergrowth below a high bluff some way up Scott's Creek that I was brought into the secret.

"How much further up to the West Sefton Bivvy?" I asked for the umpteenth time. The going was pretty rough, swags were heavy, and sweat was free.

Gillies and Rodda exchanged glances. "We may as well tell you, Paul, that there isn't any West Sefton Bivvy."

"What? You're both pulling my leg. There must be! I've heard you talk about nothing else but the West Sefton Bivvy for the last three days. 'When we get to the West Sefton Bivvy, when we climb up from the West Sefton Bivvy', you've been saying." I could see the creek running out to Welcome Flat but the hut was out of sight behind the corner of a bushy spur. Rodda and Gillies were grinning. "I suppose you think that's funny, leading me up the garden path like that?"

"I wouldn't call Scott's Creek a garden path," replied Gillies. "It's too overgrown."

"I was talking about the blasted bivvy. If there isn't a bivvy, what is there up there for shelter?" I tore a small branch from the nearest tree and pulled the leaves off one by one.

"Open ledges up on the tussock."

"Not even a bit of rock to crawl under?"

"Not a sausage. A terrific view though, squire."

"Huh!"

"Time's up," said Rodda grinding out his cigarette against a tree-trunk. "You've got a sleepingbag cover haven't you?"

From that point onward I rearranged my priorities. Shelter came first, and Mt Brunner, virgin or tarnished, was a definite second. As soon as we left the forest and emerged into a large open creek bed I was on the alert. The others had some difficulty in keeping my mind on the object of our alpine exercise—the gaining of height—for I regarded every rock that stuck above the scrub as a home for alpine waifs.

"I think Paul's got something, Rol," admitted Gillies when the mist started to crowd in. "We ought to have some shelter. No sense in getting wet if we can find a reasonable rock a few hundred feet below the open tussock."

The word shelter was enough for me, I scanned the hillside for likely places; there were enough rocks on the slope to satisfy even a bivomaniac like me. Though none of them overhung enough to keep a sandfly dry, I hunted about with the persistence of a house-wife at a fifty-cent basement bargain sale and eventually found a large overhanging rock close to the dried-up creekbed. The rest of the afternoon was taken up with preparing the place. We levered

"We arrived below the final snow slope under Ngapunatoru Pass confident that Tutoko was in the bag."
The snow ledge below Paranui leads to the crevassed snowfield falling from Ngapunatoru Pass. Our snow cave and line of retreat lay immediately below the small rock peak on the left of the photograph.

"And then Lucas was on us, roaring down from behind Mt Leary." Popeye Lucas and his Auster zoom through Wright Col to the dropping zone.

out rocks from under the overhang with our ice-axes, and sifted more dirt in two hours than a city corporation gang would dig out in a month.

"We'll have the fireplace here," I said. "Nice and handy for the cook. He can lie in his sack while he does the job."

"A bit far from water," said Rol.

"Who worries about a five-minute walk down the creekbed when he's got a dry house and plenty of firewood? We don't want it too civilised. That would take the thrill out of it all."

When the sleeping platform was finally built up and heaped with fern and springy scrub, we moved in.

We spent the late afternoon hopefully getting ready for the next day's climb, cooked a meal over the open fire, and retired about eight pm. Night didn't fall, but came with a slow transition from misty grey to a hemming black; there were no stars, no dying flush of red over the peaks, or the gradual change from things seen to those that are heard in fine weather at dusk. Tentless on the open ledges I would have found the dark and the silence of the dense mist disturbing, but under the tangible comfort of the rock where I could stretch out my hand and feel the warm hearthstones or watch the play of fire shadows above my head, I enjoyed a deep security. The thicker the mist came down, the more snug I felt. Free from any worry about wind, rain or midnight retreats, I spent the hour between wakefulness and sleep relishing the day's highlights. I'd been around the Alps long enough to realise that you didn't chase sleep, you let it come to you slowly and softly with the sound of creek water talking through the mist or the chatter of gregarious kakas swapping the nocturnal gossip of the forest. I knew that I liked the atmosphere of huts and bivvy rocks, but until this night under the overhang in the scrub high up Scott's Creek the reason had eluded me as I had been too absorbed in company and firelight to dissect the cause.

The answer came with the shock of simplicity. Shelter places meant as much to me as peaks. Whenever I'd said, "I've made the first ascent of Pudding-Bowl Peak up The Egg-Beater Arete" I'd been deceiving myself. I didn't own the unfortunate mountain; I had merely engaged in a bout of gymnastics, so demanding that I expected the world of sensation must come in to me. But when I lay, well-fed and warm in a covert that I'd worked for, I had a sense that I was going out, seeking the balance between the mountain world and me. There was time and stillness enough to observe and enjoy everything the mountains gave. I loved the hills not only for their height but also for their appearance, and their beauty was richest at the middle height where the mountain met the forest. "It's good to know where I am," I said half aloud.

"You're up Scott's Creek, that's where you are, boy. We've been listening to you talking to yourself for the last half hour," said a tired voice. "We all enjoyed the lecture, now give us a fair go, will you? We want to go to sleep."

At midnight I awoke to the crackle and spitting of the fire and Gillies shaking me with the news that "There are a few stars out but it's bound to be raining by dawn." I was my grumpy self but Rodda, as cheerful as a new boy at his first school picnic, made sure that I crawled out and went through the hollow preparations for the day; but there wasn't much poetry as we clambered by torchlight up the creek bed and reached the tussock level.

"Too warm to be healthy. There's another nor'-wester on the way, guarantee it," said Gillies, sniffing the dawn and wriggling his shoulders. "Oh, well. Better get on with it."

"Too early to say what the weather's going to do, so we may as well keep on," said Rodda, leading off up the snow that led to Welcome Pass. But just below the Pass even Rol's dogged brand of optimism was convinced that the day held neither promise nor enjoyment as rank on rank of hogsbacks, the monitory bad-weather clouds of the New Zealand Alps, queued from the Tasman Sea to the summits of Cook and Sefton. We loitered as depressed as unemployed outside a labour exchange. The clouds increased and the mountains flared with an angry red.

"Blast!" said Rol. He gave the word for retreat and Mt Brunner was safe for that day.

The next two days brought a comical but frustrating game of march and countermarch between the weather and our ambition. Each dusk the rain and mist would lift, the evening birds would sing, and we'd go to bed with boundless optimism. By midnight the murk would be down again but we'd clump up the creek and engage in the daily war of attrition between ourselves and the stormclouds. The weather won. We called off the campaign and went back to Welcome Flat and then upriver to Douglas Rock Hut.

Gillies was cheerfully philosophical, "You can't have it fine all the time."

Rol was the most disappointed, but he didn't grumble. As for me, well, I was only an alpine tramp who liked Westland. I had the least to lose and the most to gain, and Scott's Creek had given me good nights and Westland shelter. But I'd have liked Mt Brunner too.

Heavy fog followed us all the way up the zigzag, almost until we came to Luncheon Rock. When we sat down to eat we weren't in the mood of conquering warriors, but the mountains gave us entertainment where they had refused us glory and sent a flock of mating keas to take the sting from our defeat. I had seen keas often in their strength of devilry, but never before in the moments of their weakness. A hen bird flew on to the rock chased by several males who settled into a circle around her. The males bobbed and called softly and paraded before her with trailing wings. Their scaly feet slid over the flat rock in a mincing shuffle that the hen ignored with you'll-have-to-do-much-better-than-that disdain; she came from one of the best kea families in Westland and wasn't going to fling herself at the first bumbling clod just for his whistle. The eager males strove for her attention until their courtship fringed on abject clowning. Some took to the air and tried to impress her with tumbling aerobatics, others returned with pebbles which they pushed before her with lugubrious concentration. There was an air to their performance of males who will resort to the ridiculous to impress, a reluctant willingness to accept even the insolence of their rivals in the cause of love. One kea, as original as he was without pride, clowned round her in ponderous somersaults like some cheap tumbler before a haughty queen. The hen gave him a condescending inclination of her head and a bored yawn before his banishment. The rejected cock flew with a quick return of dignity to the far edge of the rock where he cursed her with strident profanity and then took wing for the celibate consolation of the misty crags of Mt Sefton. We couldn't stay to see the remainder of the bizarre comedy as we had one of our own to play out.

"It's no fun being a man, going through all that caper. Hanged if I'll let any dame get her grappling-irons on me. I'm for the hills. It's time," I said, as I got back into harness, "we shogged over the pass. Tomorrow we want to be back in the upper Hooker under Mt Cook. They say there's a hut up there. Or is that another legpull like the West Sefton Bivouac, Bruce?"

"No joke this time, Paul. Guarantee it, squire," replied Gillies over his steel-framed spectacles. "It's on a knob above the Hooker Gletscher and it's called the Gardiner Hut."

"It had better be," I said as we plugged up the snow basin toward the top of Copland Pass.

Once we were over the pass, the fog which had been our constant attendant suddenly cleared, but the Hooker Valley was grey and white, and the long ridges bare and scranny. I preferred the green and well fleshed Westland hills.

Our swags might have been lighter, but they were still awkward when we came to climb down the rock ridge that ran towards the Hooker Valley. The rock, though cleared of snow by a week of rain, was rotten and ill tempered. With Mt Brunner in our pockets we'd probably have waltzed down like satisfied old gentlemen out for a Sunday stroll; but Brunner had beaten us, and though we had left neither our guns nor the regimental standard behind with the enemy, we had the quietness of troops in orderly retreat and our minds weren't on the job. We hadn't roped up—the climbing wasn't difficult enough for that—and each of us followed a separate line of descent. Gillies, who always took his ski runs or his mountains straight, went over the top of the ridge, and Rodda went to the left and I to the right. I was mooning along a shaly ledge when a muffled shout made me look up. A shower of rocks followed by a tumbling Gillies rolled down the mountainside. The rocks kept going, but Gillies stopped a few yards from me.

I ran up to him. "What happened, Bruce?"

"Rotten filthy rock! A hold broke." He rubbed his shoulder and grimaced.

"You must've fallen twenty to thirty feet. Sure you're all right?"

"Of course. The best way to come down a ridge like this, it doesn't take nearly so long. One good thing, it's woken me up."

Rodda appeared round the buttress with a startled expression, but Bruce was up and away like a greyhound before the doctor of the party could examine him.

"There can't be much wrong with him if he can still move like that."

"He was lucky though, Rol."

"Not at all," said Rodda, "Gillies is irrepressible.

When we at last came down the scree slide near the Hooker Hut with the interminable ridge behind us, light rain was falling with oppressive persistence and the red roof of the hut was the only bright spot in the dreary valley.

We stayed in the hut all next day while the rain lashed and the thunder rolled reverberant over the summits; the upper Hooker was no place in which to wander in search of a hut above the ice.

When we left the Hooker Hut on Christmas Eve the glacier was a cheerful journey. There was sun and light along the mountain walls from Nazomi to Cook and round the glistening navigator peaks, Dampier, Hicks and La Perouse. Gillies was no worse for his fall, Rodda was chipper as a snowlark, and I, too, glad that the long spell of bad weather was over. There were peaks to climb and we were ready for them.

Three hours out from the Hooker Hut, we were well into ice country and the other two gave me a lesson on the local geography. They tossed off the names of ridges and peaks with an easy familiarity that reinforced rather than diminished the awe I felt for these mountains. But there was more than height, ice or rock to impress, the scale of time was greater. Had we suddenly come in all the desolation upon a group of climbers with long-shafted ice-axes, heavy tweed knickerbockers, belted shooting jackets, and puttees banded to the knees, I could not have been surprised: it was these early men who had given the mountains history and life, and I had only one regret, that they were for ever round the next ridge, walking in the white hollows of the neve, always ahead.

"There's Pudding Rock," said Gillies, pointing to a rounded hump of black rock overlooking the crevasse-lined glacier. "The Gardiner Hut's up there, and if we hurry we might get in before they take off the counter lunch."

The Gardiner Hut wasn't an easy place to reach in summer when the Hooker Glacier was open. There was a wire rope that dangled down the smooth and ice-worn rock if you could reach it across the gap between the glacier and the base of the rock. We went over and had a good look but even Rol, who would try most things if there was a ghost of a chance of success, shook his head and said we'd better find an easier way. I cheered up as soon as he said this. I didn't like at all the wide leap from ice to polished rock, or the hungry mutter of water hidden in the gloomy depths. We took to a provident couloir that ran steepishly up beside the rock. Rodda was ahead bashing a staircase in the ice, a slight man with a large axe and a determination that never flagged. Gillies below me on the rope exhibited a slight restlessness as the minutes dragged by.

"Get a move on, Rol. Let's get out of here."

"Keep your shirt on, Gillies. Not long now." I noticed that the ice-chips flew even faster and that Rodda was treating Gillies' remark with some urgency. His head kept lifting expectantly.

"It's a wonderful day, just look at the shadows on the glacier." I was sneaking brief glances at the wide Hooker where the crevasses ran in a wrinkled pattern and the ice walls shone green and blue and purple-brown.

"Keep your mind on your job," growled Gillies. "You can relax when we're off the ice. It's dangerous here."

"Seems perfectly OK to me. A bit steep that's all."

"When you see the ice blocks bounding down this gully, you'll soon change your mind. Last season a party nearly got collected here by falling ice."

The light and mottled shadow on the glacier lost their attraction. I was as relieved as Bruce and Rol when we reached the edge of the ice and could walk with grating crampons over the dismantled rock that littered the flat table of Pudding Rock.

The hut was a small one, a tent-shaped corrugated-iron box with heavy wire hawsers passed over the red roof and anchored to steel stanchions driven into the rock. If the Gardiner Hut commanded a panoramic vista of the glacier sweeping up to Harper's Saddle and a foreshortened aspect of the low peak and west face of Mt Cook, it was also no stranger to the west wind that poured over Baker Saddle to the flanks of Cook. The Gardiner had that cowed appearance that exposure gives some high mountain huts. The furniture was simple—three or four wire stretchers, a wooden table and two forms, and a two-burner kerosene stove. Set against the match-lining wall was the overlord of this threadbare estate, a large barometer with a black accusing finger pointing to "Stormy". In some places in the mountains, huts are more a luxury than a necessity, but this one was an essential, a shade from the snowglare in fine weather and a refuge in storm.

After the pleasure of reaching the hut had worn off, I had one thought that coloured my enjoyment: in fine weather or foul, Gardiner Hut could be a stinker of a place to get out from. It wasn't exactly the sort of hut where you could shoulder your swag and march whistling along the track.

After tea we discussed plans for the next day. "There's only one thing to climb tomorrow, eh, Bruce?" said Rodda as he set the barometer.

"Cook. It's the fiftieth anniversary of the first ascent by George Graham, Jack Clarke and Tom Fyfe. It's a mile and a half along the summit ridge, but even if we managed the low peak it would be something worth while."

At sunset the wind came over Baker Saddle from the west and the sky was scourged by whip-tailed cloud. I was too excited to sleep well and each time I awoke I padded to the door to have a look at the weather. Everytime I went out the sky was less starry, and just before dawn the wind freshened and cloud settled on the high peaks like a dull grey lid.

"What's it like, Paul?"

"Terrible. No frost, murk all over the Divide, and hogsbacks by the mile down-valley."

Rodda went out an hour after dawn but he, too, came back looking glum. "Hopeless," he said. "It's going to start thumping down any minute."

By mid-morning we had a fully-fledged storm on our hands. The wind roistered across the Hooker Glacier and burst on Pudding Rock until the timbers of the hut groaned. Sleep was out of the question and we lay with our hands under our heads, staring at the ceiling and bewailing our misfortune while the wind scoured the outside of the refuge and the barometer needle jumped forward with every gust. The only music we heard that day was the thrumming of guy wires and the trumpet voluntary of the wind. We had a sparse

Christmas dinner at mid-afternoon and made a dispirited attempt at Christmas carols.

The sanitation was homespun. You waited until the wind dropped a little, rushed out the door with everything undone and hung from the guy wire while the gale blew the clothes half-way up your back.

"One of these days," I said when I came breathless into the hut, "some poor devil is going to get lifted clean off the Rock."

"What a hell of a way to die," said Rodda.

I spent the rest of the day in a mood of enforced patience. It was no good moaning about our luck. The warmth of my bag was no consolation. This in all our holiday was the one day that I wanted for a climb, and Cook on its birthday was more desirable than all the shelter.

The weather made cynical amends on Boxing Day and we left the hut at 4.30 am for Nazomi, a nine-and-a-half-thousand foot peak near the unclimbed south ridge of Mt Cook. Freda Du Faur had made the first ascent of the peak with Peter and Alex Graham in 1912 but the name, reputed to be Japanese for "heart's desire", had no romantic ring to me that early dawn—my thoughts were set on Cook.

The climb started with the usual alpine routine, the greasy breakfast of fried bacon and ten-day-old eggs, the roping-up outside the hut and a sleepy climb over the lower neve of the Noeline Glacier until we awoke to the rhythm of the day. Bruce complained of a migraine headache and when he was in the middle of a snowbridge spanning one of the larger crevasses he stopped and vomited into the depths. After that there was no holding him as he led us up an avalanche fan at the base of the rock peak, into a cheerless gully where he cut steps for an hour in hard blue ice and bombarded Rodda and me with the spent chips of his exuberance.

The mountain company was close but cold; the long couloir up to Endeavour Col as white and as inviting as an undertaker's slab, the ice cliffs of the low peak of Cook brooding over the Noeline neve, and a wind which covered us in windblown powder snow. We left the summit about 1 pm with another nor'-wester coming in from the sea and picked our way down the route we'd come. Mt Cook, with a regard for the cleanliness of its snow, had thrown a large ice avalanche across the place where Bruce had stopped that morning. We hurried past and just before 6 pm were back in Gardiner Hut. Rodda was due out at the Hermitage that night so we had a brief snack and then committed ourselves to a two-hour shuffle down the snowed ledges and iced wire rope of Pudding Rock. The conditions were treacherous and I was quite surprised to find myself intact and more than a little chastened on the dry ice of the Hooker Glacier.

After a night at the Hooker Hut, Gillies and I returned to Gardiner Hut confident that now Rodda had taken the bad weather with him we would enjoy a spell of climbing. But the times were uncharitable and we lay hutbound for three days while the weather vacillated between rain and snow. The only constancy was with the wind, which blew intemperately, and with it went our patience. On the last day Bruce and I forced a direct way through the intersecting crevasses of the Hooker since we didn't dare face another descent down Pudding Rock.

"Well, squire," said Gillies as we clanked over the Hooker swing bridge, "it's been a funny climbing season; a fortnight in the hills and not one day completely fine. And we didn't get Brunner."

"Maybe not," I replied, "but we've something to be thankful for."

"What's that?"

"Brunner didn't get us. And neither did Pudding Rock."

Rodda's parting instructions to me had been to stalk Bruce and persuade him to join us in an attempt on unclimbed Mt Grave near Milford Sound. "If you do it the right way, Bruce might bite. Grave was named after his father-in-law. Tell him he's got to keep up the Grave family tradition of Fiordland exploration."

But when I broached the subject Bruce was not to be persuaded. "I'll stick to the Cook district, thanks, Paul. Milford's too wet for me."

11

The Remarkables

A cold in the head causes less suffering than an idea.
—*Jules Renard*

"Now, IF YOU WANT a really reliable car," said the used car sales-man, "this is the one for you." He paused impressively and looked us straight in the eye.

"Yes, but does it go?" Bill Hockin gave the old heap a kick, and the salesman a look. I felt like doing the opposite.

"Huhuh," laughed the dealer with just the right blend of assurance as he flicked the ash off his cigarette and stuck a thumb under his waistcoat. "Does it go?" His eyebrows lifted almost to the top of his head. "This is a Buick," he said, "The Car of Reliability. You could tour the world in it." And he gave the pitted chrome of the radiator a confident slap.

"We don't want to tour the world, we only want to get as far as the Hollyford entrance to the Milford tunnel," said Colin Marshall modestly.

"Is that all?" replied the salesman. "Oh, in that case, you won't have a second's worry. Brakes good, engine strong as an ox, and tyres sound. You're as good as there."

"And back again, I hope?" The one-man salesman-proprietor of YZ Motors ignored me, but his glance said, "Another crack like that and I'll bop you over the head with a tyre-lever."

"How much?" Rol cut in like a scalpel.

"You'll excuse me if I ask you your name, sir," replied the salesman, "we get a lot of inquiries about our cars from people who . . ." he dickered for the right words, "aren't . . . shall we say, always very ethical. I always think a prospective client who gives his name has established his bona fides. We prefer to start our business transactions on a basis of mutual trust, don't you agree, Mr, Er?"

"Rodda."

"Well, Mr Rodda . . ."

"*Doctor* Rodda."

"A pleasure indeed." The dealer twisted his hands in invisible soap.

"How much for the car?" said Rol incisively.

"Say, twenty-five pounds, to you, Doctor Rodda."

Rol winced, and Hockin said tartly, "We don't want to buy the thing, we only want to hire it." Marshall and I sniggered, but Rol shot us a look which said Lay-off-will-you-and-leave-this-to-me.

"Perhaps," said the salesman carefully watching Rol, "you'd prefer something a little more professional, Doctor? After all . . ."

"We've got a lot of equipment; there's plenty of room for it in this Buick. It could be what we want."

Rodda and the proprietor went into the broken-down shack that had a large sign telling passing humanity that this was the registered office of YZ Motors, the FIRM YOU CAN TRUST.

When Rol came out he said, "I took it. Didn't have any option. We've only got five days for the trip and it's too late to hunt around. Tomorrow's Easter Thursday."

"Did you manage to beat him down?"

"No. He knew he had us by the short hairs. He wanted the whole twenty-five in advance, but I told him it was half down before we leave and the rest when we got back."

"Could've been worse, Rol."

"Oh, and I also told him we wanted a test drive, tonight after tea."

We trooped down after work and piled into the old 1928 flivver. Rol insisted on driving and we went roaring around the Dunedin hills while the dealer expounded the virtues of his Buick. By the time we swept back into the salesyard I wouldn't have swapped the old girl for a Rolls.

"She's got the same rugged lines as old *Heath*, hasn't she?" I said to Colin Marshall as I ran an affectionate hand along the rakish black bonnet. "No coquetry, no tricks, just a buxom dependability. A bit blousy perhaps, but as experienced and full of staying power as a woman in her early forties."

"I wouldn't know," said Colin.

"And no gas-producing this time. No declinkering every few miles, no more char to sieve in the middle of the night," exulted Hockin. "Remember how black we used to get from the char dust?"

"It'll be a pushover this time. And refuelling? Just a matter of adding the right proportion of power kerosene to spin the petrol out. By the way, Rol, you've remembered the petrol coupons?"

"Of course."

"What about the tyres?"

"Checked them myself, and they're in tiptop order. Just as well, they're not easy to come by for an old model like this."

"Anything we've forgotten?" I asked.

"No," said Rol, "everything set. Battery, electrics, radiator, oil, tyres, all checked?"

"Yes, Rol," we chorused.

"All right then. We meet here tomorrow at three pm sharp. And nobody late please," said Rol crisply. "I want to get airborne as soon as we can. It's a long drive to Te Anau, and the Hollyford entrance of the Homer Tunnel's about sixty miles further on. That's as far as we can take the car. We'll have to walk through the tunnel and down the Cleddau to Milford."

We all arrived sharp on time the next afternoon. There seemed enough junk to fill the main hold in a large tramp steamer, but Rol directed the stowing with the critical eye of a supercargo; the rucsacs lashed to the rear end carrier with an old alpine rope, the four-gallon tins of petrol and kerosene ready for instant refuelling, the puncture repair outfit and the jack close to hand.

Hockin and I climbed into the back seat. "There's no more room than there was in *Heath*," he said, "and there was one thing to be said in favour of a bag of char. It didn't cut into your back like an angular tin of fuel."

"And we'd better not smoke for a while, not until we're sure that the fuel isn't leaking," cautioned Rodda.

"You're right, Bill," I said, knocking out my pipe, "Life with *Heath* might have been hell, but it had its advantages. At least you could smoke."

Rol got in and started the engine. "Hmm," he muttered, "sounds OK. I just wanted to be sure before I gave him the money."

The dealer came out of his office and walked slowly toward us. "I quite envy you boys," he said, stuffing the roll of notes into his pocket like a pawnbroker making polite conversation after he'd given five shillings for the Kohinoor diamond. "I can't get away. Got a big deal to transact with a wellknown city client as soon as you've gone." He walked around the car with a solemn air, "Look after her won't you? I've got a soft spot for this old Buick. They don't make them like this any more."

"I bet they don't," muttered Bill as he wedged himself between the grating fuel tins.

We were just starting to roll when the dealer stuck his head through the open window. "Pull up at the office on your way out and I'll give you a few spare tyres. You may need them where you're going, those metalled roads are pretty rough. Wouldn't want you to have trouble on your way to the Great Outback."

"That's nice of you," said Rol as he let out the clutch and the car turned into the street with a squeaking of overloaded springs. For some unaccountable reason I had a feeling of foreboding which wasn't allayed by the sight in the rear vision mirror of the salesman standing by the open gateway.

"Not such a bad bloke after all," said Rol.

"I still think it was funny the way he gave us all those extra tyres at the last minute," said Hockin.

When the overladen car was panting over Saddle Hill with a long queue of Easter traffic snaking behind we found the reason. There was a noise which sounded like a cross between the gobbling of a dozen turkeys and the explosion of a lazily descending mortar bomb.

"Blowout," said Hockin as the Buick lurched ditchwards.

While we were changing the rear tyre, Marshall stood in the roadway waving on the traffic. He came over to us suddenly. "I've noticed something. The tyres are different."

We dropped everything then and ran from tyre to tyre.

"These aren't the tyres that were on the car yesterday, when we had the test run."

"They're all the same, no tread. Smooth as a baby's bum."

"So that's why Old Greasy slung in those extra tyres at the last minute. His conscience must've got the better of him."

Rol hardly said anything, but he stood with his pipe clenched between his teeth giving a pretty lifelike imitation of an angry flourmill. "There's only one explanation. That lousy carshark has whipped off all the good tyres and stuck on old ones."

It was too late to turn back. We lumbered on with a fatalistic obstinacy as the niggardly miles came up slowly on the speedometer. Rol sat behind the steering wheel with the grim determination of a bomber pilot bringing home a battered aircraft with a triggered blockbuster jammed in its belly. No one spoke.

Ten miles south along the main road the second tyre blew like a tired old man wheezing out his last breath.

When, three hours later, the third blowout came we greeted its appearance with relief, the suspense had been too nerve-wearing. About half past midnight we limped into Gore and with the effrontery of the desperate dragged a sleepy mechanic from his bed. We hung around the garage, a cold and gloomy morgue of a place, while the garage hand crawled into the recesses of his tyre loft. Rodda didn't nag the man, he just stood behind him and puffed on his pipe with unyielding watchfulness; if there was a tyre in that service station, we were going to get it.

"Sorry," said the wearied hand, "haven't got anything that'll even look at your car. That size has been out of stock for years."

"Hmm," said Rol. "Can't you repair it?"

"Look, sir," said the mechanic as he held the shredded tyre under Rodda's nose. "Not a show. You could drive a tractor through the hole in the side wall."

"Oh," said Rodda." See what you mean." He chewed on his pipe-stem for a minute while the mechanic walked over to the doors and pointedly started pulling them shut.

"What about putting a sleeve inside it?" asked Rol. "That might get us a few miles up the road."

"All right." The garage hand was close to tearful resignation. "But it won't last you know," he said with a last flicker of defiance.

We held a council while we ate three bobs' worth of fish and chips from the piecart.

"Haven't I heard you say that you've an old ex-navy friend down this way?" said Rol. "Some name like Newby or Newton?" He gave me a stare that said don't try any funny business.

"Newman," I corrected. "Jack Newman. But I don't know where he lives." We trooped along the deserted street to the nearest tele-phone box and Rol stood over me while I thumbed through the directory.

"There's no Jack Newman listed, he must've moved," I said with relief. Knocking up hostile strangers after midnight was one thing, but dragging a friend to an early morning telephone was another. "What now?" I asked.

Hockin and Marshall stood around the car with hands in pockets and hitched shoulders. A chill wind blew a rag of paper scuffing along the pavement and the shop fronts faced each other across the street with dead eyes.

"There's only one thing to do. We'll keep on. Can't stay here, there isn't a decent mountain for miles."

When half an hour up the Te Anau road we had the fourth blowout even Rol's determination faded. "We'll camp here for the night," he said pointing to the dusty grass under some pine trees by the roadside.

"This is an utter fiasco," I heard Hocking grumble as he burrowed into his sleeping bag. "Twelve hours and four blowouts to cover a hundred and ten miles. *Heath* at her worst was better than this."

"Too right," agreed Colin, "at least the blasted wheels went round." But Rodda was already fast asleep and tomorrow was another day.

We were up at dawn and full of an impossible hope, but the only miracle of the night came from the providence of a family of wayside cows.

"That's adding insult to injury," said Colin as he wiped his sleepingbag cover.

"There's a garage a few hundred yards up the road, it may have some tyres."

Our luck was out. The proprietor shook his head and went on with work on the innards of a tractor.

"Never mind," said Rol hopefully, "we've still got two of those extra tyres left. Never know what we might dig up at the next village."

"What about getting back to Dunedin? We can't push on too far, we'll be stranded for good."

"I've thought of that," snapped Rol. The thought of a defeated retreat irritated us all.

We limped on to Balfour with a covetous eye on the hills which were creeping over the fringe of the western horizon.

"We've had it properly this time," Colin said despondently. "Old Rodda's in the garage now, ringing up every cocky for miles around and asking 'Have you got any tyres that will fit a 1928 Buick?' And he's getting some pretty terse replies." He took a disgusted swing at a stone and sent it skipping across the street.

"You've got to hand it to Rol, he's certainly persistent," admitted Hockin.

"Hey!" I interrupted brightly. "We can't leave it all to Rol, let's try ourselves. We can beat up every house in the township, keep a watch out on the road in case any old Buicks happen along."

"I suppose it's worth trying," said Hockin despondently.

Our enquiries produced a fascinating range of reactions; polite no's, indifference, incredulous stares. People told us about their backaches, their operations and the sex life of their cats, but never a word about tyres. When one vinegary lady with a forest of curly hairs on her upper lip earbashed us all the way from her front door to the gate with allegations that we were black marketeers doing the God-fearing inhabitants of Southland in the eye, we gave up and went back to the car.

"It's no good," said Rodda when we came up to him. "We'll have to forget the Milford idea. Mt Grave will have to wait till next time."

I had to admire him; no self pity, no tantrums, just a matter-of-fact acceptance of the inevitable. But none of us dared to mention that car shark back in Dunedin who was the malignant cause of all our frustration.

"What a lousy way to spend an Easter. Look at the sky over the Homer way. Clear as a bell," growled Hockin.

"What now, Rol?"

"We'll go to Queenstown and climb the Remarkables. There's a train due in after lunch," said Rodda briskly.

"Better than nothing," said Hockin. "Even if it is a bit of a come-down."

"Just as well," grinned Marshall, a revived man now that there was at least a prospect of a climb. "Silly to oppose the gods. If we'd pushed on to Homer, they'd probably have made the steering wheel jam. We'd have ended upside down in the foaming Hollyford."

"Superstitious nonsense," said Rol. "All this talk about gods and gremlins."

"Scoff your head off, Rol, but you don't know how bewitched old cars can be," I said half-seriously.

"That's right." Marshall nodded his head vigorously in agreement. "Rodda didn't serve his apprenticeship in *Heath*. After a few trips in that old bomb, you'd believe in anything."

We shared a smoke-filled second class carriage with a noisy gang of rowers bound for the Queenstown regatta. The beer bottles passed from mouth to mouth and the singing gradually acquired the comradely earthiness of the well-oiled Kiwi.

"Have a drink, pal," said a voice with the foamy bottle, "You look as miserable as four roosters with their tail feathers plucked out . . . Goin' to the regatta?"

"Climbing," said Rol, taking a token sip and staring at the road to Homer receding behind the train.

"Cripes!" said the incredulous voice. "You're not, are you? What in the name of hell for?"

The worst assault against our already tattered self-esteem came as the *Earnslaw* tied up to the jetty at Queenstown. As we flowed self-consciously with the holiday crowd over the gangway, a little boy pointed to us and cried, "Look at the men with the funny shovels. They won't be able to build sand castles, will they Mummy? They've left their buckets behind."

"The sooner we get out of town, and get up the hill the better," Hockin grated in my ear. "I can't stand much more of this."

Rol led us tightlipped and defiantly through the milling holiday-makers, Marshall and Hocking shambled along with sheepish grins, and I longed to throw my ice-axe in the lake. We were a long way from the untrodden rainforest of the Harrison River, and the un-climbed rock tower of Mt Grave. There was no shelter from the passing sniggers and we were as tender as shell-less crayfish in the moulting season.

Life, if we could have disregarded the callous fact that we were on the wrong mountain, could have been perfect. We pitched Rol's new alpine tent in a meadowy basin high above the Lake Alta side of the Remarkables. A clear stream ran bubbling in a glistening ladder down the mountainside and, behind the tussocked knob above the camp, the three rock spires of Triple Cone lay sharp against a cloudless sky.

Had the Remarkables been the true reason for our visit, that Easter would have been one of unblemished enjoyment. But always the reminder of our absurd mischance was there to mock us. For three days of fine weather the rock needle of Mt Grave taunted us with its impeccable virginity across the unruffled lake and the sleep of mountain country to the west. Even on the summit of Triple Cone there was no escape, and when we wandered down the ridge to our 4,000-foot camp Mt Grave came with us, for every time we poked our heads outside the tent we saw the distant mountain. Even through the long slow twilight there was no evasion. The black profile was still there, a satirical assertion of the strength of mountains and the fallibility of men. Dusk should have been a time of content-ment when we sat around the camp, talking or silently watching the imperceptible change of mountain angles to the curves of tranquillity. Our camp should have been a link between the sweep of mountains and ourselves, but we saw it only as a tent on the wrong peak, a cul-de-sac on the road of our ambition.

On the last morning there was a subtle ferocity, an eagerness to be gone, as we pulled the pegs from the scaly mountain earth and carefully packed the tent in its japara bag. It was as if by some magic

'Phew! That's a nice load for someone to lug up to seven thousand feet . . ."
Above: Hut-builders rest on the way to Wright Col. Mt Aspiring lies in the right background.

'The bones of the hut were standing like a dreary skeleton against the grim profile of the rain-whipped mountains . . ."
Right: Esquilant Hut builders race against time and weather. Mt Pluto is outlined behind the framework.

"The corrugated iron roof and walls . . . were more than refuge from storm; they were the nub of mountain life. The climbing day came in between."
Beyond the Esquilant Hut lies Pluto Col and its attendant peak.

the camp had lured us to the wrong hillside and the act of its destruction freed us from its thrall.

When we were down the ridge and Mt Grave had sunk behind the peaks across the lake we felt better with the constant reminder of our indiscretion gone. Mt Grave was back in the perspective of camps of the future.

"Never mind, Rol," I said, "we'll get Grave this Christmas. Easter's too short for a climb like that. We probably wouldn't have got it anyway."

12

First Ascent of Mt Grave

Company, villainous company hath been the spoil of me.
—*Henry IV*, Pt 1, Act 3, Sc 3

"THIS TIME," said Rol, "we're not going to muck about with old cars. We'll go by bus, and we're going to get Grave before someone else does." The dark eyes and the pointed chin faced Leo Faigan and me across the smoke-filled room. Rodda put a thin finger on the map and pointed. "We'll go over it all briefly once again. Now here's Cascade Camp," he went on, pushing aside the beer-mug and flicking a dreg of tobacco from the sheeny whiteness of the map. "I've arranged for the MOW truck to pick you up there as soon as the NZR bus gets in on 18th December. That'll be about 8 pm. The MOW truck will take you through the rest of the Eglinton Valley, over the divide, to Marian Camp, and up to the Homer portal of the Milford Tunnel that night. So you'll both get a good start. All clear?"

"Yes."

"The next day you and Leo pack all the tucker through the tunnel and down the Cleddau road to Milford Hostel. It's about twelve miles down the road, so try and do it in one go. We don't want to waste any time back-packing."

"Is that *all* the food?" said Faigan pointing to a large army canvas kitbag keeping the wall up.

"All except what you'll already have in your swags," said Rol.

"Gawd!" said Leo, grating back his chair. "Must go."

"Why?"

"Got to get a saddlebag and a nose-feeder if I'm going to be a packhorse."

"Funny man," said Rol.

Life, I thought to myself, is going to be interesting with Leo Faigan, even if we don't climb Grave.

"To continue," said Rodda. "When you get to Milford put everything on the *Donald Sutherland*—I've already arranged for her to take you across the fiord to Harrison Cove. That's at the mouth of the Harrison River."

"Gee, boss," said Leo, "you think of everyfing."

"I hope so," replied Rol drily.

"What then, Rol?"

"You put a camp in right among the trees near the shore."

"Ah. That's more like it," smiled Leo. "That's where we start getting stuck into all the tucker, eh?"

"No," said Rodda with controlled patience. "You put up the fly, the large one, and then you and Paul take the tent and as much food and gear as you can and push up the Harrison River. It's about three to four hours through the bush to where the creek comes in from Mt Pembroke. Pitch camp there, you'll find my old campsite, but don't go up the gorge. It's a stinker."

"That's a relief," said Leo. "I don't like getting my feet wet."

"When are you and Jack Ede coming through and when do we expect you at Harrison Cove?" I asked.

"About five days behind you and Leo. That should give you ample time to do the job, so see if you can't pack a second load up to the entrance to the gorge before Jack and I arrive." Rodda filled our glasses. "Any questions?" he said.

We shook our heads.

"Here's to Grave," he said, "the last best virgin."

"And up the workers too," replied Leo.

The rain was pounding down when Faigan and I dragged our furniture off the bus at Cascade Creek and walked over to the MOW truck.

"Good evening," I said in my best city accent to a grizzly-looking character behind the wheel. "We're members of Dr Rodda's party and I believe he's arranged for you to give us a lift through to Homer tonight."

The driver turned to his assistant. "Doctor Rodda? We don't know anyone by that name, do we Jake?"

"But he's written to you about us," I persisted. "It's all arranged."

"If there is a Dr Rodda, we've never heard of him."

I caught a glimpse of Leo making a grimace and drawing a finger across his throat. "Oh well," I said with a smile, and murder in my heart, "that's a pity. I don't suppose you could give us a lift up to Homer? Even Marian Camp would help."

"Sorry," snapped the thin mouth below the nose that was as lean as a ploughshare. "It's against Departmental regulations," and he gunned the truck and showered us with gritty mud.

"Now that's the sort of bloke," said Leo with a shrug, "who warms your heart, one of Nature's gentlemen."

It was pitch black when we shouldered swags and set off up the road; we didn't use our torches as Rodda had told us to keep them fresh for the climb.

"What do you reckon our swags weigh, Paul?" said Leo, a voice and a glowing cigarette butt.

"About seventy pounds."

"No, eighty-seven pounds. I weighed 'em myself on the steelyard at the bus depot."

"Terrible."

"Sweated labour!" said Leo. "Just you wait till the union hears about it."

By the time we had reached the curving shores of Lake Gunn a heavy thunderstorm broke upon us. The lightning flashes were so close and so blinding that we had to link hands to avoid wandering off the road. The rain absolutely hurtled down, the drops so large they stung our hands, but Leo marched on cheerfully singing exuberantly, *On to Marian, On to Marian,* to the opening bars of the Hallelujah Chorus. And so through the lightning and the rain we came to an old deserted hut near the Divide. The temptation to get under cover was too much.

"Devil take the timetable," said Leo as we booted open the door and we dumped our dripping swags on the mildewed floor.

But our conscience drove us out early the next morning. We came on our acquaintances of the MOW down at Marian Camp and hung around such doleful faces that they relented and drove us up to Homer Camp.

Heavy snow was falling as the truck laboured up the last spiral to the tunnel entrance. The two men jumped out of the cab and gruffly told us to vacate the open tray where we were sitting like two snow-covered yogi. There was a frantic urgency in the way they slung the stores inside the portal of the tunnel.

"Hurry up, they'll be here any minute," said the foreman. Before the last sack hit the concrete liner of the portal, the truck was off, hurtling down the road to the valley floor as if an avalanche was close behind it.

"Something's up," said Leo. "Have you ever seen the sunshine gang work as fast as that before?"

Within five minutes we saw a light bobbing down the misty incline of the tunnel and the sound of a horse *clip-clopping* and men's voices floated up.

"The rotten skunks have gone," said one of the Milford gang vengefully when we'd told him how we had arrived. "Now what do you think of that for a lowdown dirty trick? They're always doing that to us. They're supposed to give us a ride out to Cascade Camp, but do they ever?" and he shook his fist in the direction of the MOW camp and spat with a string of oaths that went echoing hollowly down the tunnel.

"Observe," said Leo as he picked up some potatoes from a ruptured sack and stuffed them under the top flap of his swag, "how the local branches of the Borgia family love one another."

Leo and I didn't fare much better spending the whole of that cold and snowy day ferrying two loads through the tunnel and down to the first clutter of derelict construction huts at the bushline in the Cleddau. But there was shelter at the day's end when we lit the fire and spread our sleepingbags beside the hearth while the wind moaned in the avalanche-blasted trees and the snow flurries harried the grey mountain walls.

We breakfasted on boiled potatoes which Leo persecuted to a delicate brown in a sizzling pan, lingered over the tea billy and the final cigarette until an attenuated sun came through the misty clouds.

About four and a half miles from the Milford Hostel when we were ripe for mutiny and had damned Mt Grave, our loads, and Doctor Rodda to a common purgatory, a truck came chugging up the narrow metalled road.

"Hullo, boys. Can we give you a lift?" said a plump and jovial man.

"Sir, you may, for we are footweary, forsooth," said Leo, pulling his sodden balaclava from his head with an elegant sweep as he bowed low.

"Going far?" said the man, who had introduced himself as Mr Berndtson, the manager of the Milford Hostel. We told him. "Well in that case you'd better hop in, you'll need all your energy if you're going into the Harrison. She's a wild valley."

The truck climbed back up to the tunnel entrance, collected the stores and also the remainder of our food we'd left up near the bushline. As we came swinging down through the forest and jolted over the Tutoko River bridge, Leo and I sat in the back of the truck like pontiffs.

"I'm changing my ideas about this place," said Leo. "The bush looks leprous, but the people are wonderful."

We left enough gear for a night's stay at a hut just behind the camp bakehouse and then Mr Berndtson took us down to the launch where we went aboard and stowed the rest of our gear.

The sun was shining over a Milford Sound whose placid waters curved toward the open sea like a great sheet of unruffled mica. Mist and rain had gone and the bright cliffs of Mitre Peak towered to a blue untroubled sky. To the north, far above the green forest and the steep rock ridges, the afternoon sun sparkled on the snowfield of Mt Pembroke while Mt Grave and the upper Harrison Valley lay concealed behind the glistening slabs of the Benton Ridge.

"There she is, boys. The Harrison Valley in all her glory." The skipper took a step out of the wheelhouse and sent a practised parabola of spit into the cove. He brought the *Donald Sutherland* round in a symmetrical curve which sent the wake fanning out in small hollows and crests until they broke with a racing arc on the smooth grey sand below the green forest. "I'm glad it's you going up there and not me," he said. A horny hand with large blue veins swept across a face as gnarled as an old tree trunk.

"Is it all that bad in the Harrison?" I asked him.

"Bad?" His eyes were screwed-up rocks under eyebrows as tangled and bushy as beds of bull kelp. "They say that in the old days prospectors went up there and never came out."

As we jumped out of the boat and pulled it grating up the sand, the skipper drew two bottles from under the stern sheets. "Here," he said, "grab these, you might find a use for them."

"Thanks very much, that's awfully thoughtful of you. What is it? Some of the local brew?"

"Not exactly, but it'll be more use to you than booze where you're going. It's diesoline. It'll get the old billy boiling with the wettest wood."

We pushed him off, and as he headed for the launch with an effortless flicking of the oars we heard him call, "Give my love to the sandflies and the mosquitoes, and the bush. We'll keep an eye out for your smoke signal across the sound in a fortnight's time. And don't get too wet." When he reached the launch he was still chuckling to himself.

By the time Leo and I had the tent fly up, the *Donald Sutherland* was out of sight behind the Benton Promontory. Except for the rattle of the Harrison River over the diorite boulders and the faint scuffing of sea wavelets on the beach, there was silence, a penetrating quiet as if bush and mountain were watching.

We sorted the food and gear into two piles—the stuff to be taken up valley the next morning, and the balance to be carried in on a second portage. We dined on a tin of baked beans and two slices of bread as we had been given strict injunctions not to make pigs of ourselves and gobble up food we'd need for high camps under Mt Grave. But the fire, and the peace of our surroundings made up for the thinness of our rations.

"Couldn't we have just one more slice of bread?" asked Leo. His swarthy face in the wavering firelight looked mournful framed in a khaki balaclava pulled hard down over his dark hair to shut the sandflies out. The downward slope of his eyebrows and the long creases at the corners of his mouth gave him the appearance of a dejected castaway rather than a climber at the start of an expedition of high conquest.

"You win, Leo. We'll have some dessert," I said, tossing over a large tin of peaches. "Open them up, we've got a hard day tomorrow."

"That's more like it," he said, whipping the top off the tin. "After all, this is meant to be a holiday, not a military campaign. And my motto is, when the food runs out then I run out."

Early next morning we were away with lighter swags of sixty pounds. At the beginning the going wasn't as bad as we had expected, and the forest, though silent and without any visible bird life, was open enough by Westland standards. We estimated that we'd be up to the level of Pembroke Creek in no time. But almost immediately we ran into trouble, a tangled wall of thorny creeper, hanging vines, and thick mossed trees laced into a silent entanglement. It was as if the valley, having lured us with a feint of light resistance, had suddenly decided that we should go no further.

"Leprous place," said Leo. "When we get out of it, I'm coming back with a flame thrower to burn the lot down."

We went on, silently now, each of us thinking that with the next bend in the river, packs would be eased to the ground and aching

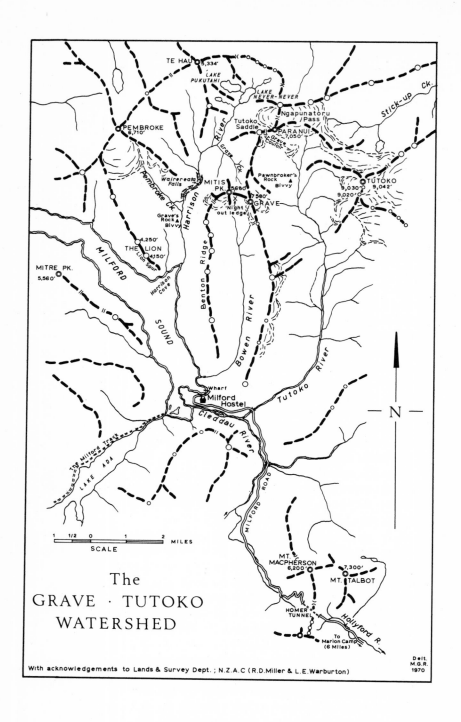

The
GRAVE · TUTOKO
WATERSHED

SCALE

1   1/2   0   1   2   MILES

With acknowledgements to Lands & Survey Dept. ; N.Z.A.C (R.D.Miller & L.E.Warburton)

Delt.
M.G.R.
1970

backs flexed with a circular swinging of the shoulders. There would be tea, smoky and sweet from the billy.

Imperceptibly the walls of the valley closed in, so that we could no longer measure our progress against the towers and notches in the serrated ridges far above.

"It's like being sucked into a green vacuum," grouched Leo.

Late in the afternoon when the valley was whispering with the insistent patter of rain, we heard the dull roar of the Harrison River in its gorge. And soon we were walking out on to the first diminutive clearing that we'd found in the valley. The forest, now unaccountably friendly, rang to the sound of our voices as we put up the tent and made ourselves comfortable for the night.

We were awake next morning just before daybreak. The night had been rather a fiasco. At supper the fire had been lugubriously stubborn as we'd left the diesoline back at the cove camp, and the soup was smoky, lukewarm and full of lumps. With no insect repellant, we'd spent much of the night vainly warding off the droves of mosquitoes which arrived from the swampy forest. About midnight the rain came, more steady than hard, but in the darkness its constant dripping on the tent was annoyingly monotonous. The roar from the gorge above the camp increased until the air vibrated in the tent.

"There's one consolation," said Leo. "The river will be too high to cross, so we won't have to stagger any further with these rotten loads. Tomorrow it's back to the cove." He stuffed a palm of tobacco into his pipe and added reflectively, "I wonder what's on the breakfast menu at the Milford Hostel?"

The thought was too much. We packed and left and we were soon back in the moss forest. The way down river was easier with empty swags, and not long after midday we were sipping tea under the comfort of the tent fly back at Harrison Cove.

"Tonight we're really going to eat," I said.

We kept a watch all the afternoon, but no launch came. Rodda and Ede must have decided to spend the night at the Milford Hostel.

The next morning we were enjoying a leisurely breakfast when I suddenly put down my mug and said, "Dinna y'hear them?"

"What?"

"It's the prince from over the water."

"You've got the relief of Lucknow and the landing of Bonny Prince Charlie all mixed up, haven't you?" said Faigan.

"Maybe, but the reinforcements have arrived. The launch is coming, with Rodda and Ede."

"Blow me down," exclaimed Leo, looking across the Sound, "the fleet's in port and not a whore bathed."

We scurried around the camp tidying up. "Caught like a Saturday housewife in a dressing gown with curlers in her hair and the vicar at the front door," said Leo as he threw more driftwood on the fire and ran down to the creek for water.

By the time Jack and Rol were ashore, we had the camp respectable, and we ambled down to the beach to meet them. "It's good to see you, Rol. Have a good trip through?" We shook hands.

"Howdy, you two roughnecks," said Ede, screwing up his eyes as the rain dribbled over the brim of his ski cap. "Not a bad day for these parts."

While they ate the rest of our overnight stew we told them that we'd taken most of the tucker up to the camp at Pembroke Creek.

"Good show, boy," said Rodda, "that should give us a good start."

Within an hour we were away. The arrival of Rodda and Ede had boosted our morale, and the day had temporarily improved. A brightening sun elbowed through the clouds, shafts of light brought the dour steeps, the still water and the gloomy forest to a harmony of colour. After a five-hour struggle we arrived at the camp opposite Pembroke Creek, but the rain was back again, harder and more persistent than before.

"What do you think, Rol? Do we go on?"

"No," he said. "Listen to the water pouring out of the gorge. We'd never get across the river." Not the least of Rodda's merits was his ability to make a good camp in the worst circumstances; this was at least his third trip into the Harrison, and he knew the tricks of the trade. "I think we'd better move the tent," he said, "the river could come up higher in the night."

Faigan and I had pitched camp conveniently near the river and we were somewhat nettled at this suggestion; all the way back up the valley that day we'd anticipated an immediate return to our sleepingbags. But Rol and Jack were indefatigable. Before we knew it, we were organised, stripping branches and bolsters of thick moss from the trees to put under the tent floor or lugging boulders from the creek for a more efficient fireplace. Faigan and I had to admit that the effort was worthwhile. We moved the tent to higher ground, yet still within a few yards of the river, and there was a deep ticking of branches and green moss under the tent floor. Like small boys playing in a pine plantation, we stretched out full length and smiled to each other at the comfort. The fire was blazing, and the tent was sited with such cunning that the smoke drifted past the entrance without filling the interior.

"A real art in that," said Rol. There was reason for his pride, for it had been he who had decided where to pitch the tent in relation to the wind and the fireplace, and he'd had the two of us holding the tent and then moving it a few feet this way or that until he'd made up his mind where finally it was to rest.

Ede, who was splitting wood with his ice-axe a short distance away while Rol worried over the niceties of windage, called out, "Hey, Rol, I think you're half a degree out. You should have brought a theodolite."

It was my turn to cook the evening stew. Everybody agreed that it tasted fine, but it had body too. Flung against the side of a concrete building it would have stuck like plaster.

At dusk the first chips of stars winked through the black lattice of the trees. The reek of woodsmoke was sharp, and in the on-coming night I had the illusion that shapes of the forest were closing in, but the tent with its taut walls and straight stretched guy ropes was a secure canvas fort against the green frontier. For a while there was much talking and sudden bursts of laughter in the tent, and we sang a few discordant lines of mountain ballad while the candle glowed. The tent sounds died and last of all we heard Rodda announce that "It had better be a bang-on day tomorrow—it's time we got up that hill."

Next morning was fine, so we left a dump of food at the camp site and roped across the Harrison River which was still running decep-tively high and swift after the rain and we all got a ducking. After a steep climb through filthy bush above the mouth of the gorge, we kept an undulating line several hundred feet above the river, often climbing or dropping down to outflank concealed oubliettes between the deep-mossed boulders, or decaying windfalls entangled with dense undergrowth. There were no deer trails, the forest contested every step. Our heavy packs and the physical obstacles of the gorge were bad enough, but the sensation of encirclement was worse. One rotting gully followed another, each ridge had a shadowy fellow beyond. I had experienced this anonymity in Westland before, but never so forcibly: the monotone of the unseen river below, the misted bluffs above, and the never ending wildwood parting briefly to the machete and then closing in behind. The forest didn't attack, it absorbed.

After three hours the tedious pounding of the river gave a deeper booming note and an unflagging Rodda enticed us down to gape at the Wairereata Falls bending in two leaps into the seething pool 150 feet below. "The worst's over. In another hour we'll strike easier going."

Leo peered cursorily down at the dark water. "Oh, the hydrophobic Harrison."

Just before nightfall we came down to the river where the beech trees hung silently over the slow moving pools. The air was soft with the smell of imminent rain, the sky heavily overcast and the valley sombre. Wet, cold and hungry, we'd had enough for the day and all we wanted was shelter. It was Rodda who urged us on, and who with a determined cheerfulness saw the gloomy river as a last challenge, an inconvenient barrier that must be crossed, for our peak lay on the far bank.

When he spoke to me I was preoccupied with the certainty that the Harrison would soak us to the chest and that, once across, we'd spend a chilly hour while we set up camp and cooked a meal.

"You're the bloke that's good at rivers. Are you willing to give it a go?"

"Do we have to?" I hedged.

"Yes, if you want to climb Grave. Camp here tonight if you want to, but if the river floods we could be stuck on the wrong side for days."

"OK, Rol, give me the rope." Once the line was tied around my middle I felt better. The current was swift but I managed well enough. The water was cold, but the comments of the other three were warm. In an hour we were all across.

We camped for the night on a mossy terrace above the river and sang our Christmas carols to an accompaniment of rain and a sputtering candle while the Harrison gave praise with a spated roar. Our singing was prompted, perhaps, more than by the habit of childhood or by a wish to keep a link with town comforts: we sang because we liked it. The noise was our defiance to the flooded river as well as our acceptance of it. But there may have been more in the lift of our voices than this. I had been pottering among mountains enough to sense that men sometimes climbed for reward other than "the view of the summit", the thrill of danger overcome or for self-esteem: mountain living has always meant mental as much as physical travel. We seldom talked about this, we were far too busy with the obstacles, the swag that was too heavy, the river and a gorge behind us, bluffs, scrub, rock and snow ahead. But when we camped we could wait a little, while our minds caught up.

We took no rest on Christmas Day. Rodda and Ede went up valley to find the end of the Grave spur, while Faigan and I prospected a route down the more rugged side of the gorge. As the Harrison was high, we wanted a line of retreat to the cove without river crossings. When Faigan and I came in to camp, all pudgy-nosed from the dense forest, and fed up after a nine-hour trip in the gorge, Ede and Rol were already home. The camp was as neat as a parade ground.

"That's all the tucker up from the Pembroke Creek camp." Faigan and I levered our way out of heavy swags.

"Good show," said Rol. "Come and have a meal."

"What's offering?"

"Harrison Special tonight," said a grin that was Ede under a once white French Foreign Legion pattern ski cap. "Stew."

"Oh, no!" protested Leo, "not again!"

"Cheer up," said Rodda. "There's plum pud as well."

"No holly, I'm afraid," said Ede. "But a sprig of beech leaves should make it look festive, don't you think? I couldn't find any rata."

"Early in the expedition to be eating bark, ain't it?" from Leo.

After tea Rol handed round cigars and we had a concert. Jack sang his favourite from *The Maid of the Mountains*, I tried to remember bits of Henry V's speech before Agincourt, Rol told some more tall tales from the hills, and Leo was himself. As a grand finale we all sang what we could remember of *Eskimo Nell*. The Harrison Valley seemed to like it, as the rain eased and the wind dropped.

Just before we turned in, Rodda said that we'd better go as canny as possible with the fuel as we'd need it all for the high camp under Mt Grave. Jack went out of the tent and fanned the fire with a billy-lid. We were still calling out to him to come and turn in as we fell asleep. Next morning as we struggled into harness, I casually asked Ede what time he gave up the firewatching.

"Oh, I just looked after it a bit until the wet logs caught," he replied rubbing eyes puffed with wood smoke.

"When I woke up once, you were still hard at it, Jack. Must've been well on towards midnight."

"Well, we saved the primus fuel didn't we?" he replied matter-of-factly.

Ede was never a selfish man.

Two hours on through the forest we dumped our seventy-pound swags near the foot of the Grave spur. While Jack and Rol made a cache of the food that was to stay as our reserve supply, Leo and I built a fire and put the billy on.

"It looks a long thirsty way up that hill to the scrub line," Leo said.

Just when the water was boiling and I was throwing in the tea-leaves Rol called out that as we'd be away at any minute, there wasn't time for a boil-up. It just wasn't our day because, for some reason, we were all rather scratchy. Perhaps the hard load-carrying and the jungle-bashing of the last few days had worn us more than we thought. Whatever the reason, Rol and I had one of those flare-ups that are the hallmark of a lasting friendship. We argued whether we should or should not have that cup of tea. I was stubborn, and made some cracks about alpine quartermasters, and this made Rol as determined as I in the opposite direction. It was a classic example of a silly situation that would not have built up had we both been less tired and more tactful.

"Good grief," said Leo. "The camaraderie of the hills! Does this happen often?"

The result was that the tea billy went flying, and the four of us went thirsty and grumpy to the hill. Mountaineers are very human.

The foot of the Grave spur, when we reached it after a comically silent half-hour, wasn't anything but a large steep slip; a mass of jumbled boulders about twenty feet high cunningly spread with deep moss, and a crisscross entanglement of shattered tree-trunks and thick bush lawyer. After four hours we'd climbed a paltry five hundred feet. The going improved, though the angle was still exhaustingly steep when we came to the crest of the ridge, but I was too done in to be cheered about it. Rol came over and took some of my load, and so did Jack and Leo. Six hours after quitting the valley floor we were at the scrubline hoping for better things.

But the scrub was as bad as the lower part of the ridge. We lost Rodda's four-year-old blazes at the end of the big bush and forced a passage up bluffs overhung with horizontal scrub whose branches, twisted by innumerable spring and winter avalanches, presented us with a maze of spiky overhangs which caught packs and tore our clothing. We tried going under the stuff instead of trying to climb over it, we pushed and hacked through it. The way each of us approached the problem was interesting and a headshrinker seated in that scabrous wilderness would have had some good stuff for his casebook. Jack singing as well as grunting, Rol going through with a quiet, controlled determination, I telling the whole of the Harrison Valley and Mt Grave what I thought, and Leo, sensibly and strategically placed in the rear, wriggling up with the least difficulty. When I was out in front and entangled swearing on a bluff, he observed dryly, "You know, I don't think Paul is on the easiest route!"

By dark we were through the scrub but hadn't found either water or a reasonable place to pitch the tent. And how we longed for them both. I don't know yet how Ede and Rodda kept going, I'd have flung my swag down and cried quits to the mountain, but they went up and up. Faigan and I could see their torches bobbing and hear their talk. They sounded as perky as two land agents comparing the relative merits of suburban building sites. At last at 11.15 pm in a night that was as soft as velvet and as dark as the inside of a seaboot, I heard Rodda's quavering voice call, "Come on up, you two. We're not going any further tonight. This site will have to do."

"That's nice to know," said Leo. "I *was* beginning to wonder."

"Any water up there?" I called.

"Yes, bags of the stuff."

The thought of water, even more immediate than the vision of food or rest, drove Faigan and me up the hill. We smelled it long before we heard it tinkling in the darkness. And then we were wading in the knee-deep pools, feeling it running clear and chill into our boots. We bent and scooped up handfuls, rolling its sweetness round our scummy mouths, splashing it over our faces. It had been a long parched climb and this was our first drink for twelve hours.

If we'd come to a camp site, that didn't mean that we'd automatically crawl into warm bags: for three hours we bumbled around carrying rocks to build up the tent platform. Leo actually went to sleep with a large boulder cradled in his arms, and I had reached the stage where the whole pantomime seemed uproariously funny. It was a crazy camp. As we threw our sleepingbags into the tent at 1.30 am I heard Faigan say, "I've always been told that mountaineers are mad; now I know they are. We ought to be in Seacliff Asylum."

Leaving Ede and Faigan to secure the camp, Rodda and I were off up the hill the next morning to prospect a route to the foot of the nor'-west ridge of Mt Grave. At first we followed the creek beside our camp, plugged steps up an old spring avalanche fan and finally scrabbled our way up very steep tussock until we reached the top of the ridge between the Bowen and Harrison Valleys.

"It's taken a lot of sweat, but it's been worth it," said Rodda. And then he was pointing. "Look at Grave!"

Through the rain scud the north-west buttress of Mt Grave was a steep black line folded in swirling mist. For days we'd seen nothing but bush and river as we'd struggled along the green floor of the forest ocean. We'd carried swags which had weighed us down like leaden old men of the sea. But now we were free, the nearest things in the sky to the keas that flew with strong slow beating wings or circled with red underwing above the silent black wall of the Bowen Face of Mt Grave. We went back down to the tent no longer mules, but mountain men.

But there was a time of waiting between the seeing and the tasting. That evening we had snow from the south-west. In the tent we were a comfortable secure microcosm in a wilderness of snow and wind and darkness. A solitary candle hung in a spiral of wire from the clothesline above our heads. When the wind gusted and the tent shook, the movement of light and shadow gave that vitality seen in the fo'c'sle of well-found, slowly rolling ships; four of us lying in our bags with our swags as pillows, the primus burring and the flame a blue corona under the blackened billy, one side of the tent stacked with food bags and fuel tins. A haze from pipes and cigarettes, a minimum of possessions, conversation, a storm outside and fair weather within.

We drank continuously the whole of the next day, and even with good meals were still hungry. Days later when our food was running low, bacon-rind might mysteriously disappear from your plate if you turned your head, or there would be subtle stealthy rustlings as unknown fingers explored the food bags in the night. Then Rol would wake with a "Wazzat, wazzat? Who the devil's raiding the tucker box?" and switch on his torch. The thieves would try to bluff it out, but Rodda would say quickly, "I know you blokes are pinching the tucker, but don't be mean about it—hand it round."

But if he kept a strict hand on the ration box, he was an endless provider of cigarettes. He was usually the first to wake each morning and nudge me with a brief, "Good morning, have a nail, boy. Have a nail."

And this was how we stirred at 1.30 am the morning we set out for Grave. We were away by three and were soon climbing steadily up the last of the snowgrass to the ridge. We bore east over easy ground along the ridge top until we reached a peaklet which Rodda called the Mitis. The rocks of Grave were cold and overlaid with snow so we waited until the sun crept over a white shrouded Mt Tutoko.

"Too cold on those Grave slabs. Let's wait for a while until the rocks warm up and some of the snow thaws."

Probably the suggestion came from me. The mountain was austere, repellent with the greenish light of dawn on the two great rock buttresses and the summit cap sloping back against a pale blue sky. Mountains, like other meals, are enjoyed best when they are warm with reds and yellows, and the valleys aren't dark purple pits but flashing with river light.

We stayed two hours during which the peak looked continually more forbidding. I was really thinking what a glorious day it would be to sit and sun when Ede said that we ought to be moving. He made the whole climb sound so easy, but I knew from the way he and Rodda eyed the frigid mountain that it wasn't going to be an easy day for a lady.

Leo, who hadn't done much of this sort of thing and had too much sense to deceive himself or others, said he'd watch our gymnastics for a while and then wander back to camp and get a meal ready for our return. "Besides," he said, "there may be moas about. They could play merry hell if there's no one round the camp to shoo them off."

We three put the rope on, and I looked hesitantly down the rock and over the small snowfield hanging over the dizzy fall into the

"Come what come may, Time and the hour runs through the roughest day."
Under the shelter of the Ruth Flat bivvy rock, David Rees-Jones reads from *Macbeth*
to John Hunt.

"It was as if future and past and present were at the same point of time. . . ."
Twenty-one years later. Under the same bivvy rock, Conway Powell looks at the
botany of Ruth Flat.

"I'd never have believed a mountain could be so beautiful and so frightening. . . ."
The unclimbed east face of Mt Fastness from Ruth Flat.

head of Grave Creek. When we clambered down to the snowfield, and so turned quite easily an evil rock tower that had been a treasury of "ifs" ever since we'd seen it in a photograph months before, I was still in a state of doubt whether I was cut out for the joys of hanging over thin air.

But when Ede shinned up a moderate pitch crannied with edelweiss as if he were a chamois, I, even with the help of the rope, baulked at it. "I can't do it. Not my day."

"Nonsense," said Rol.

"Of course you can," said Jack, and pulled me up like a bale of wool out of a ship's hold.

When my knees had stopped shaking, Rol turned to me and said, "You take over and lead the climb now, Paul."

Rodda was a wonderful man for giving you strength on a mountain and you never had anything but the greatest confidence in him. He and Jack Ede were among the most unflappable mountaineers I've met. But Grave was "his" mountain, if any man can say such a preposterous thing, and yet here he was handing over to me the privilege of leading on it. I'd known him longer than anyone else in the Alpine Club and suddenly after years I saw him quite startlingly from another angle.

As soon as I led off I was a different man. Before, I had been dreading the climb and might have turned it in on the weakest pretext, but now I was enjoying it.

The first buttress was steep and the rock exposed so we often moved singly while the other two belayed the rope. The rock meeting my fingers with a tingling crispness and the holds satisfyingly sound and deep, this became one of those days when a mountain and I were in conjunction. But as I climbed, utterly absorbed in the excitement and the technicalities of our upward passage, I knew there was much I was missing. Once, when I had reached a plausible stance on a ledge, I filched a second from the responsibility of leading and the downward pull of gravity.

In that shuttered instant I saw the fullness of the mountains as does a man who briefly lifts his eyes from a demanding problem, and in one instant fixes in his mind the slow passage of a raindrop on a window pane, or the silent unfolding of a leaf. The mountain wall was a place of strange sculpture, pinnacles, gargoyles, and flying buttresses shining in the moving angle of the sun. The cracks and small ledges in the face became more than cogs on the wheel of the alpine hours or points on a graph plotting time against height made good: they were the stations of our living. The mountain became a wonderful fusion of form and line, of steel-grey shadow and rippling light, a vast wholeness of which we were a transitory part. In that split second I saw the shadows soft on the rolling snow-fields, the attendant peaks that curved and dipped to the head of the Harrison Valley where the last green ribs of scrub and forest climbed to meet them. I saw westward, the sea purpling, and the momentary flare of white on reefs against the slow roll of the Tasman. Between my feet, the thin wisp of the river twisted like silver in the green setting of the forest, and tucked in against the lip of the mountain wall, a chin of yellow alpine tussock poised over the stubble of the valley. I was suddenly and wonderfully alive.

"What's the holdup?" Rodda's inquiry floated up.

I came back to the business of climbing. "No trouble, Rol. Just having a breather."

There was no more time for fancy. While we were shuffling across some two hundred feet of smooth, outward-shelving slabs covered with new snow, the sky became suspiciously hazy and then a white wall of nor'-west fog swirled up and over us. Close on the left, the thunder of a rock avalanche growled through the mist. We said nothing, but went at the mountain. There was no banter as feet and hands wedged in the cracks of the 500-foot second buttress. We levered over a large stone chocked at the top of a long vertical crack and three set faces moved on the mountain. By 4.45 pm, fourteen hours from camp, the summit was in sight beyond an easier curve of rock and snow, but the sky was dark with the threat of storm. Half an hour later, Ede and I stepped aside and presented Rodda with the last few feet of unbroken snow for a birthday present.

What did we feel on the virgin top of Mt Grave? Rodda and Ede were pleased; I was too, but as I looked at the storm closing in, and the ranks of the hogsbacks marshalling far out to sea, I had that get-me-down-off-this-bloody-mountain-quick sensation. Every peak from Aspiring to Tutoko had its cap of ill omen, but Rodda kept clicking his camera in endless panoramas with an unconcern that infuriated. I didn't have his brand of objective courage, I wanted to pat the summit and hurry off. Instead we built a cairn, a damned ridiculous mountain custom in the circumstances, and solemnly deposited our names and a threepenny bit.

When we left the summit at 5.45 pm I had to beat down the most difficult and dangerous of alpine urges, the temptation to hurry off a difficult peak in bad weather. We had not much over two and a half hours to get down the two thousand feet of steep rock and the descent would be a race against time and night. I didn't like racing on a mountain as too much could go wrong. So we came to the upper rim of the top rock buttress in a mood of disciplined hurry and committed ourselves to the wind and the rain with but one thought: to get down the mountain as far as we could before the storm really broke.

That night convinced me that men don't conquer mountains. If some men delude themselves that they do, we weren't among them. Outwardly we gave no hint of our individual feelings. I can't say what Ede and Rodda thought, but I knew that they were as determined as I to get down in one piece. We went down with the rope bowing in the howling wind and the rain hissing and running down the open granite slabs. The wind drowned the words we yelled, whipped them away into the closing greyness of dusk and the misty mountain wall, and separated us from each other. The sodden rope and our hand signals were our only link. Three hours below the summit, darkness caught us still on the lower slabs. We were a long way from home and there was no ledge or shelter. If we were wet, we were too busy to notice it. If we were cold, we ignored it. Even the wind was something that we accepted, but final darkness was the worst. It was as if the mountain forces, having failed to break us by wind and rain, were throwing in their ultimate and greatest weapon.

I was still leading down, Rodda behind me, and Ede last man and a faint torch somewhere above. Then we came to the open gallery of sloping holdless rock.

"Watch it," from Rodda, a call distorted and swallowed by the wind.

"Can you hold me, Jack?" from me—an alert, not an intention to fall.

"Safe as the Bank of England," came the muffled assurance.

They knew, as well as I, that if I went, all would go. But I edged down the water-gutted rock with a grate of nails stronger for Ede's defiant confidence. We were still an undivided team. The last few hundred feet took nearly three hours. I had no idea exactly where I was leading. The buttress was so featureless, just a blackness forever down and down, that we could easily have strayed left or right out on the hanging faces without return. Higher, where night had first come, my torch had slipped and smashed against the rock. It hung from the lanyard round my neck, swaying like a useless pendulum as I moved. Rodda came in close behind, shining his headlamp down to the rock around my feet. Once he stepped on my hand but I hardly felt it. We kept on, shouting and swearing in the swirling mist and the uncharitable night.

Just before midnight we were off the buttress and on easier ground, but we were so wet and tired, and the visibility was so poor, that we decided to sit the rest of the night out if we could find a ledge. We were pretty done and reaction was setting in, but we cluttered together on a shelf with our boots dangling over the sheer Bowen face of the mountain. If you asked me which was the worse, the climb down or the sit down, I couldn't say. Both were uncomfortable and both had their dangers. But I was more aware of the misery of five hours' wait for dawn on a ledge that wasn't bigger than the top of a kitchen sink. As soon as we stopped and tied ourselves to the rock in a cat's cradle of rope so that we wouldn't fall off if we dozed, I really felt the cold. The water ran down our backs and we had recurrent fits of shivering cramp. The rain flayed us, roaring in the darkness. We were alone. I thought of Faigan down in the tent, warm and asleep. The picture was so demoralising that I killed it. Faigan, for all his surface of drollery, was a deeply serious man who would be lonely with thoughts and worried about us. We'd told him we'd be back with the mountain in our pockets before dark.

"What's the time, Rol?"

"Ten past one."

"That all? I could have sworn it's half an hour since I last asked."

"Only five minutes ago."

Jack handed round a japara bag full of toffees and we chewed them between clattering jaws, paper and all. There were prunes, the shrivelled dried sort. They reminded me of another sort of misery, dead Sunday breakfasts in a Wellington boardinghouse. I let the boys know that I hated prunes. They laughed as if this was the greatest joke since Adam stubbed his toe in the Garden of Eden.

"Chocolate," said Jack.

The silver paper set my fillings on edge. "It's all full of tinfoil," protested Rodda. "How long have you had it, Jack?"

"I bought it two years ago in Zermatt. Best Swiss Toblerone."

"The tropics have melted it." We cackled again. I thought longingly of the wartime Pacific with mauve purple sea, warm trade winds and dolphins diving in the ship's bow wave.

"I'm going to get inside my rucsac," I said. I tried to pull the canvas bag over my head but I got the cramps again and gave up. Then my hands touched cold metal. "Hey, Rol?"

"Whatizzit?"

"We forgot to use the rock pitons. After all that practising on the crags round Dunedin, and then we didn't remember to use them coming down the buttress. We could've been down to camp by now. We could have banged in those pegs and slid down on the rope."

"You were carrying them."

"Fancy dragging them all that way up the Harrison. Then up Grave. Just to sit on!" That kept us cackling for another minute.

Wind and rain and more shivering. More cramp. "Hey, Rol."

"Whatizzit?"

"Let's have a smoke."

"Can't. Fags are wet."

"A pipe then."

Half an hour and innumerable matches later, we warmed our hands on glowing bowls; a small Promethean fire stolen from the mountain and the storm. Jack didn't smoke, but he was impressed: vices had their advantages.

Dawn came, and we were incredulous. We had been dreading a south snow—bringing wind change. I wanted to hobble off with the first faint glimmer, but Rodda, a man of immeasurable patience, made us wait until there was enough light for safety. It took us almost an hour to get the circulation back and untangle the swollen, half-frozen rope. Then we were moving, puppets jerking and slithering down the last rocks to the towers in the gap below the Mitis peak. A slow climb above the snowfield and a full dawn with the Harrison catching the earliest light and a great singing and awareness of life.

When we stumbled down the creek rocks to the tent, Faigan was asleep, but the stew was still warm and the embers in the fire winking in the morning breeze. Leo had kept his vigil too.

We put the primus on and made cocoa, hot sweet cocoa, and why worry about the fuel?

Leo woke and sat up with red, pouched eyes. "You're back?"

"Yes."

"Didn't think you'd make it. I saw you on the lower buttress early yesterday afternoon, moving very slowly, then the mist hid you. I heard voices shouting, then the rock avalanche fell and there was silence. I thought the rocks had got you. I called and called. No answer." This was a serious Faigan.

We didn't talk of summits or of conquering. Almost incidentally we mentioned that we'd climbed Grave.

Then we slept—it was thirty hours since we had left the camp to climb. This hollow in the scrub, beside water, with wood for a fire, was greater than the highest summit rock, and conquest.

When we left for the valley and the long shimmering Sound between the seaward hills, I didn't look back.

As the launch was rounding the Benton Promontory and Rol and I were talking about the trip, I looked down the long white wake to the receding cleft in the forest where the Harrison River flowed into the dusking Sound. Mt Pembroke held a last glow of light.

"Pretty good trip, eh, Rol?" I said. "That night-out wasn't really too bad. Quite funny when you think of it."

"It wasn't at the time; we could have bought it, y'know. Exposure.

Didn't you realise that?"

"Did *you*?"

"Yes."

"I'm glad we didn't speak of it. We'd have really been scared then."

"And what would have been the point in doing that? We were quite uncomfortable enough as it was."

When the *Donald Sutherland* came alongside the jetty near the Milford Hostel, Mrs Berndtson was there to meet us. "You're coming back again, I hope," she said.

"I'd like to, Mrs Berndtson. Very much."

I looked at Rodda. "Yes," he said, "we might. They tell me there's a mountain round here called Tutoko."

13

Retreat from Mt Tutoko

Ay, now am I in Arden; the more fool I: when I was at home, I
was in a better place: but travellers must be content.
                                    —*As You Like It*, Act 2, Sc 4

I'M CERTAIN that the idea of climbing nine-thousand-foot Mt Tutoko
came into Rodda's head that stormy evening we'd arrived so im-
portunately on the top of Mt Grave, and when he eventually brought
up the idea of trying Tutoko by a new route I was keen to join him.
The memory of our near thing on Mt Grave had blurred, and with
the optimism of the hillbilly who is compelled to return, I didn't
worry too much about storms striking again.

The plan was to walk from the Tutoko River bridge to the head
of the valley, climb up the Grave Couloir (one of the longest in
New Zealand) and follow a snow shelf we'd spotted from Mt Grave
on to a snow saddle called Ngapunatoru Pass. We decided that from

the pass a long day would get us over the unclimbed divide between the head of the Tutoko Valley and Stick-Up Creek. We'd climb Tutoko by the usual route up the north-west ridge if another way wasn't possible.

Tutoko had a reputation for being a tough nut to crack by any approach. The peak had been climbed only three times, and the unique Samuel Turner had made six attempts and spent a small fortune before he was led to the top by guide Peter Graham in March 1924. We weren't quite in the Peter Graham class, but neither were we Sammy Turners; we got along with most people and each other pretty well.

So when Rodda, Geoff Longbottom, Graham Ellis and I lay under a bivvy rock we'd discovered and made homelike near the bottom of the Grave couloir, we were confidently optimistic. Neither the fact that it had rained or snowed almost continuously for four days, nor the knowledge that the Grave Couloir had only been ascended three times in fifty-two years alarmed us. Rol was close to his mountain, and I was back where I was always at my best and happiest—under the solid protection of an overhanging rock. There was dry tussock and sweet-smelling hebe under our bags, the fire was bright if somewhat smoky, and we had food.

The nearest we'd got to an argument was over Rol saying he thought we should call the bivvy Pawnbroker's Rock because it had three clumps of mountain flax growing on it. As co-discoverer I objected. The name reminded me of the fact that I was still broke. Besides, I maintained that such a name was asking for trouble. If mountains were as tough as pawnbrokers we mightn't be able to redeem our pledges, or settle our grudge against Mt Tutoko. Graham and Geoff seemed upset to hear Rodda and me ragging each other, but they soon got used to it as being old friends, we never stopped. We'd also brought a tent along, the tent Rol had taken up the Harrison. After a lot of discussion I'd persuaded Rol that we wouldn't need the tent up high. Snowcaves were the thing, and I knew all about them. Rol, who disliked heavy swags as much as I, reluctantly agreed to leave his tent under the bivvy rock when I pointed out that lugging a heavy tent up four thousand feet of icy couloir could be the last straw that would break the mountaineer's back. I wasn't altogether altruistic when I said this. I was thinking just as much of mine as I was of his.

When the weather eventually cleared we had to spend a whole day sitting in the sun listening to the avalanches drumming down the Grave Couloir and off the west face of Tutoko, and prodding and probing the snow near the bottom end of the couloir until we'd made as many holes as the city gas department does in a pavement before it digs it up. The only difference was that the couloir wasn't like a pavement; it went up between the rock shoulderblades of the mountains like a tapering white stiletto.

"It's as steep as a hen's face." Geoff Longbottom was always frank.

"Ummmmm." said Graham Ellis.

"Forward the Twenty-seventh Light Padres," I murmured, remembering one of Leo's favourite quips.

"It should go all right, with care." Rol looked around the walls that hemmed in the head of the valley as if he were an old lag planning a breakout from a maximum security prison. "If it's fine, we'll start up the couloir at midnight."

"Gawd!" said Longbottom. "You're joking."

"That's right," said Rol. "It's safer then, the muck doesn't start rolling down until dawn when the sun first hits the hanging ice on Mt Paranui. There's a lot of it up there."

I craned my neck up at the white ribbon disappearing into the blue sky. There were some nice fluffy clouds sailing past the top of the ice gully. They looked tranquil and the ice cliffs were quiet. But I wasn't fooled, the local artillery had the whole couloir nicely enfiladed. "I bet they've got the range to a T," I said with a tingling feeling running up and down my spine.

"Grave, Gifford, and the Don brothers got up there OK in 1897–98," said Rodda, ignoring my usual gloomy forebodings. "The first ascent, *and* without crampons."

"It'll be all right if it freezes tonight," said Graham.

"If!" said Longbottom.

But it froze hard. We shouldered swags that must have touched the sixty-pound mark and walked on to the jumbled avalanche rubble spewed on to the valley floor. The stars were as sharp and unwavering as lance points, they hung like a tiara about the dark heads of the peaks, flashing red and green and white. I felt the watching-hill sensation that I'd so often experienced before, but once we were at work there was no time but the mountain's. We went up the avalanche runnels which scored the couloir, Rol as usual doing much of the hard ice work. He was as steady and as safe as if he were leading us along a city street, except that he kept throwing an eye to the pale rim of the overhanging icecliffs. We sweated for all the frost, and edged up, four dim figures in bobbing pools of light. I was thankful for the dark, which hid the steepness, but gravity told me.

There was a faint intention of dawn as we neared the first bulges of broken ice in the hollow of the couloir when the ice cliffs were nascent with colour.

"We'll have to crack it on," said Rodda, "the first train's due any moment." He went at the ice with a *whack, whack*, that echoed dully between the rocky walls and sent the fragments hissing and skipping past us in a grotesque choreography. "Doesn't he ever tire?" a voice above me murmured.

I offered to take over the step-cutting.

"No," said Rol without slackening his effort, "There isn't time to change about."

When full dawn came we were still only about a third of the way up the couloir. The watery sunrise and the hogsbacks over Tutoko depressed me. I was last on the rope, an alpine full-back with the responsibility of watching Geoff and Graham ahead of me and holding them should they slip. Neither of them had done a lot of ice climbing but they followed up behind Rodda well. They seemed as attentive as young braves behind a chief on their first scalping foray.

But mountains, for all their apparent benignity, know how to wait. Rol was cutting steps up a boss of hard blue polished ice in the steepest section of the icefall and was making a delicate move upward against the double drag of a heavy swag and gravity. Graham, tucked below, and partly out of sight from Rodda, was slowly letting out the belayed rope as Rol inched forward over the awkward convexity. Seconds before, I had been lethargic, my ears ringing, and breathing laboured, with all my willpower needed to watch the three men ahead, to dig the pick of my axe into the merest hold in the burnished ice and slowly drag myself up the next few steps. Longbottom had stopped and was taking what dubious anchorage the hard ice offered when I arrived at my station below him.

I was rather winded and was leaning over the horizontal axe-shaft anxiously watching Rol make his Agag-like transfer. Then my head cleared and I had a swift premonition of danger. Rodda was in the most delicate stage of his forward and upward move when an avalanche burst with a reverberating crack over on the flanks of Mt Tutoko. Graham, who had been the acme of concentration while he carefully paid out the rope as Rodda moved, suddenly looked away across to the spreading plume of ice dust. That one second of distraction was enough: the rope came unreasonably taut and Rodda, a burdened Blondin, was snubbed in midair. For an acrobatic second I saw him fighting to regain balance, to resist the backward pull and plant both foot and axe into the neutral ice. Then with a terrific effort he was forward in his steps and a blistering epithet went ricochetting across the couloir walls. There was no malice in the words, just the yell of a man on the lip of destruction. But it was from Longbottom and me that poor Graham received the full force of invective. We had been on the fringe of happening and had seen the involuntary circus act in slow time. Our comment was triggered by fear for ourselves as well as for Rodda and Ellis.

We went slowly up the second icefall, hugging the left-hand rock wall of the couloir, too busy with the cut and thrust against the ice to suffer immediate reaction. But later when we were at the first place where a safe rest was possible, with a droll expression, Graham said, "When I looked up and saw Rol flaying the air with no visible means of support, I thought to myself, 'What on earth will we have for breakfast if he falls? He's carrying all the eggs.' "

The rest of the couloir was a steep dragging plod in hot sun and softening snow. We were so exhausted that Rodda handed round a benzedrine tablet to each of us. This was the first and last time that any of us ever took stimulants on a climb; there was only one Grave Couloir. We reached the Tutoko Saddle at the top of the couloir half an hour before midday and immediately had lunch and as much tea as we could drink. As we sat on the sunny rocks, free at last from the drag of gravity and the threat of avalanches, I looked across the green peace of the upper Harrison Valley. We'd had to struggle for this oasis, but the Grave Couloir was behind us.

Any prospect of crossing the virgin snow shelf to Ngapunatoru Pass was out that day. The rock bluffs which tumbledhome to the shelf from the summit of Paranui were continually sending down snow avalanches which swept the narrow gallery and rumbled into the upper Harrison. We'd had enough thrills for one day, and more than a modicum of luck, so we decided to make camp. I was the snow cave fuehrer, as I'd already practised this troglodytic art on the unoffending slopes of Mt Aspiring, so I set about justifying my insistence that we leave the tent behind at the bivvy rock below the Grave Couloir. The rest of the gang slaved too and after four hours' hard digging the cave was ready, but I don't think Rol got the satisfaction I did from the work. He was a tent man, I was a dentist. Holes had fascinated me ever since the time as a child I'd first dug under the foundations of a neighbour's house. Our snow-cave on Tutoko Saddle didn't fall down either.

We were so caught up with discovery that no sooner had we finished the snow cave and had another snack when someone asked Rol if the peak immediately west of the saddle had ever been climbed.

Rol was pretty sure it was inviolate. "It won't take long," he said. "We'll be back for an early tea."

And this time we were. But that peaklet gave me a lot of pleasure, I liked rock peaks that didn't take too long to climb, especially when you could look down from their summits and see almost right up the entrance of a snow cave down on the col. I never like being away too long from the prospect of food and refuge. The half hour on the unnamed summit was pure indolence and reminiscence. Rol and I looked across the head of Grave Creek to the impressive nor'-west wall of Mt Grave and gave Graham and Geoff a lurid and suitably embellished account of our climb and night-out on that peak.

We left our crystal palace on Tutoko Saddle early the next morning and started along the snow shelf below Paranui. Though the snow wasn't very well frozen, the mountain above was quiet enough and treated us with silent indifference. I was grateful for this since I had a distinct aversion to getting falling snow down my neck. And it's not the snow that hurts most but the bits of rock that come with it. It was my turn to do some of the donkey work, so I led across the shelf. Rol, like a centurion of the Thundering Legion, was in the post of maximum glory in the rear. After his herculean efforts in the Grave Couloir he deserved a rest. The breaking snow crust did nothing to mar the picnic atmosphere of our exploration. There were a few lines of deep crevasses but we outflanked them easily enough and arrived below the final snow slope under Ngapunatoru Pass confident that Tutoko was in the bag.

"Bloody good show, boy," said Rol as we started to dig the snow cave that was to be our headquarters for the grand assault. There were smiles as big as saucers on Geoff's and Graham's faces too. The snow-shovel flew, the pot-lids scraped, and the excavated snow went flying down the slope into the upper Harrison Valley. While Graham and Geoff titivated the snow cave, Rol and I went up the steep snow to the top of Ngapunatoru Pass to spy out the unclimbed approach to Mount Tutoko.

The prospect from Ngapunatoru Pass was wilder and grander than our expectations. From the level snow hammock of the pass, the rock rampart between the head of the Tutoko Valley and Stick-Up Creek led straight to Mount Tutoko, a vision that floated behind the wreathing mist, an aerial castle of dazzling snow and brutal rock. This sudden revelation of the mountain was hypnotic. At first it was the physical immensity of the peak that compelled, then I sensed a power more than that of height or depth, something beyond visible majesty. A fragment from the Psalms of David came to me: *What is man, that thou are mindful of him?*

"The route looks feasible," said Rol, breaking our silence. Then he looked at the mist rolling in from the sea and the mountain shining resplendent behind it. "Hope the weather holds."

"It's only fine-weather fog. It looks settled enough to me."

We were so sure that the weather would be fine that we didn't even bother to climb the unnamed peak immediately north of the pass. We were tempted, but left it for a pleasant stroll the next day.

"A bit lousy if we climb it without Geoff and Graham," said Rol. "Let's leave it until tomorrow, then we can all do it together."

"Fair enough, they deserve a break. They've worked pretty hard."

"Anyway," said Rodda with a backward glance at Mt Tutoko as we dipped below the pass, "the big one's plastered to glory, we'll have to give those iced rocks a chance to clear."

Ellis and Longbottom had our snow house ready and we ate our tea with the gusto that the promise of peaks and sun gave us. We suffered a minor tragedy when one of Rol's billy-lids dropped from Geoff's hands and went skipping and bowling down the freezing slope into the upper Harrison. We laughed, not so much at Rodda's discomfiture, as at the comical antics of the disappearing pot-lid which bounded valleyward like a tumbling clown.

That night we talked, not of when we would climb Tutoko, but how, and crawled into our sleepingbags with the opulence of our assurance and Rodda's cigars. Rol and I started our nightly argument which rapidly embroiled both Geoff and Graham. The subject, commercial advertising of toothpastes and patent medicines, may not have been very esoteric, but it kept us warm and brought a feeling of homeliness. We weren't just on the mountain, we lived there.

Then the rain came. We played this off at first as a temporary reverse and even crowed that it would be just the thing to clean those dangerously iced rocks on Tutoko. By the third day we were not so cocky and talked soberly of *when* or *if* the storm passed over. Our faces grew sour and we huddled together more for warmth. The mountain was wearing us down, pushing us into a defensive silence. I was cold too, for insulation was meagre, with only a thin sleepingbag and an outer japara bag erroneously but popularly called *waterproof*, separating me from the underlying snow. The man who had the rope to lie on was envied. The storm came between us and the mountain like a slow barrier. Our talk and thoughts were more of home and warm beds than of high conquest.

Longbottom and I competed in this self-torture. "And to think that at this very minute my boy Conway is tucked up all snug as a bug in a rug, in his cot!" I lamented, in between shivering bouts. I saw home and wife and child as a paradise infinitely more desirable than this discomfort.

"Go on," said my brother-in-law, Rodda, "he's probably hollering his head off with teething or chewing his cot to bits."

"I'd settle for my little old bed in Beaumont Road with the electric blanket turned on to high," added Longbottom.

"If ever you let Conway become a mountaineer," said Ellis with conviction, "I hope he sues you for cruelty."

But Rodda wasn't going to be chased off the mountain by a tiddley-winking bit of a storm. He lay in his bag with the stoicism which would have made a fakir on a bed of nails seem like a sybarite. He was as grimly cheerful and resolute as a brigand in a cave. I admired and envied his *sang froid*.

On the fourth morning of rain I awoke from a nap. The cave seemed a lot lighter, and wetter. And there was Rodda, a thin-faced optimist in a rain-spattered parka solemnly trying to patch a gaping hole in the snowcave roof with inadequate fistfuls of soggy snow. The rain beat through the hole like water out of a shower rose. "The bloody cave's melted, boy!" His voice vibrated up an octave.

"Yes," I said inching against the wall, "I can see that."

Rodda gave a disgusted snort. "You and your blasted snow caves! Look at it, six feet of roof melted in four days. And my tent's under the bivvy rock at the bottom of the Grave Couloir."

"Better nip over and get it," said Longbottom.

"Funny man," said Rol.

"It was a wonderful bivvy rock," I answered. "I told you we shouldn't have left it."

"Well, we're leaving *this* bivvy now," said Rodda with sudden finality, "we've had our chips as far as Tutoko's concerned."

"It looks that way, Rol," I replied as humbly as I could.

We packed quickly, jammed food and gear into rucsacs, pulled on wet storm clothing and roped up inside the cave. As we went out the entrance I had a last look around the cave. There were bits of paper, cigarette butts, matches, empty tins, and a forlorn sock with a monstrous hole, all trodden in the slushy floor. We were in retreat and like a routed army were leaving behind the pathetic relics of our stay. I was sorry for that cave, it never had a chance.

The snow field and the bluffs below our cave had been descended only once before, by Marie Byles and Kurt Suter who in 1937 had come over to the Harrison from Stick-Up Creek via Ngapunatoru Pass. But we had a pretty good idea what to expect from our Grave trip and had little trouble in spite of the gale-force wind and very poor visibility. But when we came out of the scud and were threading a cautious way down the greasy snow-grassed bluffs the day still had surprises. Graham complained of gut pains and felt dizzy. He clung to the wet tussock and lost his breakfast.

A few hundred feet lower I took a shot of Longbottom on a rock with the upper Harrison as a dramatic backdrop. "Thanks, Geoff," I said as I lowered my head to wind the film, "That should be a beaut." When I looked up he was gone. "That's funny," I thought, "he must've found a quicker and easier way down."

Rodda and Ellis, waiting below on the next shelf of the bluffs, were thawing out in the misty sun. They heard a sound of metal scraping rock and, looking up, saw Geoff in full flight head-first through the air.

"Poor old Geoff's had it."

"We'll never carry him out of here. Not down that gorge."

But Longbottom fell forty feet with fortuitous elegance into the only waterfall pool on the entire gallery of rock. "Hell, that water's cold."

"Serves you right, it's not a very good day for swimming. Why didn't you wait until the sun came out?"

The day had improved so well that we talked bravely of having another crack at Tutoko from the head of the valley. We hunted among the large rocks for a bivvy but found nothing suitable. There wasn't one which gave the least pretence of habitation. The keas had been there before us and one rock in particular was thick with their droppings, orange from the berries of the alpine herbfield. The afternoon was warm with that languor of mountain valleys near the sea. Perhaps our mood was due partly to tiredness—the mountains had given us quite a hiding over the past week—and partly to the softness of the colours which clothed the scrubby bluffs and hung over the still waters of Lake Never-Never. Certainly there was a lotus-eating atmosphere which was hard to shake off until we remembered that we had no tent.

As we crossed the river just above the lake I saw two ducks, I think they were black teal, diving for food among the sedges. They went on feeding quietly and one called to its mate with a soft whistle. I wasn't only a high-climbing man, I was as much at home in the valley with its smell of grass and colour of life. It was hard to resist the invitation of this elysium, I wanted to linger beside the green turquoise lake cupped between cirque and bluff. But we had no shelter; the spell of the place would soon go when the rains came back.

The bluffs which fell sheer into the lake forced us to climb about fifteen hundred feet into the snowgrass basins below Lake Pukutahi. While Graham and Geoff made a meal, and we were getting to the bits-and-pieces stage, Rodda and I went to look for a way back down to the Harrison River below the waterfall thundering from Lake Never-Never. Though the late afternoon was calm we wanted to be sure of the way ahead. The storm had cleared with suspicious rapidity and the sixth sense that you acquire after years in the hills made us restless. Reconnaissance wasn't only a habit, it became a necessity.

That dusk was one of tranquillity. Our camp was a little tussocked bowl where we could lie and watch the day go and the night come slowly with twinkling stars and the sound of water flowing from the mountains. I made a small fire with dry brushwood just for the pleasure of smelling the tang and hearing the flames crackle and the water sizzle inside the billy. The smoke drifted purple blue across the valley in a widening fan and Mt Grave rose a dark battlement beneath a sickled moon. The night was very warm and too reminiscent for early sleep. Rodda and I lay and talked with relaxed familiarity about our days and stormy night on Grave. We relived more than the climb, we dipped into the past and brought up as pearl fishers do, fragments of conversation, of our living with the people on the hill across the valley. We didn't gabble, there were silences as each of us moved through the attic of memory.

Ellis and Longbottom were so hot in their new bags that they didn't bother about waterproof covers, lying with their bags zipped open, but Rodda and I, older campaigners and more cunning, closed our thinner bags and burrowed down inside our outer japara coverings.

At midnight we were wakened. The flash and boom of lightning-thunder hissed and rolled. Mt Grave was a white witch's face and the ridges her writhing arms. I hate lightning: it uncovers fear and makes the mountains cruel. The ground shook as sizzling blue-white shafts hit the hillside. I crawled out and threw my axe and crampons further away. Hail the size of hazel nuts rattled down.

There were cries of annoyance as Graham and Geoff woke and struggled to zip up their bags, but Rol lay curled as tight as an alpine hedgehog. I heard him call out, "Send it down, Hughie, you bastard," with a quaver, not of fear but defiance. Longbottom groaned about a pain in his belly and during the pitch-black lulls in the storm I heard him retching. The bombardment came closer. Rodda was counting the time between each flash and the whip crack overhead.

"Three seconds, that's half a mile away."

I lit a cigarette inside my waterproof cover, it would be too late when everything got soaked.

The range closed and the hillside jumped and the air had a sharp blue steel smell. *Crash-bang*. Flash and thunder arrived together.

"Damn close, that one," yelled Rol.

"Too close. Right overhead." I tried to make my voice sound unconcerned.

"Could be worse," growled Rol. "Imagine if we'd had a night-out on Grave in this."

The last of the thunder muttered away over Tutoko, leaving us with ringing ears from the shock of storm. The rain poured down. The drama had gone and we suffered the cold miserable wetness with a grumbling impatience until the earliest hint of light. "Come on, Rol," we called peevishly. "For God's sake let's get out of here."

But Rodda didn't budge, I heard his muffled reply that there wasn't any sense in moving until it was light enough to see. We were a sorry mob at dawn and stumbled through the mist and scrub into the sodden forest. Rodda was at his best. He made us cook a mess of boiled bacon which we ate standing on a rock knoll above the river. Longbottom managed a wry smile though he looked like something on an undertaker's slab, and Ellis was a stolid face with baggy eyes—a mixture of resignation and tattered defiance. I felt dejected not only by the minute's wretchedness but also by the gloomy prospect of the long bush tussle ahead. I was so cold and tired I could have howled but there was already more than enough water in the Harrison River. We went down through the forest like a procession of mourners and stood despondently among the dripping trees beside the river. Swollen by the torrential rain, the Harrison was brown and wild with tossing waves. The rocks rolled and thudded like underwater hammers.

"What do you reckon, Paul?" asked Rodda. His eyes were tired but there was a dogged set to his jaw.

"Absolutely hopeless. Too wide, too swift. If we didn't get drowned, we'd get our legs bust by the rocks."

"Oh."

Neither Rodda nor I had been into this part of the upper Harrison during our expedition to Mt Grave, and only Kurt Suter and Marie Byles had been down these headwaters before. In March 1937 they had made an epic crossing from Lake McKerrow to Harrison Cove and Miss Byles recorded that they found the Harrison worse than the tangled greenery of Stick-Up Creek.

So we mooched on, Rodda in front and, as always when things were grim or the country difficult, cheerfully determined. He was the king-pin of our retreat. I brought up the rear, stumbling along with an empty pipe in my mouth and a mind away beside the fire at home. I was beginning to feel a queasiness down in my stomach but was too tired to decide whether it came from lack of food and sleep, or the bug that had knocked Geoff and Graham. When we stopped for a meagre snack I didn't feel hungry, but Rodda made me push some sodden bread and rancid butter down. But the worst blow to my morale came when I found I'd lost my pipe bowl. It had dropped from the stem back through the rainy forest. Rain and retreat are one thing, but marches without tobacco are worse. Rodda shared the last of his cigarettes and we leaned against the mossy trees and watched the rain come down. The mist covered the mountains and the narrowing valley was a vice that hemmed us in. The river was a roaring monotony we couldn't escape; wherever we went the sound came with us.

When we had pushed down as far as the foot of the Grave spur we had another spell and ate a little more and looked across the dark river to where we'd camped that year we'd first come up the gorge. We'd been weighed down with food then and the tent had been warm and thick with the smell of cooking. Now we were wet alpine waifs pressing cold noses against the window of the past.

"Remember that stew old Jack Ede made?" I said to Rol.

"The time you knocked it off the primus, and Jack spooned it off the tent floor and Leo complained that it was bacterial and unfit for alpine gentlemen to eat?"

I nodded and said, "He did though, and then like Oliver asked for more. I can still taste it. There was just the right amount of garlic in it."

"Fair go, boy," protested Rodda.

I saw Ellis and Longbottom lick their lips. They looked like lean wolves with hungry eyes. But I couldn't stop, the recollection of that far night was reality, the shelterless present was a nightmare. While I talked it was pushed behind me. "And that plum duff we had on Christmas Day. And afterwards, the four of us lying in the tent with those cigars of yours, and Leo arguing with you whether it was spray that came through the roof when it rained extra hard or whether—"

"It was condensation. My tent never leaked," said Rol.

"What's the point in arguing about a tent we haven't got?" said Longbottom bluntly.

"It's not much good to us all folded under the Grave couloir rock." Graham Ellis gave me a wan smile with a tinge of accusation.

Rol struggled into harness and climbed to his feet. Underneath the crumpled peak of his ski cap a sharp nose ran down the thin black stubbled face to his chin. The dark eyes were deep in shadow and a muscle jumped in his cheek. "Let's get weaving. The tent's in the Tutoko, and we're in the Harrison. No good moaning about it." And he walked off toward the gorge.

"All the same," I said, determined to have the last word, "it was a good dry camp, wasn't it?"

"If you don't stop going on about it, you'll end up in the river," growled Geoff as he helped me on with my swag.

Sometimes I wondered why my friends put up with me.

The gorge was bad, wetter, rougher and more claustrophobic than before. But it had one redeeming merit: every inch through it was an escape from the Harrison. When we came out by Pembroke Creek daylight was fading and the threat of another shelterless night became a promise. We hunted irresolutely for a bivvy among the jumbled rocks but found nothing.

"We may as well keep on," said Rodda.

A climb through tangled undergrowth to avoid a deep pool with rocky sides took a long time, and we'd been going for sixteen hours and were all rather played out. It had been a wet and hungry day. I had the shivers and my knees felt wobbly, Geoff and Graham shambled along with open mouths, their jaws hanging with fatigue. But Old Man Rodda had the scent of the sea and wouldn't give up.

"Can't we have a rest? Just a minute to get our breath back?" pleaded Ellis.

"We'll stop at dark, then there'll be all night to sit in the rain."

We were more than a little sorry for ourselves but Rodda reminded us that veteran explorers of Fiordland like Grave, Talbot, Gifford, and Lyttle had spent years doing just the thing we were all belly-aching about. This brought the inevitable reply, and when we came to a mossy chute high above the river, there was mutiny in the air. We'd had to use the rope all day. Each of the innumerable side-streams had been a struggle with wild water.

"We don't need a rope on this one," said Graham. "Look," he insisted, "the water isn't higher than my boot tops. I can run across."

My eyes went down the two-hundred-foot gutter. It was steeper and more evil than the bobsleigh run at St Moritz, and that had killed a lot of people. I don't suppose it was more than twenty feet across to the bush at the far side, but there was guile in it. The softest and greenest moss covered the concave watertable which fell straight to the river churning below.

"Better put the rope on, Graham. It's safer."

"I still reckon it's unnecessary," from Ellis.

The argument went round and round until I tied one end of the rope to a tree and handed the other end to Graham. "Put it on, Ellis, and don't bloody well argue. I've had one inquest and I don't want another!"

Graham tied himself on with a tired insolence that inferred he was only doing it to placate two old women like Rodda and me. But he hadn't gone more than three feet before he was flat on his back and scrabbling with axe and grating boots high above the flooded Harrison.

We dragged him in grinning with the old Ellis flash of teeth. "Thanks. I'd have been a goner without that rope."

"That's OK, Graham, it's all part of the service."

There was no more insurrection. We levered ourselves down through the head-high fern and rotting windfalls to a sandy bay beside the river. It was now full dark; the mosquitoes and the sandflies had rolled out the red carpet and sharpened their stilettoes, and in the dim torchlight we could see them crowding for the feast.

"We'll build a mai-mai," said Rol. "It's going to be a long night so we may as well have something to do."

"Will it keep the rain out?" asked Longbottom.

"That," said Rodda, squashing a platoon of sandflies pushing through the forest on his arm, "is a question we can only answer when we've built it. Probably not, but the exercise will get us warm."

"And what the heck do you think we've been doing since dawn?" snapped Geoff.

We toiled for hours cutting branches from the trees and dragging them through the bush to the scene of our camp. The principle was simple: two branches ground into the sand with their forks at head height to support a crosspiece, then eight or more branches leant against the crosspiece to make the rafters of our shelter. The gaps between these ribs we'd fill in with smaller, leafier branches, and then top them off with a thatch of fern fronds pointed with such cunning that the drumming rain would run down the sloping watershed.

In practice it was a lot harder. We kept falling over, partly because our torches were dim, and partly because we were lightheaded with hunger and fatigue. It took a long time, with a lot of energy we didn't have, to cut down thick saplings with blunt ice-axes, a torch held in the teeth and the beasties biting and sucking. Saner men would have given up and crawled under what illusory shelter they could find. But we kept on and after we had used up all our small supply of string and taken the cord side-lashings from our swags, our Harrison Hotel was an accomplished fact. I had suggested cutting Rol's alpine rope into sections to secure the saplings, but he thought I was joking. I was deadly serious; next to stewing it, this was the noblest use an alpine rope could be put to. The first time we crawled under the mai-mai it collapsed, but eventually it was rebuilt—the zaniest shelter I've ever had in the mountains. But it did boost our morale, and we no longer felt at the mercy of the rain.

I was trying to decide whether it was wetter in a wet bag than it was under the wet rain, when Rol came up to me. "How about a fire, boy? You're the bushman of the party."

Perhaps in my tiredness I wrongly caught a suggestion that it was entirely beyond me to light a fire with sodden wood in such a downpour. I ground my teeth and took up the challenge. While the others talked in monosyllables under the mai-mai, I set to work. I took a mug, I think it was Rol's, and had everyone searching their swags for a stub of candle. This took a long time because odds and ends like this always end up at the bottom of your rucsac, and people were burrowing and cursing me because they had to drag everything else out to find that candle end. This gave me a lot of pleasure; if it hadn't been for the rain and the dark and the whining mosquitoes, it would have kept me amused until dawn. Then I went off to find some wood. Anyone who has camped in the bush knows that dry wood is best, but this was all wet, the only difference being that some of it was wetter than the rest. After feeling round in the dark half the night—my torch had long since gone out—I came triumphantly back to the mai-mai with small bits I'd culled from under logs and rocks. Then I gathered all the large stuff I could find, broke it up, and stacked it by the fireplace. The next step was the most laborious of all: I pared a small mountain of shavings from the least wet wood with a sheath knife, put the candle in the mug and struck a match.

"It'll never burn," said Graham.

"Oh, for a cup of tea," from Geoff Longbottom.

"Take your time, boy," cautioned Rodda. "Not too many shavings, or you'll choke it."

"Who's putting this fire out, Rodda? You or me?"

A tiny white flame licked the shavings and we hardly dared breathe. When the whole pile of shavings was alight I gradually fed in larger pieces split with the ice-axe. Two hours later we had a roaring fire that spat and sizzled and sent shadows dancing and showed us for pallid ghosts. We made tea, scraped the bottom of the sugar bag, and then made a skilly of soup with some bacon rind. Fortunately we still had some salt for taste. We kept the fire going all night and stood before it with steaming breeks and outspread hands. While that fire burned we no longer just existed.

When dawn came we were the most bedraggled crew the Harrison had ever seen. We were cured yellow from the smoke, the bags under our eyes were large enough to take a crayfish boat, and our faces were swollen with insect bites. "It could've been worse," said Rodda.

"Yes, Rol," I agreed, "There's no limit to how bad things can be. "It's the putting up with them that's hardest."

We had a nibble of bread for breakfast and set out for Harrison Cove. The bush relented and we struck good going, easier than when Leo Faigan and I had floundered through on the eastern bank at the start of the Mt Grave trip. And then irony of ironies, twenty-five minutes downstream from our mai-mai camp we re-discovered the bivvy W. G. Grave had found when he was returning to Harrison Cove in December 1913 after the first ascent of Mt Pembroke with A. Talbot and J. Lippe. It had lain quietly forgotten in the forest for thirty-seven years and was, as Grave had recorded, ". . . an immense rock, under which a hundred or more people could camp".

We goggled at the size and dryness of the shelter. "What mugs we've been," said Longbottom.

A light southerly was blowing when we came through the last of the Harrison forest to Milford Sound. For a while we stood gaping at the steel-grey water and the misted summits. Then we walked scuffing our feet in the sand of the open beach where the shrill cries of sea birds came strongly above the softly breaking waves. It was good to be back to the easement of the sea.

Graham volunteered to go with Rol to light a smoke signal for the Milford launch out on the nose of the Lion, while Geoff and I lit a fire and prepared a meal from our last scraps. The rain had stopped and the first sun we had seen for two days made a watery appearance. Before Rol left, he spread his sleepingbag to dry by the fire and gave us strict instructions to stow it away when the rain came back. Longbottom and I went to collect mussels. We were so hungry we broke the shells against the rocks and sucked out the fawn meat. The rest we took back and threw into the cooking pot. For a while we watched the other two scrambling around the filthy scrub above the cove and listened to their tired voices floating clear across the still water. Our heads nodded and we slept.

I woke up abruptly. The wind was raising white caps on the Sound and the sparks whirled like fireflies. "Good God! Look at Rodda's bag, it's alight."

We beat out the embers but we were too late, the brown fabric was peppered with holes.

"What on earth's he going to say?" said Longbottom.

When Rodda and Ellis returned weary from their three hour struggle, we were the epitome of industry. "How did you get on? You made a good job of the fire out there on the Lion. Enough smoke for a volcano," I said quickly but dreading the moment of discovery.

"No good, the wind's the wrong way. They won't see it from the Hostel, we couldn't get it out into the Sound."

Then Rol smelt the singeing. He picked up the burned bag and looked at us accusingly. I didn't know whether to laugh or brazen it out, seeing him look downcast for the first time in the whole two weeks.

"You stupid idiots. Fine firewatchers you are."

"Sorry, Rol."

But he was already fossicking in the back pocket of his swag and brought out a housewife of needles and black thread. Rodda had a plan for everything. He sat on a driftwood log while the dusk came and the sandflies eddied round his head. The down feathers floated about him, but he stitched and mended until the job was done. It had been a hard trip for Rodda too.

The *Donald Sutherland* picked us up the next morning and we descended on the morning tea like shaggy vultures. The passengers sat with their eyes popping out as the scones were whisked off the table.

"You lads seem very hungry, have you been far?" said a woman who shone with soap and smelled as sweet as a pear tree in blossom.

"Just up the creek a bit," we said, conscious of our grubbiness.

"You're Geoff Longbottom from Dunedin, aren't you?" asked another. "I hardly recognised you, you're so thin and pale."

That night after dinner at the Hostel we argued with the unreasonableness of men who, for the time being, have had more than enough. Rodda wanted us to go back up to collect his tent under the rock at the foot of the Grave Couloir, but the three of us were so done in that the thought of another two days of rain was too much. The tent stayed under the bivvy rock, but when Rol got it back next season the only damage was some minor mildew.

Judith and Conway were over at her parents' home when I reached Dunedin. I went there in a taxi. I'd had enough of walking for a while.

My mother-in-law answered the door with a welcoming smile. If she saw I'd lost a stone and a half in weight she wasn't alarmed. "Do come in, Paul," she exclaimed with a grin. "How well you're looking!"

14

Hut Drop on Mt Earnslaw

*For look you, the mines is not according to the disciplines of
the war; the concavities of it is not sufficient.*

—*Henry V*, Act 3, Sc 2

BOB CRAIGIE came up to me at the end of the Alpine Club meeting:
"Good talk you gave us, Paul. Tough country those Milford valleys.
You must've had quite a time of it when that snowcave washed out
above the Harrison."

"Oh, it wasn't all that bad, really, Bob. The luck of the game,
you know."

"Quite so, quite so," replied Craigie. "Just the same," he went on,
"why don't you give the jungle fighting a rest this year? Come where
you'll get some sun, on Mt Earnslaw. It's a fine-weather valley.

"What's the catch, Bob?"

Craigie gave his short quick laugh. "Something new. We want to put a hut up on Wright Col, between the Rees and the Dart."

"Uh, a working-party, eh?"

"You enjoyed all those Aspiring Hut-building trips, didn't you? And what about the fun you had that Easter helping with the new French Hut?"

"Yes," I had to admit, "working-parties can be as good as climbs."

"Well," said Craigie persuasively, "this hut on Earnslaw's going to be even better fun. There'll be a good gang of blokes," and he rattled off a dozen names of climbers I knew.

"Sounds interesting, Bob," I said. I liked the people he mentioned. "OK Bob, you can count me in. What's the plan? Lug all the material up on our backs?"

"No. We airdrop most of it. All the roof-iron, timber, nails and mattresses, everything except the floor plates. Old Popeye Lucas can't manage anything longer than four-foot-six in his Auster, so the plates will have to be carried up. They're ten feet long and six inches square."

"Phew! That's a nice heavy load for someone to lug up to seven thousand feet. What happens when the nor'-wester snores over from the Dart? Load and carrier take off like a helicopter, I suppose?"

"Quite so, quite so," said Craigie, grinning from ear to ear, "but think of the work that would save!"

"But seriously, Bob, isn't this idea of airdropping the hut materials a bit risky? Wright Col's a devilish place for wind. It'll mean some pretty tricky flying between peaks over eight and nine thousand feet on each side of the col."

"Nothing old Popeye can't handle. He's been airdropping supplies in the Alps ever since he came out of the Air Force after the war. He'll do it with his eyes closed. A piece of cake." Bob had that determined look which said that as far as he and Lucas were concerned, the Esquilant Hut on Wright Col was as good as there.

I didn't argue, recalling only too vividly how Craigie had pushed through the Aspiring Hut building campaign. "Anyway, Bob, alpine airdropping was pioneered in Otago wasn't it?"

"That's right. Way back in 1933 when Jock Sim and Scott Gilkison had that daredevil attempt in the Kitchener Cirque under Mount Aspiring. There have been terrific developments since then."

"Sounds exciting, Bob. When do we begin?"

"Things are moving now." He was so keen that the words spilled out as fast as he could open his mouth. "Plans and specifications have already been drawn up. Timber ordered, some of the materials are darned hard to come by, but we'll find a way around that one. We'll spend all the winter and spring doing the prefabrication here in Dunedin. We've got the use of a hall so we'll erect the hut there, number all the parts and then take it all to bits and pack them into parcels ready for Popeye. Probably be over a hundred separate lots to be dropped."

"Quite a job. But what about the floor plates and all the stuff that's too big to go in the Auster?"

"We've got that all jacked up too. There's a gang manhandling the plates up the Rees Valley to Earnslaw Hut in June. How about it?"

That mid-winter weekend seventeen of us lugged the ten-foot plates along the fourteen-mile porterage between the Rees River bridge and the old Earnslaw Hut. There was mud and sleet, and we grumbled happily as men do when their morale is high. But we enjoyed ourselves and I felt the same old team spirit which I'd first experienced in Tararua working-parties before the war. You didn't climb mountains on working-parties, but you saw less selfishness. A lot of the slaves were ex-servicemen and one of them put the spirit of the weekend very succinctly. We had just dumped the wet loads of timber inside the old Earnslaw Hut. The wind was creaking the hut and the hail rattled on the roof.

"You know, Paul," he said as he flexed tired shoulders, "I spent four long years in the army. The war was bad enough, but being away from the mountains was worse. And now I'm back it gives me one hell of a kick to be building something up. I got to hate knocking everything down."

We went back to Queenstown in the steamer *Earnslaw* and crowded down into the boiler room to dry out. We draped our wet clothes on the steampipes, took over from the firemen and heaved the tax-payers' coal until the old ship trailed a smokescreen down Lake Wakatipu that would have made a fleet destroyer black with envy.

Back in Dunedin we worked on the hut week-nights and weekends for the rest of the winter, the whole of spring and early summer. When the last package had been carefully wrapped and the job number stencilled on the side, Bob Craigie put down his hammer and said thoughtfully, "It's been a long job. Thanks for your help, you blokes. Now the rest is up to Popeye and the weather."

But the weather didn't cooperate. Early in December the advance party who were waiting on the dropping zone on Wright Col saw nothing but ten days of rain and mist. Even Popeye and his Auster couldn't fly in storm.

Leo Faigan told me when he came back to Dunedin, a few days before I went in with the main wave, that they had been able to do nothing but some metaphorical alpine housework: "We swept all the couloirs and tidied up all the snowfields in readiness but Lucas never came. The weather was leprous," he said with a laugh that was part resignation and the rest just Faigan.

Then more trouble came. There was a nationwide railway strike and some of the main party were marooned in Queenstown. The *Earnslaw* lay tied up alongside the jetty. It seemed that I'd be stuck in Queenstown for the next week. The people were hospitable and the pubs legendary for their hospitality, but I liked the mountains even better. I spent the night in the draughty shed alongside the lake steamer and was up early and breakfastless the next morning. I was going to get up that lake if I had to swim. Fortunately there were several private launches running. All were besieged with holiday-makers standing in patient queues. By judicious but not brutal use of the ice-axe I melted my way through the throng and after some persuasive talking stowed myself among the lucky passengers of the *Muratai*.

"No manners, these mountaineers," I heard some disgruntled tripper say as the launch pulled out from the jetty. He was quite right of course, but I soon got over qualms. I was hungry, and there was a hut to build.

At 10 pm that night Jim Brough, Ray Stewart and I reached the Earnslaw Hut after a sodden walk from Glenorchy. As soon as we pushed open the door and called loudly for tea we were greeted with a warmth which told us we belonged. Even the phrases that the incumbents hurled at us were those of servicemen. The war was only five years dead but the spirit of comradeship still lived. We hadn't yet had time to be spoiled by the unquestioned acceptance of peace.

"Reinforcements," cried somebody, as he filled our mugs.

"Didn't think you'd get through," said Bob Craigie where he sat at the fire with a Bersagliere hat cocked on one side of his head.

"I had to get here tonight, Bob. A matter of tactical necessity. You blokes have got all the tucker."

"Tomorrow," he said, "we'll really move things along. All the timber's at five-thousand feet near the fenceline on the slopes of Mount Leary. It'll clear by morning after this thunder and Popeye's bound to be over. I want you to get up the Birley Glacier to Wright Col as soon as you can. Got to give the Air Force some ground support. The rest of us will back pack the thousand pounds of timber and tucker to the col."

"But there are only fifteen of us. That's over sixty-five pounds each apart from the weight of our swags. And four of the party are women."

"You do what Bob says," interrupted Gwen Mitchell, "and get up to that col. You needn't worry whether we can do our whack. We will."

"Well," laughed Craigie, "that's one in the eye for you, Paul."

"A direct hit," I admitted, looking at Gwen. She was as quiet as a mountain pool and as clean and straight as a forest beech.

"And seeing you're so concerned about the girls," said Bob with a straight face, "you three men had better take a few lengths of timber with you."

We were away from the Earnslaw Hut straight after an early breakfast. By the time we reached the scrubline the day was bright and perfect for flying. Stewart, Brough and I worked across the tussock hollow of Kea Basin and were soon on the lower slopes of the Birley Glacier. The Rees spread below us in a quiet estate of green forest and winding river but it was to Wright Col we looked where the East Peak of Mt Earnslaw soared in rock tiers to the blue sou'-westerly sky.

While we were still upon the upward snow trail we heard the sound of Popeye's Auster, a faint recurring buzz caught and flung back from shining summits and rock walls. Lucas was on the job. Caught in the excitement of the day we raced toward the rendezvous. He beat us. With glinting wings, a quivering day moth to the mountain candle, the Auster crossed and weaved between Mt Earnslaw and the lion shape of Leary Peak. The mountains roared and the receptive col took falling sticks of timber thudding and bouncing like shining darts. And then the drone was gone and the mountain silence washed back along the col. There was light on the river, and far below the patient ant-like crawl of bearers, each with its wisps of wood.

All that day Lucas came and went with a casual ease. By night six hundred pounds of hut were gathered in a dump and Craigie was told by runner that the opening phase of the battle of Wright Col was swinging in our favour.

But Boxing Day brought the appropriate climax. We knew that Lucas, a man of wit as well as élan, would be eager to steal a march on us. At first light he'd be lifting the weighted Auster off the improvised Glenorchy strip and nosing across the mountains to the col. There was necessity as well as pardonable bravado in his rivalry: early morning gave the most stable mountain-flying conditions, for when the sun warmed the rocks and cirques and the wind came, he'd be bucketing in the cross-currents of the alpine sea and accurate dropping would be difficult and dangerous. Popeye, with a war behind him and many peacetime backcountry flights in his logbook, was a fantastic flyer, but he wasn't a rash fool. He knew the mountains too well for that: he'd told Craigie and me when we met him in Queenstown before the drop that he aimed to be "an old pilot, not just a bold one".

And so the mountain war was on. The sky already held the threat of wispy cloud. Lucas would get our stuff down, we didn't doubt that; but the hut still had to be built when the excitement and the drama of the airdrop was over. And we couldn't build it until every stick of timber was on the site and the whole party gathered on Wright Col. Some of those foundation-plates were still two thousand feet below the col.

Those of us camped on the col were up before three in the morning and away down to the foot of the glacier to help with the last carry. I doubt if the main party had much sleep that night for we met them in the first tint of a frozen Christmas dawn not far below the col. Craigie was in front, just as we had expected him to be, with that preposterous Italian alpine corps hat, a square-jawed grin, and a metaphorical whip that he used more on his own back than on others. He spurred us timber-laden back to the col and across to the dropping zone.

And then Lucas was on us, roaring from behind Mt Leary to the north. We had expected him to approach from the south with a growing drone that would have given us time to disperse with dignity before the first sticks fell. The dawn with rising light on peak and snowfield was peaceful, and then there was noise and the shape of scythe wings. The tea billy and the primus went flying. We scattered like troops surprised in some quiet rest-area miles behind the line.

Popeye told us afterwards, "You looked like a gaggle of Jerries caught at morning ersatz coffee. It was so funny I nearly hit the bloody mountain."

The attack had been almost too realistic, for the first bomb had thumped home close to where we'd been standing. We crept out ruefully with a healthy admiration for Popeye's shooting. "That's not my idea of a joke," I said. "I got such a fright that I darn near ran all the way up Mt Leary. I'm going to claim it as a new ascent."

His fun over, Lucas settled down to a methodical day's flying. There was a fascination in watching the way he did the job. He'd first appear around the high rock shoulder of the East Peak of Mt Earnslaw and burr across the col against the light wind.

"Any minute now," we'd say and then, as the plane steadied against the unseen turbulence, the first load appeared. For an instant the bundle seemed to float like a wisp of tussock against the brown and grey rock walls and then it would arrow down in a lazy parabola toward the target zone. At the beginning we watched from a safe distance and took cover behind rocks on the flanks of the col, but Lucas was so accurate that we soon loitered under the falling bolts and could estimate almost as accurately as Lucas where they would land. The lengths of timber were the most predictable as well as the most spectacular: they curved down with a tired swishing until they hit the snow with a hollow thud and a brief eruption of white. The area of the drop zone was small, no more than a shrunken patch of icy snow on the Leary side of the col some thirty yards by seventy, yet Lucas, a gossamer speck a thousand feet above, planted eighty-five per cent of his tulips safely.

"I wouldn't like to be on the receiving end of Popeye's visiting cards if this were the real thing," said Craigie.

When the odd salvo fell short and crashed into the rocks the air was full of splinters and our faces were as long as beanpoles. After each initial drop from the east, Lucas flicked past 9,000-foot Mt Earnslaw until the Auster was a flash of quicksilver high over the dark obelisk of Mt Pluto, then it soared in a climbing turn and dived down toward the col before steadying for the next bombing run. Out came the rolled roof-iron, cutting the air in wide scallops, and the rubber mattresses bouncing with Falstaffian drollery down rocks and snow to the Doll Tearsheet hollow of the col. When the last bundle had been dropped, the Auster dipped low over our heads and swooped over the rim of the western end of the col until we lost sight of it in the depths of Bedford basin. But momentarily as he passed we caught a blurred glimpse of Lucas sitting in the doorless cockpit like some puckish gremlin, a nose and balding dome, his face all smile behind a waving hand.

Then came the frantic rush to gather the manna before the Auster came back with the next load from Paradise. Craigie was usually first there. We streamed behind him, scurrying like agitated slaters from pocket to pocket in the rocks and lugging the bundles to a central dump near the building site. Sometimes the mountain won and pulverised the less fortunate timber-lengths to twisted kindling.

But Craigie was never upset for long. "We're winning, chaps," he'd say. "I've allowed for ten per cent breakages and so far we've got a good credit balance."

But our greatest disappointment came when on one run we saw two small dark objects fall direct for the rocks beside the snow. Hands were raised in horror as the bottles flashed briefly in the sun and flew to brittle shards. The liquid foamed but was soon swallowed by the thirsty rocks. "Of all the rotten luck," we moaned as we stood sorrowfully in a bereaved circle.

"Never mind," said the practical Bob, "it was a nice surprise. At least we can say the hut has been christened." And he urged us back to work.

The sortie and return went on all morning. Even in the rising wind Lucas shuttled back and forth between the peaks against a dulling sky.

"Well," said Craigie, checking the bundles against the tally in his note book, "that was the last of them." And Lucas and his Auster droned away back to Paradise.

"A good show, eh, Bob?"

"Very satisfactory, very satisfactory," was all he replied. "Time we had lunch."

We were sitting happily in the sun near the hut site when Lucas came back. There was no roar of motor this time, just an insistent sighing of wings which we didn't hear until he was almost on us. For the second time that day he had caught us by surprise. This time he was so low that the undercarriage of the Auster could have parted our hair, and he slung out a bulging sack which hit the snow in front of us and bounced over our heads. Popeye had a practical sense of humour; he had brought us spring onions, green peas, lettuces, and farm fresh carrots to eat with our biscuits and bully beef. Tied round the neck of the sack was a hastily scrawled note: "Thought you'd like these—they're fresh from Paradise."

"Now that," said Bob, as he snapped his way through a succulent carrot, "is what I call service. Ground to air cooperation at its very best."

By dark we'd chosen the hut site and those floor plates that we'd sweated up the valley to the col were laid. The hut was started.

We awoke to a dawn that spilled an angry red over the Earnslaw peaks and rolled westward across the green-sea floor of the Dart Valley to the Darran peaks. Madeline, Tutoko and Grave were high rocks in a threatening cloud surge.

"It's coming up dirty," muttered Craigie, "we'd better get cracking."

I looked at the cloud wedges splitting the lustreless morning and thought of storms without shelter in the Tutoko and Harrison. There was the same soft smell of rain, the same slow piling-up of storm. The waking rocks fell down the slashed gullies on the Earnslaw wall with hollowed thuds. On fine mornings stones sing and whirr and the snow is moving with light, the mountain battlements are manned by sun-glinting towers and overhanging barbicans, the sounds are sharp and the hills have clean crisp words. But that morning as we raised the first hut-frames our hammers were muffled and the saw-rasps dull. The air was heavy and the mountain ridges stolid and brutish. Even the water music from the river and thawing snow galleries came to us with a lifeless monotone. Colours were flat and the peaks indifferent; they brooded and waited. But we had no time, and no shelter.

We sawed and hammered and carried, and measured our time

against the mountains. We worked with careful haste, one eye always on the sky. The lighthearted excitement of the airdrop changed. Sullen clouds piled in from the Tasman Sea and shut us into a small dark world where we were aware of one urgency: we had come to Wright Col to build a hut for others, but first we must make it for ourselves. We were no longer whooping spectators on the aerial sideline but in the centre of the drama. The mist wreathed among the rock towers of Mount Earnslaw and crept lower. In the arc of the col we were exposed to both southerly and nor'-west storm. When the gale came trumpeting through the col work would become impossible and the hut skeleton would disintegrate. Timber and roof-iron would litter the wind tunnel between Leary Peak and Mt Earnslaw.

We worked, and there were no passengers. Ralph Glasson and Bob Craigie were our overseers, and they toiled magnificently. The men hammered and sawed and measured and nailed while the women carried timber and coils of wire and kept us fresh with frequent snacks and hot drinks, and the weather kept on closing in. By late afternoon the wind was moaning through the col and our hands and faces were shrammed with cold. There wasn't time to sit down and eat; we grabbed a sandwich or a mug of tea and kept on the job. Our talk was terse and clipped, and when the wind gusted Craigie and Glasson had to yell their instructions.

I felt the same defiance I'd known on Atlantic nights at sea or when pitching tents on a score of stormy mountainsides. We were alive, we were struggling with our enemy and were determined to win. There was a fierce joy in that.

We had our anxious moments. The numbered sections for the four walls were assembled and then each framework lifted into position and secured to the floor. But the wind was so unruly that all hands, cooks, and rouseabouts, dropped whatever they were doing and rushed to support the frame. We pushed and heaved to keep it in alignment.

"Why do men always holler for help at the most annoying times?" asked Lois Aldridge as she helped us to keep the wall from being blown over in the wind. "If I don't get back to the primus soon your stew will be all burned and horrible."

Craigie grunted something about the hut coming first, through the four-inch nails between his teeth.

"Well, I just hope you'll remember that, Mr Craigie, when you're eating your supper."

"If the hut blows away you'll have more to worry about than supper, Lois," replied Bob with a troubled eye on the rain-squalls wafting down the Dart Valley.

The business of joining two walls was difficult. Just when the skewed nails were ready for the final blows that would marry them, the wind gusted and the master-builders dropped their hammers and joined the rest of us who were battling to stop the hut from becoming airborne. Then, as soon as a lull came, Craigie and Glasson scrambled up the wooden spars and after a quick check on the alignment of the two walls drove home the nails with rapid blows. When the four walls were eventually up, and the bones of the hut were standing like a skeleton against the grim profile of the rain-whipped mountains, we all trooped around the perimeter.

"Amazing," said Craigie as he checked the angles, "quite amazing. The four walls are really square. I half expected that they would've formed a parallelogram."

"Just as well, Bob. Imagine what old Popeye would think if he saw it all skew-whiff the next time he flew over. He'd probably reckon we'd been drinking."

When the roof frame was up we wrestled with the lining paper. The stuff rattled and cracked in the wind like frozen canvas. One wind flurry, more vicious than anything the mountains had yet thrown against us, tore the paper from the walls and the free end whipped like a prayer flag across the desolate col. Hut-building at 7,000 feet had its problems, but by night the roof was on and all but one of the side walls closed in.

"If the wind changes direction now," said Craigie grimly, "the whole lot will go. The flying sheets of roof-iron could cut a man's head off."

Eight of the team bedded down in the doubtful security of the partly-open hut. The other four of us spent a wild night holding down a bucketing tent while the wind blustered and roared through the col. But in the morning the hut and the entire party were still there. New snow lay over the sharpness of the ice-glazed rocks. The mountains were austere under a drape of white linen.

It was rather cold. I shuffled over to where Craigie was already at work. "Quite a night, eh, Bob?"

"A bit rugged." His hammer never stopped.

We worked without rest all day. There wasn't any point in stopping, work was good, it kept us warm. But the women had the worst job. They cooked and fed us while the snow fell and the ground-drift blew white across the col. Their kitchen was a low wall of rocks where the primus flames coughed in the searching wind, and water was frozen in the billies. But they were unendingly cheerful. Their singing rose clear and thin above the wind, and once I heard them discussing vigorously how they were to keep the food warm. They were more troubled by the minor tragedies of high-altitude cooking than they were by the snow-black sky and the cruel wind. They were magnificent, and we couldn't have built that hut without them.

By dark on the third night after the airdrop the hut was closed in but we laboured on until midnight by the yellow flare of a kerosene pressure-lamp. When the sleeping bench was at last completed we flung down our hammers and crawled into our bags. The hail beat angry little fists against the roof and the wind growled around the hut walls, but we were secure.

There was the warming satisfaction that we'd achieved something, not just for ourselves but others. And that sometimes is a rare commodity upon high hills.

But we weren't left in peace to enjoy the first morning when the wind dropped and silence folded over the Earnslaw peaks. About eight the door was pushed open and for the next two hours we were bombarded with the garrulous chatter of four visitors who sat on our legs until we got cramp. With the unthinking egotism of those who take housing for granted they berated us that we weren't already hotfooting for the summits. At last they went—a clutter of jumbled voices back over the col—and left us ringing-eared.

Later that day the last flat rocks were piled around the hut and the peaks stood temptingly close and clear. We looked up and thought about climbing: even labourers have their days off.

Bob Craigie could see that we had the hill itch. "Now that the hut's almost completed, why don't you boys go off and climb something?"

We made a show of protest, but our eyes stole to the peaks on both sides of the col. "We don't want to run out on you, Bob. . . ."

"Nonsense." Craigie was determined. "We built the hut for a climbing base didn't we?" We nodded.

"Well, what are you waiting for?"

We didn't argue, but shot off straight up the rock gully behind the hut to the top of Mt Leary.

If the peak lacked difficulty, it made amends as a viewpoint. It was an alpine armchair. I looked south-west to where the gleaming notch of Ngapunatoru Pass hung like a tenuous spiderweb between the pillars of Mt Tutoko and Mt Grave. Westward was the sea and, in between, the green flexed muscles of the lower hills rippling to the Olivine summits. Closer, all sheeny with new snow, East and West Peak of Earnslaw were scarcely beyond our fingertips. And in the scaly hollow of Wright Col, the tangerine hut lay as a ladybird in the calloused palm of the crags. North, over the shoulders of the Dart headwaters, there was only one peak for me: Aspiring. It rose like a great white sail from the blue haze of the alpine sea. But the minute hut down in the col was my link between Aspiring and the past of Tutoko. It was a telergy that bound me to them both.

"I think we should go and elect trial by Sir William," said Brian Wilkins, pointing to the peak with the knife edge ridge that reared up like a guillotine from the flanking snowfields. "He looks severe but just."

"Suits me," agreed Ian Bagley, "provided he doesn't give us a life sentence."

The south ridge of Sir William, named by Jock Sim after his father who was a judge, was at that time still unclimbed. We made a new and respectful approach to the peak by a route which we scratched out among the temperamental gullies of Mt Leary but when our fourth, John Carruthers, was nearly decapitated by falling rocks, we weren't quite so sure of Sir William's impartiality. Those rocks came down with the full swift majesty of the law, but Wilkins wasn't in the least troubled. He stood safely under cover and sang *I've Got a Loverley Bunch of Cokernuts* in a rich defiant baritone. But I thought the peak a crusty old curmudgeon: he bowled you out of court before you had a chance to state your case.

We tiptoed back early a few days later. In the faint daybreak both judge and court orderlies were still in fusty sleep. The long nose of the south ridge went up in a series of scaly buttresses to the summit ridge. On each side the thin wing of the nose fell down to the rat-trap slits of crevasses' mouths. Sir William wasn't the kindest mountain I had seen. I had the feeling he was watching us through hooded eyelids. But we kept on for three hours by holding the shattered dignity of the mountain together with our hands as we climbed over the book-like plates of rock. In one place we let ourselves down from the witness-box coping on a rope which we tied to a large rock and flung down over an airy gap. But when we at length came to the true base of the nose we'd had enough. The place had too over-awing an air of instant committal. And when Bagley knocked an ill-tempered rock spinning down to the glacier, Sir William awoke at once and answered us with a fusillade of smoking rubble.

"I think we'll go back," I said, "and find an easier way. It's too early to return to the hut, it's only eight o'clock."

We found a way down a steep rock shute to the Frances Glacier and, while Sir William was looking the other way, sneaked up the conventional green chlorite schist ledges to a clouded summit.

"He's not such a bad-tempered old buffer," said Wilkins tolerantly, "provided you don't tread on his dignity."

But Sir William exacted a deferred punishment toward nightfall when we were in the chops of the sulphurous gully on Mt Leary. Wilkins had performed an awkward shuffle along a ledge below a jostling overhang. Bagley was behind me with the afternoon sun glinting on his massive spectacles. He looked like a night owl dozing in its rocky hide.

"Don't know why you made such heavy weather getting round that ledge, Brian," I called confidently, "I reckon I could *run* round it." And I did just that. As a circus act it would have brought the ringside spectators bravoing to their feet; as a piece of mountaineering mummery it nearly sent us all to the limbo of the upper Bedford cirque. But there was nothing wrong with my running technique, and just when I was preening myself for my undoubted agility and devil-may-care head for heights, the rope suddenly tautened and I was swinging upside down over the ascendant gully.

Even in my peculiar position there was no mistaking either the alarm or the fire in Bagley's remarks. When eventually his face appeared round the proboscis of the overhang, it was as white as the bandeau over his forehead. "You nearly dragged me off," he raged, "you of all people doing a stupid thing like that!" Then in a quieter tone he added: "Next time you want to do aerobatics, for God's sake tell me. Then I'll be ready with some slack rope."

I didn't venture with Brian and Ian on their east-west traverse of Mount Earnslaw, my ribs were still too bruised. But I was there by proxy. Before they left, Wilkins asked me if he could borrow my rope.

"You're welcome, Brian. But I'm not so keen on lending it."

"Why?"

"Too much responsibility. How do you think I'd feel if it broke on you during the grand tour up there on Earnslaw?"

Wilkins held up a rope that was rubbed smooth. It was so thin I could just about see daylight through its strands. "I see what you mean," I said. "Take mine then, and may Saint Christopher go with you."

Apparently Saint Christopher did, for they had a slip coming down off West Peak, but Wilkins, the rope and the wobbly boulder round which it was belayed held firm. Bagley was very impressed with the steep snow and ice wall of the south face.

But the kernel of the story came some weeks later, when Wilkins met me back in Dunedin. "You'll remember that old rope of mine? The one I swapped with yours for our climb of Earnslaw?"

"Yes, what about it?" I scented a story.

"Well," laughed Brian with a smile as broad as his Irish face, "the other night I used it to leg-rope the cow while I was milking; old Strawberry's the most docile beast between Mosgiel and Taranaki but she gave one twitch of her hind leg and the rope broke." And Wilkins shook like a laughing Buddha.

"And what did Bagley say when you told him?" I asked.

"Oh, he just gave a gulp and then said something rather unprintable. But it was funny, really."

The last day of my stay at the Esquilant Hut was thick with fog. I was due out at Glenorchy the next morning to meet Judith when the *Earnslaw* pulled in from Queenstown. We'd parked Conway with relations and I was keen to introduce my wife to the pleasures and the mysteries of the mountains. I hung around the hut waiting for the mist to lift, but it kept so low that I wasn't very happy about going down to the bottom of the Birley Glacier alone. Brian and Ian saw me to the edge of Kea Basin and after a quick trip down the Rees Valley I finally clumped down the road to Glenorchy.

The next day the mountains were at their glistening best and Judith and I took all day to swag up to the Twenty-five Mile Hut. She seemed to be impressed with the grandeur of the mountains and the nobility of mountaineers, but as we stopped before the weathered door of the old stone hut she asked, "And where's this new hut you've been telling me so much about?"

I pointed proudly up to Wright Col, a high snow notch far above the green valley floor.

"Poof, that's not far. From all your yarns I thought it would be at least on the top of the mountain."

We spent a night with the mice which gambolled through the ragged lining of the Twenty-five Mile Hut and we survived the smoke which filled the place as soon as I started the breakfast fire. "Now I understand how your clothes get that distinctive smell," she said.

"OK then, we'll go straight back to Glenorchy."

"Don't be daft," she replied, "I'm enjoying the trip. Every smelly bit of it. When do we leave for Wright Col?"

We took our time over the easy climb up to the Earnslaw Hut. Judith insisted on a leisurely pace. "I'm not one of your madmen that rush uphill with their heads inside a bag. This is new to me. I want time to take it all in. We've got all day, so poofty to you and your hurry."

From the valley floor of the Rees, the trail zigzagged up through old burned forest. Wild foxgloves grew around the charred grey stumps of dead trees and when the wind passed the hillside lived again with swaying waves of red and white. At the top of the burn scar a pair of grey warblers fluttered among the stripling beeches. They rested briefly above our heads and sang their wistful trilled lament and then flew off to search the lichen-draped branches of a stand of nearby ribbonwoods.

I knew all about ribbonwoods, they clung to gullies where the going was hardest and the scrub was most obstructive, but I didn't recall that I had ever bothered to notice their blossoms. If I had, the impression was rejected in the hot pursuit of peaks. But we had time that Earnslaw day. The entire ribbonwood grove was white with large flowers of exquisite fragility and the fern about their trunks was carpeted with the shed petals.

We arrived about dusk at the creaking assortment of swinging roof-iron that was called the Earnslaw Hut. But we didn't have the chance to listen to the hut's old tale. Just as I was lighting the fire a clutch of two women arrived fresh from the conquest of the East Peak of Earnslaw. They had apparently had their moments of adventure, for the repetitive story that assaulted our ears with shrill exclamations was one in which a bounding stone persistently recurred. After we'd heard the horrific tale for the sixth time I lost my patience and said tartly, "What a pity that stone didn't clobber you just enough to stop your tongues."

The atmosphere was rather tense after that, so Judith and I cleared out for a walk up into Kea Basin. It was cold but quiet. When I awoke back at the hut next morning Judith had disappeared. With my usual hankering for an early cup of tea I went down to the creek for water. There, under the waterfall that ran through the cool forest and over a mossy spillway, was my wife.

"Hey," I called, "Come out of that at once. Cold water's bad for you before a climb."

"Rubbish. You mountaineers have one thing in common, a pathological hatred of water. You don't know what's good for you."

I filled the billy and left her to her spartan toilet.

The sun was well up by the time we had climbed through Kea Basin and were wandering across the scree toward the foot of the Birley Glacier.

"Is it always as hot as this?" asked my wife: "I always thought of the mountains as terribly cold places."

"We'll have a spell then. And when we get to the hut on Wright Col I'll brew you a nice refreshing cup of tea."

"Can't wait that long, Paul." And in an instant she had shed her clothes and was splashing in the ice-cold melt of the glacier.

"You're daft, woman! And I'm even more daft for having persuaded you to come to the hills."

"Stop your blethering," she said as she danced up and down on the rocks beside the pool, "and hop under. I bet you haven't had a decent wash since you left town."

"In that water? It's straight off the ice. Not in your life! And it's against the rules of the Alpine Club. I tried it thirteen years ago on Whitcombe Pass. No thanks, it's a hell of a way to die."

I watched her all the way up the glacier and was ready when she suddenly went for a skate on the steepest part of the climb. I fielded her without difficulty and then gave one of my most pontifical lectures. "I knew that would happen. That's the trouble with you women, you'll never listen, will you?"

"Don't you come the male superiority line with me, Mr Powell," she replied defiantly: "I'd do the same thing again. It was worth it to feel clean."

We came to the hut in the early afternoon and spent the rest of the day pottering about the col taking photographs and basking in the sun. The sun went down a lurid red over the Darrans, and the darkness rushed out of the trenches of the valleys. Then the stars came and the inquisitive evening breeze. We walked out of the hut and watched the last glow along the summit ridge of Mount Earnslaw.

"Do you want to climb tomorrow?"

She paused and said, "I just came up here for curiosity: I don't want particularly to be a smelly mountaineer."

We left it at that. Next morning as we went through the col where the rocks of Earnslaw and Mount Leary climbed lightfingered to the blue sky, I suddenly halted. "Look, there's Aspiring. Isn't it wonderful?"

She didn't say anything until we were well down the glacier. Then —"It's really got you, hasn't it, Paul?"

"Yes."

"Well, that makes two of you," she said quietly.

"Two of us?"

"Yes, you and Conway."

I looked at the white *skean-dhu* away to the north. The sun was bright on the intervening green valleys and the plaided pattern of the tussocked hills. As we went slowly down to the shining river, the rope bound us to each other and the future.

15

Return to Ruth Flat

Come what come may,
Time and the hour runs through the roughest day.
                                —*Macbeth*, Act 1, Sc 3

RUTH FLAT at the head of the East Matukituki River and east of
Mt Aspiring has always been one of my favourite places. It was
from there that Marshall, Riddiford, Sage and I reached the Volta
Glacier and made the first circumnavigation of Aspiring in 1945.
And twenty years later during the ten days of storm on the Volta
we had sometimes had a yearning glimpse of the flat from the Volta
icefield. We could see the flat, green and infinitely desirable in
occasional patches of sun, but we couldn't get down.

There wasn't a moment during those ten days that I didn't think
longingly of the rock bivvy in the dracophyllum scrub. Once I was
sure I caught a glimpse of it, a small grey pinprick in the green of
the alpine scrub only three-quarters of a mile away. Lying in the cold
darkness of the snowcave with the wind roaring and the thunder
knocking, my mind went again and again to that bivvy rock. I put
the thought away, but I vowed that if we got out of the Volta trap,
I'd go back again to Ruth Flat and to the bivvy rock where the
dracophyllum stung the eyes with its smoke, where the scrub
scratched against the rock overhang when the wind came over the
Main Divide, and where there was laughter and warmth as the billy

hissed on the fire and our shadows danced on the rock behind us. Just over three years later I was there. With me was my son, Conway, eighteen years old and eager for the hills.

He had only a few days before he went back to his job during the university holidays. On 14 January 1968 I rang the office of Tourist Air Travel in Queenstown and asked them if they could turn on a plane tó fly the two of us into Ruth Flat.

"Nothing doing today, it's too windy for a landing on a small mountain airstrip. There's a lot of cloud about too."

"Oh."

The pilot on the Queenstown end of the line must have heard the disappointment in my voice. "It may be better early tomorrow morning. Ring the airfield then and we'll see what we can do."

Conway saw to it that I was on the 'phone to Queenstown before eight the next morning.

I walked back along the road beside the Clutha to our cottage and before I had turned in the gate, Conway raced across the grass and vaulted the wire fence.

"Are we going, Dad?" There wasn't any doubt what he wanted that day.

"It's on, Con. The pilot said he can get us down on Ruth Flat, but I don't know whether it'll be good enough for a fly around Aspiring first."

Conway's face fell a little. We'd flown around the peak together before but Aspiring is the sort of mountain that you never tire of seeing from the air, or the ground, and Conway's appetite was as avid as mine.

"Cheer up," I told him, cocking an eye at the sky over the Minaret Peaks across the other side of Lake Wanaka, "we might get round Aspiring yet. I reckon it's clearing back all the time."

Without asking me, Judith knew we were going off. She hadn't lived with a mountaineer for twenty years for nothing; she could read the signs with uncanny infallibility.

"When do you leave?" she asked as soon as we went in through the glass sliding doors.

"We're meeting the plane at the Luggate airstrip in an hour's time. No hurry," I said, settling myself down at the table and pouring out another cup of black coffee and ladling in the sugar.

"Oh yes?" Judith replied with pleasant disbelief. "If I know you and Conway, you'll sit down gassing and arguing and then take off in a last-minute panic."

"They won't be late, Mum," said Reda innocently. "It's only six miles from Albert Town to Luggate, and their gear is all ready packed."

"Reda," said Judith, laughing as she washed breakfast dishes at the sink, "if you're going to marry a mountaineer when you grow up—and there's every unfortunate chance that you might—you'll have to learn that climbers are *always* late."

And that time Judith was right; we were late. Cessna ZK-CHK, a six-seater, was waiting on the airstrip with the engine ticking over when we shot in through the half-opened gate and stopped beside the tin shack and the red forty-four-gallon tins of aviation gas.

"Hullo—I'm Paul Powell," said I to the pilot with my usual modest greeting. "Who are you?"

He was greying at the temples, lean, tall, with a weathered face. "Tex Smith," he replied quietly.

So this was the great Tex Smith of whom I had heard so much. I felt a real chump. Tex had flown over more Main Divide ice than I'd ever walked over.

As we headed west and followed the bends of the Clutha river towards Albert Town I was rather silent; I'd already said too much. Tex put the Cessna into a bank over our house where I could see Judith beside the bright green of the two willow trees by the front verandah. She had been quiet when Con and I left but I had now learned enough sense to make no comment. After the frights she had had from my climbing over the past twenty years, I didn't wonder she was sometimes subdued at my going. The Volta episode in 1965 had been the worst, and here I was off to the same place again. This time two of her eggs were airborne in the same basket.

As we headed up the lower reaches of the main Matukituki and the valley closed in, Aspiring grew and grew, clouded and austere in banked rolls of sou'-west weather. Avalanche Peak looked most impressive, just like a fearsome trident with angry cloud wreathing between the rock prongs that form its three summits. Far below, the small red rectangles of the Mt Aspiring station were set where the dark green of the forest met the lush, brighter green of the riverside pasture.

"I wonder what Phyllis and Jerry Aspinall are having for breakfast," said Conway, looking down.

As soon as we entered the sloping palms of the hills which form the east branch of the Matukituki, the flying became a little lumpy and as always I was a bit apprehensive. Not scared—stimulated perhaps—and very conscious that the mountains were so great and I so small. I had another look at the mist and cloud swirling around Aspiring and its attendant peaks. I decided there and then that our jaunt among the peaks and icefields of the Waiatoto side of Mt Aspiring could comfortably wait for another day.

Conway looked disappointed, but when I said to Tex, "Don't

bother about going round the west side of Aspiring, it's not the best for photography," he gave me an understanding glance and held a steady course up the bushed valley. It was both wonderful and bewildering to fly so effortlessly over ground which I knew so well and which had been the scene of so many adventures over twenty-five climbing years; Junction Flat, where the mountain tree stood on the flat at the meeting of the Kitchener River and the East Matukituki; Mt Sisyphus from where I had first seen the Volta ice; Moncrieff Peak and Col, Aeroplane Peak, Fastness, and the wide white plain of the hanging Aspiring glaciers. Names came too, and the faces of people with whom I had climbed and had shared so many stormy nights and brilliant mountain days.

"There's Ruth Flat, Dad. Tucked right up there above the top end of the Bledisloe gorge. Just like it is in your photos." Conway leaned forward and pointed. I came back to the present.

Tex took us up valley at a fair height, somewhere between six and seven thousand feet, until we were right over Rabbitt Pass and could see the starting point of the Pearson River (a tributary of the Waiatoto) and the head of the south branch of the Wilkin. Mt Ragan was there too, a flat-topped chunk of rock flecked with bands of dull snow and its base covered with brooding mist. I thought of Charlie, Mr Explorer Douglas, climbing the peak in his stockinged feet in the 1890s, and the other men who had wandered over and explored this country. Very much in the present (Conway saw to that), I couldn't ignore the links of the past.

The Cessna came round in a tight bank, pivoting above Mt Lois and Mt Aspinall until we were losing height and scraping past the ice on the valley side of Mt Pickelhaube. I caught a brief glimpse of the Volta Glacier rim where we'd been marooned three years before. Mist and cloud were rolling in from the west up the funnel of the Waiatoto just as they had then.

"It certainly looks a mean place." Conway was staring out the starboard window at the blur of mountain slipping past the dipping wingtip. "You just can't keep away, can you?" he said.

I didn't reply. I was too busy watching and remembering as Tex spiralled the plane down through the shafts of sun that came through a provident break in the cloud. The bush and scrub suddenly came to vivid life, green, yellow and brown. Then I saw it, a passing smear of grey clung about with spindly scrub, a solitary rock in a sea of vegetation.

"There it is, Conway," I was yelling, and jabbing a finger against the perspex panel. I had a sensation of excitement, greater even than the revelation of a cloud-haggled Aspiring. There was more to it than that, but in the flurry of our arrival there wasn't time to register

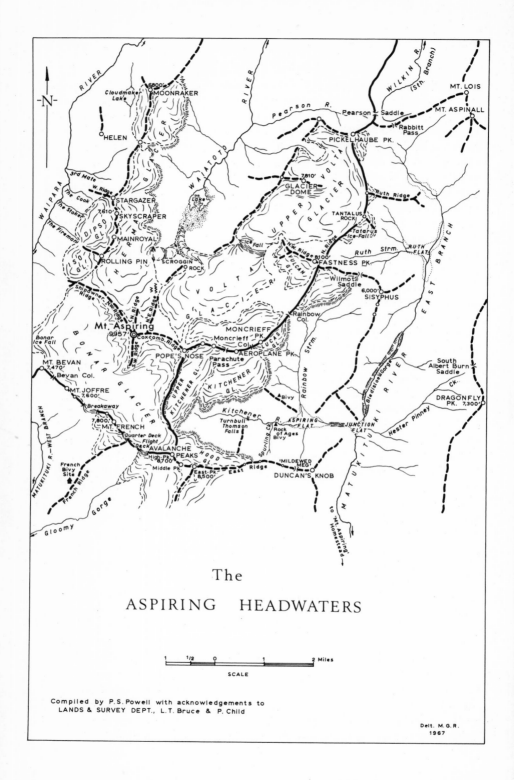

The

ASPIRING HEADWATERS

SCALE

Compiled by P.S. Powell with acknowledgements to
LANDS & SURVEY DEPT., L.T. Bruce & P. Child

Delt. M.G.R.
1967

more than an indefinable pleasure that we'd arrived. The aircraft touched down with a gentle come-back-to-reality bump and rolled with a scuffing of shingle toward the hut tucked into the forest at the end of the airstrip. We threw our swags and axes out and Tex revved the motor and was away. As Conway and I stood watching the Cessna float over the grassy flat and the grey river shingle, I had the same sensation that I'd felt so strongly the morning that Harry Wigley had landed us on the Volta Glacier in January 1965: a bewilderment at the quick transition from Albert Town to the heart of the hills. It was as if future and past and present were at the same point of time, meeting on a common ground of my experience. Con told me that he felt the same thing, an odd porridge-headedness, a lethargy that was mental rather than physical. Whatever the cause I came down to earth with a thump when I realised that Tex and the Cessna were flying happily down the Bledisloe gorge with half my camera gear still in the plane.

"You lug around far too much photographic junk, Dad. You must have at least ten pounds of the stuff, all of it uneatable." So we went over to the hut and brewed a strong cup of tea. The place was very clean, just as Alan Reith and I had found it when we'd come over Wilmot Saddle from Rainbow Valley the previous January. There were two tiers of single bunks aligned against the sacking which insulated the corrugated iron wall, a small table with a kerosene primus stove, the customary collection of half-rusted tins of food, and candles with little white avalanches of melted wax placed at strategic intervals at the head of the bunks and around the small four-paned window. At the far end of the hut, a long-handled shovel, a pickaxe—all with spit-polished hickory handles—crowbars, ropes, and a large tin trunk with a gargantuan brass lock, leaned against the wall in half darkness. There were bullets with soft noses, bottles of gun oil, a tin of detonators, a sackful of fuse and plugs of gelignite, and a long two-man bush saw with ferocious blades, all stowed as neatly as in a bosun's store. The meat-shooters who lived here were clearly neat, methodical men.

But the hut was more than tidy. It had an air of homeliness which I had seldom seen before in a mountain hut. The smell of the place was pleasantly musty, not the sharp twinge of sweat and dirt which makes your nose wrinkle in so many outback shelters as soon as you lift the latch and push open the protesting door. There was an atmosphere here of men who had been contented and cheerfully happy in sun as in the long days of rain. But it was the chair beside the table which attracted me. There wasn't a nail in it; legs, back and seat were of beech saplings. The joints, carved with a sheath-knife, fitted with exactness, and the frame was strengthened with tight twists of fish-cord lashings. Whoever made that chair was an artist as well as a craftsman. I could see him on a wet day, when the river was high and dirty and the schist boulders knocking as they rolled toward the mouth of the gorge, carving the parts with a fag of roll-your-own stuck in the corner of his mouth and the smoke curling round his face as he frowned in concentration.

"It's a beaut chair, Dad," said Conway, easing into its comfortable curves and sipping from a mug of tea.

"It's a masterpiece. Just as wonderful as the finest Chippendale."

"Just shows you what can be done if you have time," replied Conway, helping himself to another doorstep of bread topped with half an inch of butter and honey. "You know, I wouldn't mind at all if we got stuck here for a week. We've got plenty of tucker—and the bunks look good."

"Same here, Butch." And I thought of cold wet snow caves on the inhospitable Volta and windswept huts, spartan and high above the woodline. "What say we spend the night here?"

"We'd better move on," said Conway with a reluctant eye on the bunk. "Besides," he was all resolution, "I want to see your old bivvy rock up in the scrub, and you promised we'd go up the valley toward Rabbitt Pass and have a crack at Mt Aspinall."

The sun was flooding down when we came out of the hut, crossed the small creek that ran from the forest, and walked leisurely out to the open flat. The air was bright and the tussock glistening with raindrops so that the whole expanse seemed to be dancing with light in the south-westerly breeze. The flat was as I had remembered it, a large equilateral triangle bounded to the west by the high rock wall running from Mt Sisyphus and Mt Fastness. The sprawling end of the Ruth ridge which ran up through beech forest to snowgrass and a last rock and snow blade to the Volta Glacier rim formed the northern boundary. To the east, where the river ran placidly over ribs of grey and black silt and stone, the beech trees rose at a gentle angle to alpine scrub and herbfield cut with deep creekbeds leading to rounded basins below the final summits. If the western walls were grim, those in the east were soft to the eye, a pleasant relief of yellow-gold tussock and undulating ridges of glinting schist and screes.

The bivvy rock was half a mile from the hut somewhere among the boscage of scrub that ran down an ancient rubble fan from the base of the four-thousand-foot Fastness-Volta wall. I knew there was a twisting avalanche chute nearby where the spring snow fell churning and often spread well out on to the valley grass, and that a runnel creek half-hidden with overhanging tussock curved around the tumulus on which the bivvy rock was set. Conway and I separated, each of us taking a different line through the overgrowing deer trails that wound through the thicket, and calling to each other as we went.

"Anything over your way, Con?"

"No, not a sign. I think it's another of your stories."

"You've seen my photo. It's round here somewhere. Can't be far away."

"It's probably overgrown with scrub. Twenty-one years is a long time."

"Keep looking."

I stopped and sat on a mossy rock. The afternoon was warm in the shrubbery, full with peaceful drowsiness. Gradually I was aware of the tingling that comes when you know that you're not far from home and you turn from the street and walk down the drive toward the house with the gravel crunching under quickening feet. I looked up, quite suddenly and on impulse. There, only thirty feet away was a rusty tin jammed in the mottled fork of a turpentine tree. Beyond were the overhanging bluffs and far above a slick of ice bright in the sun on the Volta rim. I sat very still and looked at the relic, not too sure that it was real, wondering if it might be a play of light on the slowly weaving branches, perhaps a trick of a too-hopeful imagination. I looked away and then sharply back. The tin was still there. Faintly I could hear the grate of branches against the metal.

I somersaulted back down the years. It was a fine morning after heavy overnight rain and three of us had forced through the curtain of scrub and stepped on to the grass. I'd put the bright tin between the fork of the turpentine tree and wedged it home with short blows from my ice-axe.

"What the hell are you doing that for, Paul?"

"So I can find the bivvy rock again."

"You won't come back here again. Pickelhaube'll be climbed long before you do."

"You never know," I replied. "You never know in the hills."

The incident came back with photographic sharpness, even the joking inflexion in the long-forgotten voices; the feel of the tin in my hand, the dull sound of the metal driven home.

I got up from the rock and walked over to the tree. When I touched the tin, the pitted surface, corroded by twenty-one summers and winters, broke easily and left a red flake on my finger.

"Where are you, Dad?"

"Over here."

"Have you found the bivvy rock?"

"Yes."

"Good, I'm coming over."

"Give me a minute, Conway. I'll call when I'm ready."

"You OK, Dad?"

"Of course."

"All right then. I'll get some specimens. The botany's pretty interesting round here."

And so are many other things, I thought, as I pushed aside the sharp spindles of dracophyllum and walked crouching in the tunnel that the overhanging branches made against the sloping rock. I came under the arching ledges of schist where the screening trees shut out the brightness. The light was green and soft, and the bivvy very quiet. It seemed just another rock, one of hundreds that men have used in the Alps for temporary shelter in storm and then have left gratefully enough but with no particular urge to return. As my eyes adjusted to the subdued light I looked around again. The place had changed. There was neglect, a faint quality of melancholy, of things felt rather than seen. Thick fern curled over the flakes of rock and grey dirt where we had once slept. Under the far end of the overhang yellowish grass sprouted lank and untrodden round the stones of the fireplace. A rusted billy lay upended where there had once been flame and glowing embers. I bent down and picked up a leaf of the snowgrass we'd strewn over the sleeping-bench to soften the bite of the rocks; it went to powder in my hands. I felt that by coming back I had broken a link with old mountain days, and with the moments of our living under the rock with the trees. A kea called then somewhere from the scrub below Wilmot Saddle.

"You silly idiot," I muttered, "It doesn't do to live too much in the past."

I turned to go and then my eye caught something. High up on the back wall of the rock and partly hidden under glossy broadleaf branches were three names. I remembered scrawling them with a blackened stick from the fire the morning we left the bivvy: "J Hunt, D R-Jones, Paul P." The other two had chiacked me and said that people who littered their names on bivvy rocks were on the same literary level as those who wrote on walls in public lavatories. "There's only one difference," I'd told them. "This is a private grot and we found it. There's no law against artwork in your own house."

Curiosity as well as nostalgia had me rummaging around the bivvy, lifting up rocks at the back of the sleeping-bench, turning up the stones of the fireplace and running a searching hand along the rock ledges on the back wall where we'd sat propped in sleepingbags watching the billy come to the boil or the stew bubble on the hearth. When on a high mantel overlaid with the rock-dust of over twenty years my fingers touched metal, I nearly dropped the tin in my

eagerness to retrieve it. Inside the tightly-pressed lid was an assortment of things left as talismans rather than as necessities for a return;
a tarnished 1939 penny, two stubs of candle, a primus pricker, four
small boxes of wax matches. I took out one of the matches and
fingered it. The brick-red head was dry and the wax stalk smooth
and white and flared strongly as I rasped it along the sandpaper
and held it to the candle. As the light strengthened I sat with my
knees drawn up and my back against the roughness of the rock.
Time slipped. I was back to a stormy day in December 1947 when
the rain poured down and thunder burst and echoed in the hills.
John Hunt was standing in front of the fire drying out his clothes,
his head turned to where David Rees-Jones sat hunched up in his
sleepingbag reading from *Macbeth*.

"Read that bit again, Dave. It's very appropriate, isn't it? Wild
words for a wild day."

And David repeated:

> *Hang out our banners on the outward walls;*
> *The cry is still, "They come": our castle's strength*
> *Will laugh a siege to scorn.*

John rubbed his stomach and looked ruefully at our dwindling cache
of food. "But that passage about hunger; what was it again?"

"*. . . here let them lie, Till famine and the ague eat them up,*"

repeated David with measured solemnity. "Is that the one?" he
asked.

"Yes, that's it. Don't care for it much—too realistic. If this rain
keeps up the way it has for the last four days we'll be cooking the
soles of our boots."

I was still chuckling to myself when I looked up suddenly and saw
Conway. Present and future were back again.

"It's not much of a bivvy," he said. "You should see the one in
the Beansburn. That's terrific."

"Come on," I said, blowing out the candle and getting stiffly to
my feet, "It's time we got cracking. We want to put a camp in under
Mt Aspinall before dark. And let's hope we'll get a fine day tomorrow.
I want our first real climb together to be a good one."

We didn't look back as we walked down the gentle incline of the
old tree-covered moraine and round the edge of the beech forest
to the hut.

The afternoon was still young and the day warm and sunny when
we left the hut for the head of the East Matukituki Valley. After an
hour's easy travel over grassy flats and several crossings of the

river we came to where the creek from the south side of Mt Aspinall ran down through burned-out scrub. We dumped our swags there and continued up the main valley for another half to three-quarters of an hour until we were at the bottom of the tussock slopes leading to the summit of Charlie Douglas's quaintly-spelt Rabbitt Pass. Fortunately for me, Conway was botanising all the way or rock scrambling on inviting morainic boulders, some of them twenty or thirty feet high. Though the sun had dulled over and gloomy wisps of cloud were weaving over Rabbitt Pass we ignored the chill sou'-west wind and strolled around the flanks of the pass, Conway to pounce with eager concentration on some new specimen while I watched the mist ebb and flow over Pickelhaube and the Ruth Ridge to the Volta.

We camped for the night a few hundred feet up the steep creekbed that ran down from Mt Aspinall. There was plenty of dry scrub, and the creek gave us water, and music. We had no tent and no knives or forks, so we stood eating blackened sausages with twigs while the flames leaped and the acrid smoke fishtailed across the gully. When it was full dark I let off a firework I'd been carting around in my swag for the last four years and we danced like dervishes in the golden rain.

I woke several times during the night, not because I was cold or because the mass of young green fern—Conway reckoned it was something called *Polystichum vestitum*—wasn't soft or deep enough. Perhaps it was the loquacious creek, maybe the old excitement of a new climb. The moon came up over the Albert Burn tops and sent mottled patterns scurrying along the valley floor and across the scrub and tussock of the Ruth Ridge. The south-west clouds were moving faster now and when we roused a shade before four, I wasn't very optimistic about the chances of a climb, but after breakfast we stuffed our sleepingbags and unwanted impediments under a rock near the creek and faced the hill, bearing to the west and towards the ridge that ran up from the head of the valley towards Mt Aspinall. About six am we were near the ridge crest and I was getting a little breathless from the pace that Conway was setting. He had the enviable ability to talk, and pluck and stuff plants into a plastic bag while he was on the move.

Another hour on and the summit seemed pretty close.

"We'll be on top soon," I said, "And it's been easier than I thought. Usually the best of mountains has a trick or two up its sleeve. This one's very well behaved." I looked up at the summit touched with the first rags of mist. "Nothing that'll stop us—just a climb about half a mile along the ridge. The rock's steep enough to be interesting, not so rotten as to be dangerous."

I must have sounded a trifle pompous, for Conway, who was a few yards in front, laughed and called to me: "Come and have a look at this lot."

I shuffled up to where he sat swinging his legs and picking lichens off the rock.

"Ummm." I didn't like the look of the next section of the ridge at all. There was a wall-sided slash in it about a hundred feet deep. Beyond the upridge side a rock tower glowered, its friable ledges covered with stringy lichen. "Not very nice is it? Take a lot of time that, Conway."

"I'll go down first," he said, getting out the 120-foot length of white nylon.

Little as I liked the idea of Conway swinging his way down there on a double rope, I was even more perturbed that I would have to follow him. "This isn't the Eiger. No point in looking for trouble."

I cast a rapid eye over the mountainside. A continuous snow slope ran on the south side of the peak giving promise that it led to a less dramatic and vertical approach to the top. "Now, if we retrace our steps two hundred yards or so we can get on to that snow slope. A bit steep at the top, but there's a good run out at the bottom and no nasty bluffs to go sliding over."

I went first down the snow slope, facing outwards and kicking steps in the hard snow with my crampon spikes. Conway fed the rope out round the shaft of his axe where he was comfortably set on the reverse side of the slope. It was an easy enough place, but I was very conscious of the responsible as well as the stimulating side to our partnership. If Conway felt it, he never said so. It was, apart from the times we'd crossed rivers together, the first time we'd ever had a serious rope between us in the hills. I watched him as if we were high on the ice ridges of Mt Tasman. He came down like an old hand, a study in concentration, and a full smile at the end of it.

"I haven't ever heard you silent for so long. Bloody wonderful. The mountains have their uses."

"The same could be said for you," said Conway over his shoulder as he led along the snow below the rock towers of the summit.

We crossed a wide crack where the snow had shrunk from the base of the peak and soon stood in the rock gap overlooking the north branch of the Albert Burn.

It was now very cold as occasional flakes of sleety snow came whipping down with the wind. I ferreted around until I found a staircase of red rocks up the north side. With the wind bowing the rope between us, Conway led on to the top just before midday. He tried to look blasé—this wasn't his first summit—but Balboa couldn't have been more pleased with himself when he first saw the Pacific.

It was twelve years since Conway and I had first argued our way to
the bushline and shot a deer on the Cattle Face opposite the old
Aspinall homestead, a long apprenticeship for Conway, but a good
one.

"What's the height?" he asked.

"Not too sure. Somewhere around 6,500 feet."

"Quite high enough for a day like this," he said. "I'm glad we're
not on the Volta."

"So am I."

The cloud was over the peaks across the valley like a purple weal.
I blundered around the summit block taking photographs, but when
in abstraction I nearly fell off the mountain and Conway went into
hoots of laughter, I knew I'd made his day.

We sheltered from the worst of the wind behind a large rock and
shared the last of the chocolate. "Has Mt Aspinall been climbed
before?" Conway asked hopefully.

"I'm afraid so. By Howard Boddy in the early thirties. Maybe
not by the way we came."

"Oh. But it doesn't matter, does it? I've had a beaut day."

And that remark, I thought as we clattered down the rocks to the
niche, is the beginning of alpine wisdom.

Snow and stinging hail chased us down to our camp in the creek
and by mid-afternoon we were back under the shelter of the hut on
Ruth Flat.

While Conway boiled the kettle, I went for a quick look at the
river. It was still low but heavy rain was falling in the head of the
valley, and there was prospect of a dirty night.

"Are we going out tonight?" said Conway, handing me a mug of
tea.

I listened to the wind in the trees, and rubbed my hands with the
sheer pleasure of being snug under a roof in a well-found hut. I
hadn't any doubt about my decision. "Not much point in rushing
down valley now, Conway."

"Why not? It's only half past four. We can be away by five," he
replied seriously.

"We've got good quarters. I want to spend the night here just to
lie in my bag in a warm bunk and listen to the rain hissing down.
It's a wonderful sound on an iron roof."

"That's all very well for you, you're still on holiday, but I'm due
back to work in Dunedin early on Friday morning, and today's
Wednesday."

"Sure, but what's the hurry? We can get from here to Jerry
Aspinall's in six hours, eight hours at the most. There's all day
tomorrow."

"All right, we'll stay."

There's nothing so pleasant as preparing the evening meal in a back-country hut. You're relaxed and you know that for a few hours at least you're free from important decisions. Let it rain, thunder or snow. Provided the roof stays on the hut and the cooking-pots keep bubbling you don't worry. You don't care if the river floods or the wind blows itself inside out. The worse the weather, the more you revel in your temporary home. Like small boys safe from bullies in a favourite hideout, you rejoice all the more. The dangers of storm and rough travel, always respected, often feared, aren't for you tonight, and tomorrow's another day. Someone looks out the window through the streaming pane. "Just look at that river, glad we haven't got to ford that tonight. Never seen it so high."

"Thank God we're not sitting on a rock ledge at ten thousand feet. Hell of a night to be caught out. Bet someone's getting it in the neck. I wonder if so-and-so are off the mountain. Hope they'll be all right."

You exult in safety tonight because of danger to be faced tomorrow.

Con and I lit the candles and served tea on hot clean plates. The rain beat harder and the wind blustered around the hut. We yarned as we washed the dishes and then had a game of ludo on a board I'd brought in with me. It was the same board on which Allan Evans, Geoff Milne, Jack Ede and I played in the first Aspiring snowcave in December 1947. Every time I pushed around the counter I thought how well the years had treated me. Maybe it was still a lucky board. For once I beat Conway.

At eight I went to the hut doorway and had a quick look at the weather.

"What's it like?" said Conway, getting into his sleepingbag. "Still raining?"

"Raining? Heck, it hasn't really started yet. When it starts punching holes through the corrugated-iron roof, then you know it means business."

"You always did exaggerate. Do you think it'll be fine tomorrow?"

"I don't know."

"Oh, well," he yawned. "G'night, Dad."

I sat for a while at the table listening to the hut noises and the storm outside before I blew out the weeping candle and crawled into bed. "Am I glad I'm safe and snug down here?" I thought for the umpteenth time that day. The Volta Glacier had left its mark.

In the darkness just before dawn the hills clanged with thunder and the tops shone with lightning. The rain came bucketing down. As the light filtered slowly into the hut, I got up and looked out the window. The East Matukituki was enjoying itself. The placid ford was high with dirty grey waves and flashes of off-white.

"It doesn't look too good," growled Conway, thinking of his vacation job in Dunedin and the watery miles between.

"But a good day for the sack. Wake me with a cuppa at eight o'clock, will you?"

"Your turn to put on the tea boat—and to make the breakfast. Can we manage two eggs?"

"Hadn't we better ration them?" I replied by force of long habit. Shortage of food always worried me more than a surplus of water.

"Why? It's a holiday isn't it? Not a ruddy war."

At eight I was still snoring so Conway got up and made a weird concoction for breakfast; two eggs, bacon minus rind and chopped very fine, and four small tomatoes beaten to a frenzy with the heated relics of the previous night's tea. He was exuberantly cheerful as he mixed the mess in an aluminium bowl and I wondered if it was just his usual boisterousness. When he served me with the lifeless mess I had thoughts of melodramatic murder, but it tasted and smelled like the best Soho goulash. I ate it Roman-style, reclining in my bunk. As far as I was concerned it could rain for a week or until the tucker ran out.

About three in the afternoon we went down to the ford across the river, about four hundred yards below the hut. The water though still swift, high and discoloured, didn't have the malevolent and hungry appearance it had had a few hours earlier. We built up some rock cairns at the water's edge as markers so we could tell whether the river was going to fall. After tea Conway had a sudden burst of activity—not that he had been anything but active all day—but there was a purposefulness now that made me ask, "Why all the flurry?"

"Getting everything for a quick getaway in the morning. If the rain stops in the night the river might be low enough to ford at first light. We could be down to Aspinalls by early afternoon. Somehow or other I've just got to get back to Dunedin to start work the morning after tomorrow."

"That's very conscientious of you. But aren't you forgetting one important thing? Remember? We left the car on Luggate airstrip, so how are you going to get down the thirty miles to Wanaka? And then you've got to get all the way back to Dunedin. No buses by the time we get to Wanaka and I don't fancy the road walk to get there."

"I'll worry about that when we get to Jerry's. Shouldn't be any trouble; there are plenty of cars going to Wanaka from Cameron Flat this time of the year. And if there aren't, well, I'll just hitch a ride from a passing kea."

"OK then. If the river's at all cooperative, we'll give it a go. But with one definite reservation: I'm hanged if I'm going to let us get ourselves drowned. I've been down this gorge three times before. It can be a real stinker."

"Mum will be worrying. We're a day overdue already."

"I appreciate that, Conway, but after twenty years she's not going to get in a panic because we turn up a day or so late. She'd rather we rolled in a week late than be fetched up down at Wanaka as a couple of stiffs."

"Of course."

"And don't worry how you're going to get back to Dunedin. Once we get to Albert Town, I'll drive you down myself."

"Thanks, Dad. Wake me up at 3 am will you? We could be away by four."

As it happened I woke up a lot earlier than he'd intended. I'd gone to bed with the problem on my mind. I dislike having to *push* things in the mountains, especially when conditions are doubtful, so for some time I lay in my bunk chewing ideas over. It was a simple enough problem, I'd faced far worse ones over the mountain years, but in the darkness with the wind pulsing and the rain whispering on the roof thoughts become exaggerated. I wished it was dawn and time to go.

I was woken by the moonlight streaming in the solitary window. The hut shapes had changed and for seconds I lay there confusedly wondering where I was. The roar of the creek beside the hut was louder and at first I thought the flood was worse. Then I realised that wind and rain had stopped and that the noise of the creek accentuated the stillness that had come upon the hills. I looked at my watch, 1 am, and crawled out to investigate.

A dramatic alchemy had transmuted Ruth Flat and its encircling peaks. The impact was one of great contrast; a stern whiteness where the moonlight slanted on the flats and the mountain walls, an absolute darkness in the gullies and clefts seaming the rock faces. But the stars were sharp and splendid, Orion's Belt hung over the Volta and the Southern Cross above the tenebrity of bush and bluff across the river. The only sound was that of water shuffling down the river gravel and the distant rumble of the Bledisloe Gorge. The marvel of the night was like the first line of Genesis: *In the beginning God created the heaven and the earth.* I was seeing valley, mountain and sky for the first time. Frost hardened the wet shingle, and every leaf, every grassblade, hung burning. The air had that nip which comes with sudden freezing after rain, but I stood watching Fastness, too captured to move. I had seen that mountain many times before, climbed it twice, flown round it, and spent days when it came and went behind storm clouds, but this was compelling. The moon well in the north passed shadows across the east face as if the mountain was slowly altering shape. New snow covered the steep rocks and where the many overhangs jutted there was no snow. I shivered. The mountain was beautifully ethereal and sinister at the same time.

I went back to the hut and rooted Conway out of bed and brought him out to see it all. He came out rubbing the sleep from his eyes, stumbling over the silvered tussock, his feet grating over the freezing schist silt the flood had brought down from the head of the valley and laid in curves and ribs over the grass.

At first he said nothing, which I thought was very temperate of him. Then, after he had looked around the peaks, "I'd never have believed a mountain could be so beautiful and so frightening. Look at that east face—it's more three-dimensional than in daylight. And how impossible! I can see how it impressed you the first time you saw it in 1945." There was a real bite in the air. He rubbed his bare legs and stamped his feet on the tussock and went incredulous back to his bag.

I was caught by the magic of the hills; the ringing silence, the air of little knives, the white waves and dark hollows washing toward the insubstantial summits. I danced and yodelled and called to the mountain and the ridges. Sleep was quite out after that revelation, so I put the primus on and brewed up a pan of cocoa with a whole tin of condensed milk and plenty of sugar—no rum worse luck. As I sipped I thought over what Conway and I had said out in the moonlight on the Ruth Flat. "You'll be back here again, Con. These mountains and Aspiring have got you too."

"Yes, I think they have."

We tidied up the hut, left a note of thanks to the owner that we were homeward bound and were going to take our chance with the gorge, and pulled the door behind us.

I don't like the feeling when you shut a hut door for the last time. There's a finality when the shaft of the padbolt grinds home into the galvanised bracket on the door frame. The empty hut echoes and you sense that you've finished with a part of your mountain life, that you're locking it up and leaving it behind. You hurry, you almost run across the flats in the first of the light. Once you're across the river and well started on your journey it's safe to look back; the hut and the hours of shelter it gave you are already in the past. The immediacy, the tension of leaving have been drawn out and have broken. You think you're free, but already you're planning to return.

The grass was very frosty, the sky clear with a few stars, and the first sun creeping down the east face of Fastness as Con and I hurried down the east bank toward the mouth of the Bledisloe gorge.

An hour downstream from the hut we had to make the major decision for the day: would we go down the five-mile gorge, or would we play safe and go over the high-level route by bush and snowgrass?

"If the weather holds the gorge will be quicker." I looked at the swirl of the current, the rock walls choking the river, the trees silhouetted high on the grey-white bluffs of Sisyphus. "And once we're comitted, there'll be no turning back."

"What happens if there's a cloudburst while we're in the middle of the gorge?"

"Too bad, Conway. We could get rather wet—for keeps."

"What do you reckon?"

I took another look at the river, down the green gutter falling away through bluffs and bush, to the forested ridges which climbed steeply and incalculably distant to the south. Behind us at the head of the valley, there was some wispy stuff, high up in the sky and very innocent-looking. "Let's try the sewer shall we? Besides, it'll be good experience for you. And when you're an old man you'll be able to frighten your grandkids with stories of how you and their great-grandad came down the Bledisloe Gorge in 1968."

"We'll have to get down it in one piece first," said Conway with a sober eye on the white and green flurry.

I led off and straight away made the first mistake. We crossed the river before we really needed to. I went across first with Conway watching me, feeding out the rope as I came to the deepest and swiftest part. The slightly turbid water was chest-high, and I suddenly realised that the river was at least a foot higher than it was when Alan Reith and I had crossed in the same place a year before. Conway came over like a veteran. Because we'd made our first crossing far too early, we were then forced into a series of attempts to regain the east side of the gorge. But reasonable places were not many. All the way down I had been giving Conway the benefit of my thirty years of accumulated river wisdom, and in particular I'd been stressing how important it was to pick the best place to cross to avoid taking unnecessary risks.

I suppose I'd got fed up with looking and had lost the sharp edge of judgement. The sky was definitely overcast now and I could think of little else but getting down and out of the gorge before the rains came. I spotted a likely place where the river narrowed and foamed between a series of flattish rocks and was clambering down a greasy moss ledge when I heard Conway yell.

"What is it now?" I was getting peevish. After a few hours you tire of the continual roar of broken water and the sensation of being in a twisting, enclosed spillway which never seems to end. "I can't hear you. You'll have to come down to me."

We waved our arms and mouthed as Conway was fifty yards behind me up the gorge. I waited, stamping my wet legs impatiently.

"I wish you'd keep up with me," I yelled in his ear.

"You're going far too fast. You'll miss the best of the crossings if you do that."

"I know what I'm doing. I found my way in and out of this gorge before you were born." I gave him the rope and tied on. "Get the other end round your middle, and stop arguing. We're crossing here."

Conway had another swift glance at the river. "You won't make it."

"Why not? I've crossed in far worse places than this." But I wasn't so sure now.

"That's what a certain bloke once told you on Rob Roy. Remember?" The words brought me up smartly. I saw that he was worried, not for himself, but for me.

"I think we could do with a rest, and while we're resting, I may as well have a fag. You have some barley sugar."

Conway didn't smoke and he'd been nagging at me the whole trip about what cancer-sticks, as he gloomily called them, did to you. Instead, he was supposed to have an extra ration of barley sugar, but it didn't often seem to work out that way.

"Well, what do you think of your crossing now?" He pointed to the rocks I'd proposed to leap from, and the churning water between. The longest leap was about six or seven feet and the rocks at both ends smooth and periodically swilled over by the pulse of the gorge.

"I must've been barmy. One slip and I'd have gone over that water chute and then twenty feet down to that white pool. And there's a nice sharp tree-stump in the way. Thanks, Con."

"A pleasure. And we're quits now."

"Quits? What for?"

"For that time when I was five and I argued that I could cross the Hawea River in the days before the dam ruined it."

"I remember. You got really shirty because I said you could have a try if you let me put a rope on you. You went two feet and were swept off your feet. I played you like a fish."

"That's right," he said as he got up and went toward the better crossing he'd found a quarter of a mile back upstream.

We crossed easily here to the east or Albert Burn side. The weak patches of blue sky disappeared and the first heavy drops of rain fell. We looked at each other. Without a word Conway led off at a cracking pace. By now we were on the worst section of the gorge, the part I'd always referred to as the "Vice-Regal Gut". It was darker,

more shut-in here, for the river twisted down a rocky tunnel. The sides were concave, continually dripping and hung with moss beards. In a flash flood, escape from the river would have its thrills; on the Sisyphus side where the high walls came straight down for two thousand feet from the scrubline, it looked even more difficult. We'd been on the move for five hours and were wet through, hungry and cold.

"I'll be glad to see that tree on Junction Flat."

"Not long now. Just around the next bend." But I didn't believe it.

"That's all you've been saying for the last hour. I'm beginning to wish we'd taken the high route. At least we'd have seen something."

We went on, grumbling, watching the beech trees perched high on the Sisyphus bluffs. When they started to dip down we could be fairly sure that the next bend might be the last.

We had waded chest-high round yet another rock ledge and had emerged with water cascading from our windproof clothing when I heard a deeper note above the river clatter.

"Can't you hear it?" I yelled in Conway's ear.

"Of course. You've been making the same prophecy for the last half hour, 'That's the last fall, the big 'un, just ahead. We'll be out soon.' " Conway lifted his hands and shook his head. "Let's hope you're right this time. I'm getting fed up with the noise."

"It is pretty monotonous, isn't it?"

"Oh," he said with a half smile, "I don't mind the gorge or the water. I got used to them hours ago."

"What's biting you then?"

"Nothing much, really. Just that for the last three hours you've been murdering Handel's *Water Music*. I don't ever want to hear it again."

We waded on tiptoe and with hands clinging to the rock wall until we rounded the corner. In front of us and not more than a hundred yards downstream was the prophetic slip. Below it thundered the largest waterfall in the entire gorge. The water smoke filled the narrow canyon and the rocks shook.

"Must be a fantastic sight when there's a real old-man flood rampaging down the gorge," said Conway as he flung me a rope to help me up the last steep into the trees.

"Never mind the speculation, mate. Just give a bit of a heave will you? When I'm up there with you all snug among the botany, I'll chatter like a chimp."

We sat well back from the eroded overhang and nibbled a few wet squares of chocolate. For the first time for over six hours we had the chance to relax and look about without wondering about what lay ahead.

"Well, there it is, at last: Junction Flat, and the mountain tree."

"I was beginning to think that it was running away from us. When we were down there," said Conway, hooking a thumb in the direction of the gorge where the water shone dull in the faint sunlight, "did you get the sensation that the gorge didn't want to let go?" He stopped, as if embarrassed that he'd revealed too much of his thoughts.

"Yes. I know what you mean. On a fine day, with the river low, the trip down the gorge is a pleasant ramble. With the threat of bad weather and rain it's a different matter."

"I've never been down a gorge like that before. It's a new experience for me. I began to wonder what on earth was going to happen next."

I let him unwind.

"And when we came to that last part, the bit where the river ran through the rock tunnel and we had to wade up to our chests, I looked up and saw the driftwood from the last big flood stuck twenty feet up in the rocks. Twenty feet! Imagine being caught there. You'd never get out of it, the walls are too overhanging. And then when it started to rain—" He hesitated.

"Go on."

"Well, I felt quite windy."

"So did I."

"You didn't show it. Did I?"

"No." I was glad I could answer truthfully. "Not a bit. You were abominably cheerful—annoyingly so."

"Sorry about that."

"Nothing to apologise for. You did the right thing."

Conway laughed and said, "Lesson number two, eh? Once you're committed, never let on you're scared."

"That's right. Too late then. The time to speak up is before you get into trouble. Once you're in, you're in. If everyone starts wringing their hands and panicking, then," I flicked a stone high over the gorge, "the party goes to pieces, and you've had it."

"And," I said, as I dug my ice-axe into the ground and levered myself to my feet, "we haven't had a decent meal since we left Ruth Flat. Let's wander down to Junction Flat and have a feed. I'm so hungry I could eat the boots off a dead swagger."

We went down through the moss beech forest and regained the river through a mass of tangled vines and ribbonwood. Here, just below the falls, the river suddenly became more reasonable as if it too was tired and wanted to relax after the rampaging of its last five miles. We crossed easily to the western bank, certain now that Junction Flat lay only twenty minutes on up a spectacular exit through the bluff which Alan Reith and I had first discovered three years before. Though only half a mile from the gorge entrance, the last pools are far too deep to wade, and the bluffs are still too high and too straight to climb—except in one place, where a cunning ledge works upward and runs hard against an overhanging impasse of bluff at the rim of the gorge wall. A rocky chimney leads through a notch in the rim and the benches of deep mossed beech forest lead softly down to Junction Flat.

Conway led off, but rather prematurely had us involved in a tired argument on a false ledge which petered out to nothing more than a view of the dark river straight down between our boots. He wanted to *burn on* ahead, as he called it, but I was stubbornly determined that we weren't going to separate at that late stage in our journey. We were tired and the gorge might still have the last, and final word.

He came down reluctantly and we went down the gorge another hundred yards until I found my old blaze, now a three-year-darkened scar on a large beech tree which leaned over the water. In five minutes we were standing on the rim with the gorge below and behind us.

We looked back briefly and then walked luxuriously down the carpet of moss whistling and singing. The confines of the gorge and the constant hammer of the wild water were behind us.

As we walked gladly from the forest and through the browntop grass to where the mountain tree stood waiting, Conway turned to me and said, "It's been great. You know, Dad, I think I'm just as mad as you."

I looked across the grassy flat where the Kitchener River came down from a rainswept inner cirque. Avalanche and Aeroplane were somewhere up there in the stormclouds and the flat and the mountain tree were just the same as they'd been twenty years before. "Come on," I said, "Let's get down to Jerry's, there's still shelter down there too."

We strode through the well-remembered forest, two men in the rain.

Appendix 1

Chapter 3: THE HUT ON MT ALPHA

At the inquest following the death of Arthur Fredric, Dr P. P. Lynch, pathologist, gave evidence that "The deceased's condition of the heart was such that
it might have caused death at any time, quite apart from any question of effort
or strain . . . I don't think anybody could have behaved any differently, or that
there was anything further they [the party] could have done that would have
made any difference. If you had had an army of doctors there they could have
done nothing."

The Coroner returned a verdict "that the deceased died near Alpha Hut in
the Tararua Ranges on 14th August 1938 from coronary sclerosis and infarction
of the heart".

Appendix 2

Chapter 4: CAVE CAMP

The following made the Rakaia-Whitcombe Pass crossing and climbed Mt
Martius:
Bruce R. Banfield, Kathleen Boswell, Muriel Broughton, Bob Coates, Stan E.
Davis, Derek Freeman, John Gabites, Bernard D. A. Greig, Mavis Hunt (David-
son), Ruth Jones, Arthur P. Oliver, Paul Powell, Don Viggers, Chas Watson-
Munro, Roy Wilson.

Those who made the ascent of Mt Thorndike were:
Kathleen Boswell, Muriel Broughton, Stan E. Davis, Derek Freeman, John
Gabites, Bernard D. A. Greig, Paul Powell, Chas Watson-Munro, Roy Wilson.

Appendix 3

Chapter 14: HUT DROP ON MT EARNSLAW

The Esquilant Hut on Wright Col was named after W. R. Esquilant who was killed in a climbing accident on the Weisshorn in Switzerland on 24 August 1946.

Bert Esquilant, a member of the New Zealand Alpine Club and the Canterbury Mountaineering Club, had a distinguished mountaineering record and it was fitting that the Esquilant bequest was used to build a hut on Wright Col, for the West Peak of Mt Earnslaw (9,261 ft) was among the first of his many major climbs.

Many members of the Otago Section of the New Zealand Alpine Club helped with the prefabrication of the hut during the winter and spring of 1950. The members of the Wright Col building party in December 1950 were:

Lois Aldridge (Glasson), Ian Bagley, J. F. Brough, John Carruthers, A. R. Craigie, Eileen Elliot, Graeme H. Fyfe, Ralph Glasson, Margery Macaulay, Gwen Mitchell, J. Parcell, Paul Powell, Ray Stewart, Colin M. Todd, Brian J. Wilkins, Owen L. Wynn.

Index

Early morning on the Mt. Hector track